CW00550983

Far From
EUtopia

Far From
EUtopia

How Europe is failing –
and Britain could do better

ROSS CLARK

abacus
books

ABACUS

First published in Great Britain in 2025 by Abacus

1 3 5 7 9 10 8 6 4 2

A CIP catalogue record for this book
is available from the British Library.

Hardback ISBN 978-0-349-14696-6
Trade paperback ISBN 978-0-349-14697-3

Typeset in Baskerville by M Rules
Printed and bound in Great Britain by
Clays Ltd, Elcograf S.p.A.

Papers used by Abacus are from well-managed forests
and other responsible sources.

MIX
Paper | Supporting
responsible forestry
FSC® C104740

Abacus
An imprint of
Little, Brown Book Group
Carmelite House
50 Victoria Embankment
London EC4Y 0DZ

The authorised representative
in the EEA is
Hachette Ireland
8 Castlecourt Centre
Dublin 15, D15 XTP3, Ireland
(email: info@hbgi.ie)

An Hachette UK Company
www.hachette.co.uk

www.littlebrown.co.uk

Contents

Introduction

At 4.40 a.m. on Friday 24 June 2016, David Dimbleby stiffened in his chair in the BBC studio and announced: 'The British people have spoken and the answer is clear: we're out.' Britain was waking to a terrifying new future. Or so it seemed to some. When markets opened a little over three hours later, the FTSE 100 plunged 12.5 per cent in minutes. Barclays Bank was down 35 per cent. Half an hour later, the prime minister, David Cameron, resigned and Mark Carney, governor of the Bank of England, announced that he was making £250 billion of emergency funds available to any banks which needed propping up. Back in the BBC studio, Conservative MP Anna Soubry proclaimed to the world: 'Yesterday we were told this was scaremongering. Here we are, can you believe it, this morning talking about an economy which is in this terrible shock. We have made a very, very, very bad mistake.'

Thus began a narrative that Britain had self-harmed; that the UK had doomed itself to an impoverished, isolated future while the rest of Europe forged ahead to prosperity without us. It got worse. Within hours, a smashed window in a Spanish restaurant in south London had been interpreted as the beginning of a wave of xenophobia and racism (the police later said they thought it was a burglary). As if an omen of our new place in the world, four days later the England football team was knocked out of the Euro 2016 championships in a 2–1 defeat by Iceland (population 380,000, the size of Coventry).

The belief that the EU represents the epitome of human civilisation, and that Britain divorced from it in a moment of petulance, has become embedded in the ideas of those many diehard Remainers who have refused in any way to accept the leave vote. They wear a pair of differentiated spectacles: one side of which has a rose-tinted lens with which they gaze longingly across the Channel, while the other side has a blackened, blinkered lens through which they view their own country.

It is a conceit that is amply demonstrated, for example, in John Kampfner's 2020 book *Why the Germans Do It Better: Notes From a Grown-up Country* – the inference of which is that Britain has reverted to childishness. Finished during the early weeks of the Covid-19 pandemic, it compares the German and British approaches to the gathering crisis. Germans, writes Kampfner, were suspicious of state control but nevertheless had submitted to being tracked and traced to stop the infection from spreading. Britain, on the other hand, had 'provided a case study of how not to deal with a crisis'. Its care homes had become death traps, while the government had overlooked what was coming because it was consumed by 'pseudo Churchillian self-delusion'. For Kampfner's German friends, 'Britain's travails have been the object of sickness and sympathy. So many conversations begin with the same sentence: what has happened to you, my British friends?'

If only Kampfner and his friends had waited. In the end, it wasn't just the UK government that was caught napping by the virus. When a *Lancet* study of excess mortality rates across the pandemic years of 2020 and 2021 was published in April 2022, it revealed that Britain and Germany's experiences were virtually indistinguishable. Britain had suffered an excess death of 126.8 per 100,000 and Germany 120.5 per 100,000.[1] While Germany did some things better, Britain did better with others, such as the procurement and rollout of vaccines. One reason Germany might have had better outcomes in the early weeks of the pandemic is because elderly people were already sheltering from a flu outbreak which had swept the country in the winter 2019/20, involving 80,000 cases and 130 deaths by the third week of February.[2] Covid was a tragedy that struck both countries – indeed, all countries – and confounded both healthcare systems. The idea that Covid showed up the inferiority of Britain's public health system compared with others in Europe is bunk.

That is just one example of the blinkered view of Remainers who live with the fantasy that post-Brexit Britain has been reduced to a crashing and burning satellite of a wealthy and successful EU. There are many others. In 2022, Mark Carney, by then the former Governor of the Bank of England, made the extraordinary claim that, 'In 2016 the British economy was 90 per cent the size of Germany's. Now it is less than 70 per cent.'[3] As other economists quickly pointed out, Carney had appeared to use nominal figures (i.e. not adjusted for inflation) for the size of the German economy but inflation-adjusted ones for the UK economy. Moreover, he had used statistics that simply compared the size of the two economies in current exchange rates, ignoring that the pound was very strong at the beginning of 2016 and very weak in 2022.[4] When comparing the two economies on the basis of purchasing power parity – which compares the buying power of a currency within each country – the UK and German economies moved pretty much in lockstep between 2015 and 2022, with the UK economy around 70 per cent of the German economy in both years.[5] A year on from Carney's claim, it would have been harder still to present the German economy as much more buoyant than Britain's – it had fallen into recession, almost uniquely among major economies.

The German economy continued to shrink into 2024, with GDP shrinking in the second quarter by 0.1 per cent – to the point at which it was a little smaller than it had been on the eve of the pandemic, nearly five years earlier.[6]

I should lay my cards on the table now and say that I voted Remain in the 2016 referendum. I was one of the 48 per cent, in other words. While I was attracted to the idea of Britain trying to escape Europe's low trajectory of growth and become a more dynamic economy – a Singapore on Thames, as it was often called – in the end I fell for the 'better the devil I know' argument. I could see that Brexit would be very disruptive, especially with the many families – including my own – who have established bonds across Europe. Not only that, I feared a British withdrawal would break up the EU, with serious repercussions for Eastern Europe, perhaps culminating in some countries being drawn into Vladimir Putin's sphere of influence.

But I accepted the result – unlike the elderly dog walker I met on the morning of 24 June 2016, who told me, 'It'll be war, now.' It didn't have to go quite so badly, I said in response. I started to look forward to Britain forging its own path, maybe even to Singapore coming to the Thames. At no point did I feel inclined to do as so many frustrated Remainers started to do and see support for EU membership as a paradigm of liberal virtue. It is remarkable that in the first forty-two of Britain's forty-seven years of EU membership I never remember the organisation attracting much sentiment in Britain. I don't recall people waving EU flags, going dewy-eyed at the thought of European integration or showing any other kind of emotion towards the bloc. It was treated as a rather humdrum body, which even its supporters saw as somewhat ponderous and bureaucratic. Only when our possible departure hove into view did a kind of pan-European patriotism suddenly emerge.

On EU departure day, 31 January 2020, the BBC trammelled its archives for what had happened on the day that Britain had joined, 1 January 1973. Had there been national rejoicing? All it could find was a clip from the Devon village of Ivybridge which, almost uniquely, had celebrated the occasion with a week-long 'Fanfare for Europe'. The local folk dressed up, drank, danced, planted commemorative trees and sang the Ivybridge European Community Song, which began with the words: 'Why is Grandma chewing garlic, why is Grandad pinching bums?'[7] – not, I think, necessarily the associations with things European which the 2016 Remain campaign sought to promote. The clip ends with a darker sign of dissent to come: overnight, persons unknown had vandalised the newly planted saplings. But that was it: only one village in England had bothered to respond to a letter sent by Edward Heath's government to every parish council in the land suggesting that we mark the occasion with some kind of national celebration.

I will also say that I am instinctively very much of Europe. I have no desire to live elsewhere in the world. I admire the US for its sheer originality and capacity for wealth creation, but I wouldn't want to live in a country that is afflicted every other week, it seems, with a school shooting. I have no wide-eyed regard for the US, which I can see has deep problems in it social structures, race relations and many other areas. I wouldn't want to be reliant on its expensive – and under-performing, when looked at on a national scale – healthcare system. I would find its sprawling cities alien, being used to walkable European ones. I would find its consumerism cloying. But it is hard to ignore the gulf that is opening up between the US and European economies; the bounding growth and dynamism of the US compared with the decline that is evident over so much of Europe.

Neither would I care to live in Southeast Asia. Singapore will crop up again and again in this book as an exemplar of how to create wealth and improve the living standards of its people; nowhere on earth has made such a rapid journey from a third world to a first world country, all in my lifetime. But

I wouldn't want to live there, either; aside from the climate, I couldn't live in an authoritarian state, even a benign one. Even less, would I want to live in China, obviously. Again, however, it is hard to overlook the drive of Southeast Asia, contrasted with the stagnation of Europe.

Now the dust has settled a bit, it is hard for anyone to argue convincingly that Brexit has been the disaster which was widely predicted. Even the *Guardian* seems to have its doubts. 'Britain's economic performance in the seven years since 2016 has been mediocre but not the full-on horror show that was prophesised by the remain camp during the weeks leading up to the referendum,' wrote the newspaper's economics editor, Larry Elliott, in December 2023.[8] That seems a pretty fair assessment, because although the tumbleweed isn't quite blowing through the streets, it is hard to argue, either, that Britain has really seized the opportunities presented by Brexit. We have simply become a different breed of European social democracy and trotted alongside the EU.

On the other hand, since 2016 the EU seems to have descended into a sulphurous mire. Relations between Brussels, Poland and Hungary have been poisonous at times, with the EU deciding that their elected governments are not acting in tune with its own values and threatening them with the loss of billions of euros in grants. The European parliament elections of 2024 saw a dramatic rise in Eurosceptic parties – which are not necessarily in favour of their countries departing the EU but are keen to trim its powers. Meanwhile, angry citizens in Western Europe have started taking out their frustrations directly on the EU, complaining about the same things that persuaded a majority of British voters to plump for Brexit: regulatory overreach, a democratic deficit – and migration.

Quite what John Cockerill had done wrong is hard to fathom. The nineteenth-century Lancashire-born industrialist was credited with sparking the industrial revolution in what is now Belgium, using British know-how to open an iron foundry in the town of Liege in the year 1817. He followed it up with a blast furnace and a factory turning out steam engines, diversifying into garments and helping to found the Bank of Belgium, before dying, aged forty-nine, of typhoid while returning from St Petersburg in an attempt to raise capital for his, by then, struggling business empire.

But his contribution to the life and wealth of the emerging nation of Belgium counted for nothing when, on 31 January 2024, a mob of angry farmers tore his statue off its pedestal in Brussels' Luxemburgplein and threw it on a fire made from burning crates. In its place they put up an amorphous rag doll and a sign declaring: 'People of Europe say no to Despotism' (in spite of Brexit, English remains an official language of the EU and also, it seems, its malcontents). They then threw eggs at EU buildings and blockaded much of the centre of the city with their very large and expensive tractors – many of which had presumably been bought with EU agricultural grants (€52 billion worth was handed out in 2023 alone). You can't please some people, especially when you are trying to bribe them with their own money.

At least the campaign for Brexit was calm and, for the most part, polite. It was played out in debates in village halls. Not so the farmers' protests which erupted across Northern Europe at the beginning of 2024. For French farmers, not to mention many other groups of workers, it is forever 1789. There is nothing new about latter-day Robespierres taking to the streets, erecting barricades or blocking motorways and setting light to lorries. But what has changed is that they seem now to be treating the EU, as much as their own governments, as the enemy.

During the final years of the UK's membership of the EU, there seemed to be conceit in Brussels that recalcitrant Britain was alone in its lack of enthusiasm for European integration;

any dissent elsewhere was minor and unlikely to lead to other countries leaving the bloc. That has now been shown to be false. With Britain gone, the mantle of Euroscepticism has been taken up with relish by French farmers, Polish Catholics and many others offended by what they see as an increasingly arrogant EU.

But this book is not just about the EU, which should not be conflated with Europe as a whole. For all the EU's failures and objectionable aspects, there is a wider malaise in Europe. The continent as a whole – Britain included – has lost its self-appointed place as the world's keeper of civilisation, along with its reputation as the slightly less wealthy but more cultured and self-restrained twin of the United States of America. Its economies are stagnating, its quality of life fading, and the reputation for freedom and democracy it has tried to establish since 1945 is rapidly becoming lost.

Take away the noise of Brexit and you can see that Britain and the EU are both locked in the same cycle of decline. They are like a bickering couple, each moaning about the other's inadequacies while failing to see that they are themselves very little different. Both have lost their spirit of innovation, their momentum, all the qualities which once made other parts of the world emulate us. Europe has become a macrocosm of Athens: a place of culture and history, but where the glories of the past tower over the tawdry reality of the present.

In so many ways, Europe is becoming a backwater. For innovation and scientific advancement, look to the US. For economic dynamism, look to the US or to Southeast Asia. For the highest education standards and the best healthcare, look to Southeast Asia, or to Australia. But to what would you look to Europe? Culture? Rather less than in the past. The freest societies on earth? Depends on your concept of freedom. An agreeable holiday? That is the problem. We have had too many good holidays there (assuming, as we shall later see, we haven't fallen victim to Europe's growing intolerance of tourists).

We idolise Europe because of holiday syndrome. We think the Italians all live in agreeable stone villas in sumptuous countryside because that is where we stayed on holiday – we don't see the pokey high-rise flats in crumbling and graffitied concrete suburbs, which are home to far more Italians. We think the French all eat well because we found a lovely restaurant in the Dordogne; we don't see the fast-food outlets which increasingly feed the French. We think it is always sunny in Benidorm because that is how it was when we went there in August; we don't see the lashing wind and rain at other times of year. We think Bulgaria is deliciously cheap because our spending money went a long way; without stopping to think how the locals get by on much lower incomes. In Greece, we read novels, guidebooks or even Homer; we don't read the local paper to read of the road accidents. In Germany, we see beer and bratwurst, not idle factories. We might take a peek at the ordered seediness put on for the tourists in Amsterdam, but we don't see the misery and crime which goes with drug addiction and prostitution.

In summer 2023, I walked along Corsica's GR20, a mountain path with 50,000 feet of vertical ascent that takes you 120 miles across the island, over precipitous cliffs, through pine forests and maquis alive with cicadas, in almost unbroken sunshine. It seemed the most perfect place on earth; Europe at its best. At no point in the nine days it took to complete the route did it remotely occur to me that I was crossing one of the most violent places in Europe; Hackney, Moss Side, Handsworth – none can touch it for its murder rate. I only found that out when I got home, and started reading about the cycle of mafia-style violence and the code of omertà which sustains it. That is holiday syndrome for you: obliviousness to what is really going on beneath our noses; a lack of curiosity, even, to find out. We don't want to because we have gone away on a holiday from reality. Then we come home and the multiple problems of our own country reassert themselves in our consciousness. We return to seeing the bad things. That is why we – or some of us – think Britain is wrecked, a miserable and impoverished isle which, in a fit of madness, chose to cast itself away from civilisation.

However, it isn't true. There is much wrong with Britain. But whatever you think is bad this side of the Channel, you can almost always find worse on the other side without having to look too hard. The more you look at the rest of Europe through the same lens as you view Britain, the more you start to challenge the notion that Britain is some embittered divorcee reduced to living in a tawdry bedsit after marching out of the family home in a fit of pique.

1.

Sclerotic Economy

One of my favourite jobs every December is to look back at what the psychics had predicted would happen during the preceding twelve months. It is a weird alternative universe of wars that never broke out, meteorites that never fell, victories that were never celebrated and celebrity marriages that were never toasted. But in 2023, it wasn't the crystal-ball gazers that amused me the most but the IMF (International Monetary Fund). In January of that year, it predicted that of all the world's economies just one would be plunged into recession during the following twelve months: the UK, which would see output contract by 0.6 per cent, weighed down by fiscal and monetary policies eating away at household budgets. The euro area, by contrast, would expand by 0.7 per cent.

There must have been a flaw in their crystal ball, because when the growth figures for 2023 began to emerge in early 2024, it wasn't Britain that came out as the laggard, it was Germany, whose economy had slumped by 0.3 per cent over the course of the year. Household consumption was down

0.8 per cent, the public sector had contracted by 1.7 per cent and the manufacturing industry – the pride of the German economy – was down 2 per cent.[1] The UK economy, by contrast, grew – just about – by 0.1 per cent during 2023, with two quarters of negative growth in the second half of the year nearly cancelling out growth in the first half.

It has been a familiar story ever since 2016: think-tanks and worthy international bodies have talked down the UK economy, citing the damage they assume has been done by Brexit. Anyone who aspires to a career in economic forecasting should first take the trouble to read a paper published by HM Treasury on 23 May 2016, exactly a month before Britain's EU referendum. 'A vote to leave would represent an immediate and profound shock to our economy,' declared the then chancellor, George Osborne, predicting that within two years the UK economy would have shrunk by 3.6 per cent, relative to what would have happened had Britain not voted to leave. Unemployment would rise by 500,000 during the same time.

And that was just the 'shock scenario'. The Treasury's analysts had also drawn up a possible 'severe shock scenario', in which the economy would have contracted by 6 per cent within two years of a vote to leave, and unemployment would have risen by 800,000. Unlike many of the economic forecasts in advance of Brexit, which were couched in terms of relative growth several decades into the future, these predictions can be measured against reality. In the second quarter of 2018 – two years after Britain voted to leave – UK GDP was £548 billion, 4.2 per cent up on what it had been in the second quarter of 2016.[2] Over the same period, unemployment fell from 1.668 million to 1.362 million.[3] The Treasury's forecast, in other words, was not just wrong but laughably so.

None of this should make anyone think all is well with the UK economy, still less feel pride. In 2023, seven years on from the Brexit vote, and three years on from Brexit itself, Britain's economic growth was pretty stagnant, having struggled to recover from the Covid-19 pandemic, during which it had shrunk by an unprecedented 20 per cent in a single quarter. But was it worse than other European countries? In the second quarter of 2023, the UK economy was 1.8 per cent larger than it had been in the fourth quarter of 2019, the last before Brexit (and also the pandemic). That compared with 1.7 per cent growth in France, while the German economy had expanded by only 0.2 per cent.[4]

While the UK economy dipped into a shallow recession in the latter half of 2023, it then rebounded in the first half of 2024 to become the fastest-growing in Europe, with expansion of 0.7 per cent in the first quarter and 0.6 per cent in the second quarter. Germany, by contrast, grew by 0.2 per cent in the first quarter and contracted by 0.1 per cent in the second quarter. The Eurozone as a whole expanded by 0.3 per cent in each quarter. So much for the theory that Brexit has led Britain to under-perform the rest of Europe.

Is Europe's long stagnation an inevitable result of a pandemic that closed down large parts of the economy for months on end and disrupted global supply chains? Not at all. By contrast, the US economy quickly resumed growth. By the end of 2020, it had already rebounded strongly, so that the contraction across the year as a whole was limited to 2.2 per cent. It then expanded 5.8 per cent in 2021, 1.9 per cent in 2022 and 2.5 per cent in 2023.[5] In other words, by the end of 2022, the US economy was already 5.4 per cent larger than it had been at the end of 2019. By the end of 2023, it was 8.1 per cent larger. The strength of the US economy continues to surprise. January 2024 saw the number of jobs expand by a massive 353,000, twice as much as analysts had been expecting. US stock markets duly rose because increased employment indicates more output and greater profits. European stock markets fell back, by contrast, because investors calculated that the good economic news from the US would keep global interest rates higher for longer, depriving Europe of the stimulus it needs to wake it from its stupor.[6]

It isn't Britain that has the problem; it is the whole of Europe. This is recognised even by many advocates for the EU. Writing in the French newspaper *Le Monde* in February 2024, Stéphane Lauer declared that 'Europe's economic stagnation is no longer a risk but a reality that needs to be urgently tackled' (he went on to suggest that further integration was the answer, a conclusion with which others may disagree).[7] The fact that the whole of Europe has been underperforming is lost, however, on those who continue to try to claim that there has been some kind of calamitous collapse in the UK economy caused by Brexit. In a Mansion House speech in January 2024, Mayor of London Sadiq Khan made the extraordinary claim that the UK economy is £140 billion smaller than it would have been had Britain not left the EU, a claim based on research he had commissioned from analysts Cambridge Econometrics.[8] He was asserting, in effect, that Brexit had stolen 6 per cent from UK growth. Yet the above figures show what a nonsense that is. Khan was saying that had there been no Brexit then the UK economy would have surged ahead in line with the US economy. But our neighbouring EU economies have not performed even nearly as well as the US. Indeed, Britain has slightly outstripped them since Brexit.

Economic output in Britain and Europe has never really recovered from the 2008–9 financial crisis – growth in GDP has never been anything other than lukewarm since. There are many people who like to blame this on government 'austerity' – by which they mean cuts (or rather a slowdown in growth) to public spending made in an effort to balance the books. Yet, when you look at the trajectory of growth in the public sector, productivity in UK public services is back to where it was in 1997, marking a whole quarter of a century without improvement – it is hard to escape the conclusion that a larger public sector would compound Britain's growth problem.[9]

Britain's sluggishness is not the result of leaving the EU. The malaise merely reflects what has been happening across Europe for many years. Over the period 2000 to 2022, according to World Bank figures, economic growth in the EU averaged 1.53 per cent per year. In the US, it averaged 2.03 per cent. That might seem a small difference but, over twenty-three years, it means that the EU economy grew by 41 per cent while the US economy grew by 58 per cent.[10]

Alternatively, to measure Europe's relative decline globally over the past six decades we can turn to the Maddison Project, a Netherlands-based database that collates economic statistics from across the world over a long period and presents them in a comparable format. It adjusts GDP for local spending power – thus removing the distorting influence of short-term currency movements – and presents all figures at 2011 prices.

In 1960, it tells us, Western Europe accounted for 26.8 per cent of global GDP. By 1980, that had fallen to 23.9 per cent and, by 2000, 21.0 per cent. Then the slide accelerated, so that by 2018 Western Europe was producing only 14.7 per cent of global GDP. Meanwhile, East Asia grew from 10.6 per cent of GDP in 1960 to 15.5 per cent in 1980 and 20.3 per cent in 2000. By 2018, it had firmly overtaken Western Europe on 23.3 per cent. South and Southeast Asia has travelled in the same direction: growing from 7.8 per cent of global GDP in 1960 to 16.3 per cent in 2018. It is perhaps inevitable that the European economy should shrink in relative size given the rapid industrialisation of China, India and much of the rest of Asia, as well as the fact that the population has been growing more slowly in Europe than in Asia. Yet Europe has done significantly worse than a group of countries collectively known as the 'Western Offshoots' – the US, Canada, Australia and New Zealand. In 1960, they were just a little ahead of Western Europe, on 27.9 per cent of GDP. They then declined to 24.4 per cent in 1980, grew slightly to 24.9 per cent in 2000 and had fallen back to 18.7 per cent in 2018. In other words, they have held their own much better than has Western Europe.[11]

But what about Britain's performance within Western Europe? This time, let's look at some figures which adjust for population growth/decline and are therefore not distorted by high levels of migration from Eastern to Western Europe. Between 2000 and 2018, GDP per capita in the UK grew by 19.1 per cent, slower than Germany (38.4 per cent), the Netherlands (25.2 per cent) and Sweden (33.1 per cent) but faster than France (15.3 per cent), Spain (16.7 per cent), Belgium (17.9 per cent) and Italy (5.0 per cent). Over the course of this century, Italy has become the real laggard of Western Europe, and almost unique among peaceful countries in failing to raise the living standards of its people by an appreciable amount during the first two decades of this century.

By contrast, EU membership has worked for former Soviet bloc countries, at least at first sight (we will look at that more later). They have seen rapid growth this century, albeit from a low base. Between 2000 and 2018, GDP per capita in the Czech Republic grew by 72.1 per cent, in Hungary by 95.1 per cent and Poland by 115.6 per cent.[12] Those growth rates might explain why there is little public appetite for abandoning EU membership in Eastern European countries, in spite of frequent clashes with Brussels on matters of democracy.

Britain, then, is pretty mid-table in terms of Western European countries this century. It lagged behind Germany over the two decades prior to Brexit, yet has done a little better than Germany in the years since. The caveat to this is that the Covid-19 pandemic has robbed us of the chance to judge the performance of post-Brexit Britain against the grim prophecies. It so distorted the economies of all countries that it is impossible to sort out what was due to Brexit and what was due to Covid.

One thing, though, is for sure. Since Covid/Brexit, it is Germany, not Britain, that has become Europe's economic also-ran. In the words of the country's finance minister, Christian Lindner, in January 2024, Germany has become like a 'tired man after a short night'. That is one way of putting it; others might conclude that Germany was suffering a nightmare.

It might not seem so when you take a ride on a graffitied train through the suburbs of East Berlin and see the abandoned factories which, more than three decades after reunification, remain the haunt of urban explorers, but for decades German industry has been the powerhouse of Europe. Where other EU economies underwent deindustrialisation, Germany seemed to manage to stay on top, accounting for just over a quarter of all industrial production in the EU in 2022.[13] The country's industrial sector employed 7.5 million people. In particular, its car industry carried the prestige of the nation. No company summed it up better than BMW, which made its first venture into car-making in the 1920s by manufacturing the British-designed Austin 7 under licence. By the 1960s, BMW had outgrown the now-declining Austin both in sales volumes and quality. By the 1980s, the company produced some of the most popular luxury cars sold in Britain. In 1994, it was able to perform a triumphant turning of the tables: it bought the Rover Group, which had consumed the now-defunct Austin brand some decades earlier. That wasn't the end of the humiliation: six years later, BMW decided that the Rover Group – and with it the remnants of Britain's mass-market car industry – weren't worth saving. It jettisoned the lot, save for the latter-day reinvention of the Mini, which BMW continues to manufacture in Oxford.

Yet, suddenly, Germany doesn't look nearly quite so immune to industrial decline. Indeed, it seems to be embarking on a ride down the same precipitous slope that Britain and other European countries have already ridden. In 2018, German industry entered a prolonged recession, with output sliding even before the Covid-19 pandemic. While production initially recovered from the deep hole of 2020, it never saw a full recovery, and, in 2023, the slide grew steeper. By the end of that year, German industry was producing just 92.7 per cent of the volume of what it had been producing in 2015.[14] The decline of automotive production has been especially acute. At its peak in 2007, the German car industry produced 6.2 million vehicles. It still managed to produce just over 6 million in 2015, before suffering a sharp and sudden reversal. By 2022, Germany was down to making 3.7 million cars.[15] Worse is almost certainly to come. In September 2024, Volkswagen announced that it is to close factories in Germany for the first time in its eighty-seven year history.[16]

'*Vorsprung durch Technik*' ran the Audi slogan that was first used in 1971 and plastered across the company's adverts for the next twenty years. Few in Britain ever knew quite what it meant – 'advancement through technology' – but we realised what it was saying: lots of people make cars but only Germans use their brains. It might have convinced us at the time, but a little less so now as German cars have become synonymous with the gas-guzzling, overpowered executive car stuffed with microchips and other gadgets liable to leave you in the lurch by the roadside when they fail. German cars no longer shine for reliability. In the annual reliability survey conducted by *What Car?* magazine in 2023, based on the experiences of 22,000 owners, too many recently introduced German

cars occupied lowly positions, while Japanese cars shone out
as the ones least likely to cause their owners trouble. Lexus
and Toyota were revealed as the most reliable brands, with
Volkswagen 22nd, Mercedes 24th and Audi 26th out of 32.[17]
The lousy fuel efficiency of German cars somewhat contrasts
with the country's environmentalist image. In the magazine's
tests of real-world mpg (as opposed to official figures), bottom
place went to the Audi S8, which achieved just 21.7 miles per
gallon. In all, six out of the bottom ten places went to German
cars, while six of the top ten places went to Japanese cars.[18]
Nor – and this is a personal opinion – do German cars exactly lead the world on comfort, something I found out the
day someone gave me a lift in some BMW sports coupe. It
felt like being dragged along the road as every single bump
in the tarmac jolted through my buttocks.

At the moment, the clever thing is to convince your customers that your cars are economical and clean, and German
cars are lagging behind on this. As the global industry began
to tilt towards electric cars, German manufacturers were
caught napping. They were late to bring new vehicles to the
market, with US-based all-electric Teslas becoming the new
darling of better-off UK motorists. Not even the opening of
a Tesla factory in Berlin in 2022, however, has managed to
revive the German car industry. At the cheaper end of the
market, it is Chinese-made cars that are beginning to muscle-
in. Germany – and Europe as a whole – has been throwing
money at the battery industry, and failing. By 2023, 60 per
cent of batteries for European-made electric cars were being
manufactured in South Korea and a further 30 per cent
in China. It is the same with other car parts. Meanwhile,
Germany lost nearly a hundred companies which had been
supplying its motor industry, along with 30,000 jobs.[19] In 2023,
Michelin announced the closure of three German plants.

Remarkably, the failure of the German car industry to

involve itself in the growing market for electric cars happened in spite of Germany's legal target for reaching net zero carbon emissions by 2045. On the one hand, Germany, like the whole of Europe, is trying to set the world an example by committing itself to one of the toughest carbon-reduction targets anywhere in the world. Yet, in reality, it is making little real progress in achieving them.

But surely Tesla must have received a warm welcome after choosing Berlin as the hub of its European operations? At first, the plan seemed to go well. The factory at Grünheide, in the old East Germany, was designed and built in just two and a half years, opening in 2022 and bringing 11,000 jobs to one of the poorest areas of the country. Within two years of opening, however, German environmentalists were trying to run it out of the country, setting up camps in the surrounding woods and throwing paint over the company's Berlin showroom as they protested against traffic and the loss of trees.[20] The factory also suffered an arson attack which took out its electricity supply – an extraordinary act in a country whose population until recently has seemed to take pride in being Europe's industrial powerhouse.[21] Other potential investors in Germany will be taking note: Europe's once economic champion has become a hotbed of Luddism. It wasn't the only European resistance to Tesla, either. In the Netherlands, investigators rounded on the company after a German newspaper received data about company employees which appeared to have been leaked by a company whistleblower. Tesla was accused of not taking sufficient care to protect such data – although surely every company holds data on staff and customers which could be leaked by an insider, if they wanted to. In Sweden, a labour dispute between Tesla and a small group of its engineers erupted into a full-scale picketing operation, with dockworkers refusing to offload the company's cars and postal workers refusing to deliver its post.[22] It all rather fits a growing pattern, as we shall see, where Europe tries to frustrate the activities of large US companies whose success it has been unable to emulate.

Overzealous net zero targets are a large part of the problem in driving industry away from Europe. In spite of claims by the renewable energy lobby that wind and solar are going to save consumers and businesses a fortune, there is scant sign of any benefit so far; rather, energy prices in Europe have raced ahead of those elsewhere in the industrialised world. In 2022, industrial users in the UK were paying 18.55 pence per kWh for their electricity, including taxes. In Germany, it was the equivalent of 16.51 pence, and Italy 25.55 pence. In the US, it was just 7.21 pence, and South Korea 7.73 pence.[23] It certainly isn't 'cheap' renewables that were giving the latter two countries their low-priced energy, because they have markedly lower proportions of their electricity mix made up by renewables than do most European countries. In 2022, the UK generated 41.4 per cent of its power from renewables (which includes biomass), Germany 43.5 per cent and Italy 36.2 per cent. In the US, it was 22.4 per cent and South Korea just 8.7 per cent.[24] Wind and solar might seem cheap on the face of it – or at least they did until a surge in commodity prices and interest rates in 2022. But they have to be backed up either with expensive storage or by gas – which itself becomes much more expensive when used intermittently to balance wind and solar output because it means plant is standing idle a lot of the time. Germany's energy policy in recent years has been based on wind power combined with Russian gas – the supply of the latter going pop after the Ukraine invasion of February 2022. The countries with the cheapest electricity in 2022, by contrast, were those which had high shares of that reliable trio: gas, coal and nuclear. In the US, the heavy lifting was done by gas (39 per cent), coal (19 per cent) and nuclear (18 per cent). In South Korea the corresponding figures were gas (28.5 per cent), coal (34 per cent) and nuclear (28 per cent). In Europe, only France and Finland, with their high shares of nuclear energy, avoided the crunch in energy prices. Germany intensified its own energy crisis by closing down its nuclear industry, with well-functioning power stations closed prematurely in a panic reaction by former Chancellor Angela Merkel to the 2011 Fukushima disaster in Japan. Germany went ahead with the closure of three of its six remaining plants on New Year's Eve 2021, in spite of the fact that Putin's tanks were already amassing on the Ukraine border. Fifteen months later, it closed the remaining three, undeterred by having just limped through a winter of soaring energy prices.

High energy prices in Europe are already having a drastic effect on the fortunes of the industrial sector. In 2022, German chemicals giant BASF announced that it would no longer invest in Europe owing to high energy prices – EU carbon levies being a large part of the problem. Instead, it will build a new £10 billion plant in China, where electricity is cheaper – but 60 per cent of it is generated by burning coal. BASF is also planning to invest €3.7 million in the US by 2027, expanding petrochemical plants in Louisiana and Ohio at the same time as shrinking production capacity in Germany. 'Europe is increasingly suffering from over-regulation, slow and bureaucratic approval procedures and above all high costs for most production factors,' said Michael Heinz, chief executive of the company's North American operation.[25] Germany's emissions aren't so much being cut, they are in effect being offshored to Southeast Asia – and jobs and wealth with them. As Siegfried Russwurm, head of the BDI – which represents German industry – put it in February 2024, Germany's policies for trying to cut carbon emissions are 'more dogmatic than any country I know', with the uncertainty over future energy prices driving manufacturers away.[26]

Is French industry doing any better? In January 2024, the

country's newly appointed prime minister, Gabriel Attal, used one of his first addresses in that role to draw attention to industrial decline in Britain: 'Last week, because of Brexit, the last blast furnaces in Great Britain closed. Steel is no longer produced in the UK. In France, on the contrary, thanks in particular to investment from Europe, industry is coming back.'[27] I don't know what France he was talking about, but not the one depicted in his own government's official statistics which show that French industry has stagnated, with industrial production showing no growth between 2015 and 2022; vehicle manufacturing was down 20 per cent on that period.[28] We think of Britain as a deindustrialised country where manufacturing in 2022 accounted for just 8 per cent of GDP, but it is no less true in France where manufacturing accounted for 10 per cent of GDP, down from 23 per cent in 1960 and 14 per cent in 2000. In fact, this century the UK manufacturing sector has expanded a bit faster than that of France. In 2000, French manufacturing output was a little higher than in the UK: $228 billion compared with $218 billion (at 2015 prices). By 2022, the UK was out-manufacturing France, by $286 billion to $256 billion.[29]

A Ford gearbox factory near Bordeaux, a glassware factory in Orleans, a tyre factory near Bethune; these are just a small selection of the industrial plants closed in France in the past few years. They don't even play at engineering any more in France; the last Meccano factory closed in Calais in 2023. This is all despite the French government's efforts to keep factories open for political reasons. Any company that wants to close a factory in France, or even just amalgamate two small and inefficient factories into one new one, can expect merry hell. But it doesn't help anyone in the longer term; it merely makes things worse by keeping unproductive plants limping along, causing companies needless expense and undermining their long-term future. In 2020, the state-owned car company

Renault was reported to have a production capacity of 1.9 million vehicles a year but was in fact only making 655,000.[30] However, it was struggling to close any of its surplus capacity because its numerous small factories – which had been built in various locations over the decades as job-creation schemes – were strongly defended by unions and local politicians.

Unions, indeed, have quite a lot to do with Europe's economic stupor. It's easy to believe that Britain is strike-bound, with train drivers, doctors and nurses all holding multiple walkouts in 2022 and 2023. True, it often seems as if Britain has returned to the bad old days of the 1970s when poor labour relations became known as the 'British disease'. But things could be worse. Actually, during the decade 2010–19, Britain was one of the least strike-affected European economies, with an average of 17.9 days lost to strikes per 1,000 employees per year. That put it on a par with Germany, often portrayed as a European country with especially good industrial relations. It was far less than Spain (49.1), Belgium (97.7) or France (127.6). It was less even than Norway with its image as a calm and sensible, if sometimes a little dull, place. It is true that British labour relations have deteriorated severely in the past four years with an average of 88.9 days per 1,000 workers per year lost to strikes between 2020 and 2022 – mostly on the back of long-running disputes in the rail industry and the NHS. That puts Britain among the worst countries in Europe, though still not nearly as bad as Belgium (163.9).[31] But the tendency to down tools should really now be known as the Finnish disease – given that a shocking 433 days per 1,000 workers per year were lost to strikes in 2020–22. The Scandinavian model of social democracy has collapsed in Finland, which has entered its own permafrost of discontent. In one week in February 2024, 300,000 workers were estimated to have walked out on strike, paralysing public transport, air traffic control, nurseries, shops and hospitality, chemicals works and – especially worryingly – nuclear power stations. Nearly all trains were stopped and many supermarkets closed, with one exception: Alko, the Finnish government's monopoly on alcohol sales was open as usual, which in a way made the whole business seem even more hopeless. All you could do in strike-bound Finland was drink yourself blotto. The striking workers were reacting to economic reforms which would see benefits reduced and the right to collective bargaining subjected to greater control.[32]

European workers do love not to work. German employees lead the developed world for the number of days they take off for sick leave – an average of 19.9 in 2019, even before the Covid-19 pandemic had a chance to impact the figures. Among OECD (Organisation for Economic Co-operation and Development) countries, only Mexico, on 30, was higher. The Czechs, on 17.2, and Slovaks, on 16.9, were not far behind the Germans. In Britain, the corresponding figure was 4.6, and in the US 6.[33] Germany's work absence problem was little better by 2024, when an average of 19.4 days were lost per worker, adding up to a total of 158 million working days. According to pharmaceutical group VFA, sickness absence is costing the German economy €26 billion per year, taking 0.8 per cent off GDP. In other words, had German workers managed to go to work just for half the days they lost to sickness absence in 2023 the economy might have grown rather than shrank.[34] It is not a great compliment to Germany's healthcare system – of which more later – if workers are needing to take a day off work nearly every other week.

Even when they do turn up, German workers have the shortest working hours of any OECD country, averaging 1,341 hours a year in 2022. It is France, with its official 35-hour working week, which has the reputation for long lunches and knocking off early, but its workers are relatively industrious compared with the Germans, working an average of 1,511 hours per year. Among others at the low end are Denmark, on 1,372 hours, the Netherlands, on 1,427, and the Swedes, on 1,440. The average worker in the UK manages 1,532. It is a step up before you get to the world's fastest-growing developed countries: the average US worker puts in 1,811 hours and the average South Korean worker 1,901.[35] The OECD average is 1,752. It isn't just the overall lack of working hours that marks out Germany but the speed at which they are falling – the average employee worked 67 fewer hours in 2022 than they did in 2012. That is two whole working weeks which seem to have gone missing. It is little wonder that economic growth is so sluggish. The German workforce claims a high rate of productivity per hour, but there is only so much you can get done if you are knocking off after thirty hours a week.

We rightly decry the failure of infrastructure projects in Britain, which invariably seem to get delayed for years and escalate in price multiple times. But are things really much different in the EU? When Tony Blair's government decided to revive nuclear power in Britain, a decade after the last new plant, Sizewell B, went online, French state energy company EDF seemed a good bet to build a new plant at Hinkley in Somerset. Britain, in typical fashion, had squandered a pioneering role in nuclear power. The world's first nuclear energy plant opened at Calder Hall, Cumbria, in 1956 – yet, by the 2000s, no more plants were being built and the country's expertise in the field had dissipated. Unlike Britain, France had stuck with nuclear power throughout the 1970s when the technology generated large environmental protests, and carried on with it in spite of the Chernobyl accident in 1986. EDF seemed keen to help out. In 2007, the company's then chief executive promised that Britons would be dining on turkey cooked with nuclear power from Hinkley C at Christmas in 2017. Another company involved in the design, Areva, declared that Hinkley would be able to generate electricity at just £24 per megawatt hour, about half of the then market rate for electricity.

Yet, by 2013, before EDF had even committed to the project, the UK government was having to offer four times as much – in that year EDF agreed to a 'strike price' of £92.50 per megawatt hour, rising with inflation and guaranteed for thirty-five years. By 2017, work had at least started, but there wasn't much more than a hole in the ground – and Hinkley C was itself beginning to look like the turkey. EDF was struggling to complete two other plants of the same novel design, called a European Pressurised Reactor (EPR). The one at Olkiluoto, Finland, was supposed to open in 2009 but finally started generating electricity only in 2023. Flamanville, in Normandy, was supposed to be open by 2013 but as of 2024 was still not generating power. Weaknesses in the steels and welds had held up the project for years, sending costs soaring from €3.3 billion to €19.1 billion.[36] As for Hinkley C, in January 2024 its completion date was put back to 2031 and its estimated costs had risen to £46 billion.[37] Meanwhile, China has managed to build two EPRs at Taishan, in the south of country, the first of which took ten years to construct before it opened in 2018. True, you wouldn't want a nuclear power station where every last engineering detail has not been checked over many times, and safety must be the first priority, even if it means long delays. But that doesn't explain why it is taking twenty-five years to get a nuclear power station from the planning stage to completion. Nuclear power forms a large part of the plans of European governments to reach net zero by 2050, but it is not going to make much of a contribution if power stations conceived today are not going to be up and running by that date, which is of course now itself only twenty-five years away.

It is not just bungling, though, that explains why the European economy is falling behind the US and Asia. There has been a fundamental loss of ambition, a failure to explore new technologies and novel ways of doing things. Europe just isn't innovating nearly so much as are the US and, increasingly, China and Southeast Asia. In 2022, according to an assessment by the European Commission of spending by the world's largest 2,500 companies, the EU accounted for 17.5 per cent of the world's £1.25 trillion spending on research and development, down from 23.4 per cent in 2012. The US's share was up a little from 40.1 per cent to 42.1 per cent over that period, while China's share had surged from 4.3 per cent to 17.7 per cent. South Korea invests more than any European country apart from Germany. Even after three decades of relative decline, Japan still invests more than Germany.[38]

Another measure of the liveliness of an economy is the number of mergers and acquisitions in the markets – a sign that ideas generated by business startups are translating into growth. In January 2024, for example, there were $227 billion worth of mergers and acquisitions globally – $177 billion worth of which were in the US and only $18.2 billion worth of which were in Europe.[39] Or we can judge economic vitality via the number and value of initial public offerings (IPOs) – new companies launched on the stock market. London has been a big loser in recent years. In 2023, no European stock exchange featured in the top ten for IPOs, either for the number undertaken nor the total amount of money raised. Tokyo, Saudi Arabia, Indonesia, South Korea and Turkey all had more companies launching on their stock exchanges than any European country. In total, European exchanges raised $13.0 billion in IPOs in 2023, behind the US ($22.3 billion) and Asia/Pacific ($69.4 billion).[40]

Come Brexit, and several EU countries started to eye up London's financial business. Paris, Frankfurt, Amsterdam; all had designs on London's position as Europe's financial capital. In terms of stock markets, at least, London has certainly fallen back in recent years. But there is little sign of any other European financial centre stealing its mantle – on the contrary, the whole continent is beginning to look like a financial backwater.

Where are the European tech giants to rival Microsoft, Apple, Google? They don't exist – unless you count the French data services company Atos, whose shares collapsed by over 90 per cent before it proposed, and then withdrew, an emergency fundraising share issue in February 2024. Or there was Wirecard, the German fintech company which collapsed spectacularly in 2020 after irregularities were found in its accounts. Britain's biggest claim to a tech superstar is the chipmaker Arm Holdings. Except, that is, it is no longer listed on the London Stock Exchange. In 2016, it was bought by Japanese Softbank for $26 billion. Softbank put it back on the market in 2023, though chose to float it not in London but in New York, on the NASDAQ exchange. By the end of its first day trading, Arm Holdings was worth $60 billion,[41] and within five months its value had doubled as US markets surged ahead of the stagnant UK market.

In the list of the world's largest companies by market capitalisation in January 2024, the highest European company came in fifteenth – that was Danish pharmaceutical company Novo Nordisk, whose weight-loss drug Wegovy has proved a huge hit with the world's healthcare systems. There were just four European countries in the top thirty, nine in the top fifty and seventeen in the top hundred. For a continent which has aspirations to become the world's leading economy, that is a sign that things are going very wrong.

2.

Regulating to Death

For some people the EU will forever be associated with a directive banning straight or unusually bendy bananas. For some, it epitomises the pettiness of Brussels' mad officials; for others it is symptom of the anti-EU brigade's shameless capacity for malicious invention. 'A Brussels ban on bendy bananas is one of the EU's most persistent myths,' declared Jon Henley in the *Guardian*, for example, a month before polling day in the 2016 referendum. Except it isn't. Indeed, a more persistent myth is that the directive on bendy bananas was a myth. It was called EC 2257/94, passed on 16 September 1994, and quite clearly states that all classes of banana – I, II and 'extra' – must obey a set of minimum standards including that the fruits must be 'free from malformation or abnormal curvature of the fingers'.

The ban on overbendy bananas is, thankfully, long gone – the European Commission repealed it in 2008 after fears that it was leading to too many bananas being thrown away. But that was not, needless to say, the end of EU over-regulation. On the contrary, the bloc's desire to control every aspect of commerce, to be driven by precaution rather than opportunity, remains undimmed – and in far more serious ways than laying down standards outlining which bananas were allowed to be sold in European shops.

Where America innovates, Europe regulates. America, with an important contribution from Tim Berners-Lee, gave us the internet, Europe the General Data Protection Regulation; the US gave us the smartphone, Europe the Digital Markets Act; the US gave us Google, the EU an antitrust case against the company for paying Apple to make it the default search engine on its devices. It isn't that big tech doesn't need regulating, or that the US isn't sometimes a bit slow at protecting consumers, but it is hard not to wonder whether there is an element of sour grapes in the EU's constant pursual of US tech companies. We didn't manage to get these things going ourselves, so let's try and clip the wings of the companies that did.

While the rest of the world explores and embraces novel technologies, the EU sees them principally as a threat. Nowhere was that clearer than with genetically modified (GM) crops, a technology in which Britain was in a good position to take a lead during the late 1990s. Then came the scare stories about 'Frankenstein foods', including a later discredited study about GM potatoes damaging the immune systems of laboratory rats. Environmental activists pranced around in fields in hazmat suits and destroyed crops. An attempt by the Blair government to take the debate over GM crops to the people via town and village hall meetings ran into hostility from a public that had been fed little but scare stories. Green groups lobbied the EU hard for a ban and, in 1999, the EU came up with a typical fudge. It didn't ban the growing of GM crops outright but it made it so difficult to gain regulatory approval that research was driven overseas. Even if a crop was granted approval, its creators would be forced to reapply after ten years. As a result, only one GM crop – a form of maize with inbuilt resistance to the European Corn Borer – ended up being grown in the EU, mainly in Spain. And that only sneaked through because it had been approved slightly ahead of the new rules.

As well as making life all but impossible for companies developing GM technology in Europe, the EU also tried to restrict imports of GM foods – something which the World Trade Organisation (WTO) ruled against in 2006, on the grounds that there was no scientific justification for such bans. In vain did the European Commission's scientific adviser, Professor Anne Glover, try to make the case that the rules against GM could not be justified by the risks. In 2014, Greenpeace and other environmental groups wrote to the president-elect of the commission, Jean-Claude Juncker, expressing their hope 'that you will decide not to nominate a chief scientific adviser'.[1] In other words, we don't just find the current incumbent's advice inconvenient; we would rather you didn't have anyone advising you on science, and that you would listen to us, environmentalist activists, instead. Juncker fell for it, and Glover found herself out in the cold.

Meanwhile, the commission came up with a new way to frustrate the GM industry. Even when a GM crop did manage to leap through the required hoops in order to gain approval to be grown in the EU, individual member states would be allowed to ban it – and indeed all – GM crops being grown in their territories. By the autumn of 2015, half of EU member states had passed outright bans, and the technology was back where it started – in Europe at least.[2]

Here is what Europe is missing as a result of its suppression of GM technology. It is now a global industry worth $22.3 billion in 2023, with North America gaining most, followed by South America.[3] No one has had their immune system suppressed like the fabled rats, but GM technology has, for example, allowed US cotton growers to reduce by 45 per cent the amount of pesticides they need to protect their crops against insects, in turn reducing the run-off that pollutes water courses. Growers of GM maize have managed to decrease pesticide applications by 30 per cent. Cotton-growers in India and China have saved 304 million kilos of insecticides. While GM technology has not been without the inevitable sort of issues that come with any new technology – there were some cases of evolving weed resistance, in the early days, now controlled through better management – GM technology has helped increase yields of corn by 17.7 per cent, cotton by 14.5 per cent and soy bean by 9.3 per cent. Had it not been for the technology, soy bean cultivation would have required an extra 11.6 million hectares of land, corn 8.5 million hectares and cotton 2.8 million hectares. To put that into context, this is as much agricultural land as exists in Vietnam and the Philippines. You might think environmentalists would approve of a technology that has reduced the need for wild land to be turned over to intensive agriculture, but that is not how the minds of European environmentalists seem to work.[4]

Most unforgivably of all, an irrational fear of GM food on the part of EU regulators helped to block the approval and worldwide distribution of golden rice, a variant of the crop genetically engineered to be fortified with vitamin A. Had it been embraced, it could have been saving millions of children in the developing world from vitamin A deficiency – a condition estimated to contribute to the deaths of 2,000 people globally every day, as well as causing blindness in many more. Yet, scientists developing the crop, according to science writer Ed Regis, encountered a 'byzantine web of rules, guidelines, requirements, restrictions and prohibitions'.[5] While this wasn't all the fault of European regulators – it was imposed through a UN-backed protocol signed in Canada in 2003 that established a precautionary principle for novel foods and crops – Europe was a big influence. Golden rice could have been a European achievement – it was first developed by the Swiss Federal Institute of Technology and the University of Freiburg, who published their results in 2000. But, after the EU's virtual block on new GM trials, the research moved to the US, who eventually approved the crop in 2018, followed by the Philippines and Bangladesh.

Europe's refusal to embrace GM hasn't even saved European consumers from eating the dastardly foods – for the past two decades GM soya has been mixed with non-GM soya and sold as a global commodity, not least for the many vegan foods which are based on that crop. So, if eating GM really did make you grow two heads, Europeans would be as affected as anyone. We just haven't been allowed to profit from the technology or enjoy the environmental benefits.

GM technology could have allowed European farmers to reduce pesticide use. Instead, they have been subjected to EU limits on pesticides without adequate alternative means to fight the pests. When farmers protested by blocking the streets of central Brussels with their tractors, in February 2024, the EU ended up dropping its limits for pesticide use – putting the control of pesticides back to square one.

And still the EU is slow to learn the lesson. Genetic engineering has moved on. Gene editing – or New Genomic Techniques (NGTs) as it is alternatively known – offers a much more precise way of altering plant species, directly editing genes to achieve the desired characteristics. The US has had no problem allowing trials, and nor have China, Brazil and several African countries. It is being used, for example, in Kenya to produce sorghum that is resistant to a pest called witchweed, which can devastate the crop. Banana growers in the Philippines are using the technology to produce fruits that stay in good condition for longer (maybe one day they will solve the problem of overbendy bananas, too). But, once again, the EU has been caught out prevaricating, allowing environmentalists to rule the roost. In 2018, the EU Court of Justice ruled that plants produced by NGTs should be subject to the same rules as GM crops – which effectively meant they couldn't be grown or developed in Europe. Three years later, the European Commission began to wonder whether this was really such a good idea, given the rapid progress of the technology elsewhere in the world; it produced a report suggesting that the rules should be relaxed. Even so, it took until January 2024 for the European parliament to debate and vote on it. In the event, they voted narrowly in favour of liberalisation, but at the same time they voted to ban the patenting of crops produced in this manner, which would prevent developers of the technology profiting from it – a move certain to deter private investment. Scientists shouldn't hold their breath for the technology ever to take off in the EU. There is strong lobbying against NGTs from environmental groups and vested interests that threaten to strangle the liberalisation efforts. But at least in this case, the UK – or rather England– has managed to deviate from EU regulation and allowed the technology to be tested.

That doesn't mean, however, that a British industry for gene editing is yet sailing ahead of Europe's. In spite of the government passing a Genetic Technology (Precision Breeding) Bill, which became law in early 2023, businesses working in this field were still complaining that regulators were throttling the business a year later. One, Hoxton Farms, trying to manufacture laboratory meat in an east London warehouse, was still waiting for approval for its product from the Food Standards Agency (FSA) and was thinking of moving to the US to take advantage of swifter regulatory approval there. Other companies were still waiting, too. In three years, the FSA had managed to approve just sixty-three out of 450 applications for novel foods. A further 1,500 applications were stuck in a queue while the regulator sought further information.

In other words, an industry that had been singled out by the UK government for post-Brexit opportunities was still being thwarted by regulators, only this time British ones rather than EU ones.[6]

Having deprived itself of a GM industry, Europe went on to repeat the folly with shale gas. In 2010, Europe seemed to be on the cusp of following the US in developing an industry based on the horizontal fracturing – or 'fracking' – of shale rock to release reserves of natural gas. France, Poland, the Netherlands and the UK were all found to have large potential reserves. But then came the scare stories. Fracking, it was claimed, would cause earthquakes and pollute water supplies. A US documentary film, *Gasland*, purported to show a man lighting gas coming from his kitchen tap, the inference that it had got there because of fracking – a claim later debunked by an engineering professor who noted that the shale gas was separated from the water supply by thousands of feet of impenetrable rock, but that gas was known to leak naturally from coal deposits much closer to the surface.[7] Yet campaigns by green groups succeeded in persuading France and Germany to ban fracking in 2011. While the UK never imposed a complete ban, it effectively strangled the nascent industry by passing, in 2012, a regulation demanding that companies must stop drilling if they trigger a tremor which measures 0.5 on the Richter scale – a size of tremor that occurs naturally many hundreds of times a year in the UK and is neither capable of causing damage to buildings nor felt by human beings on the earth's surface. Efforts to get a UK industry going dragged on for several years until the government imposed a moratorium in 2019, by which time environmentalists were opposing any new fossil fuel development.

As with GM foods, there has been a price to pay for failing to develop a fracking industry. It has become fashionable among environmentalists to argue that shale gas produced in

Britain would never help to secure national energy security or reduce prices in Britain, because gas is an international commodity and so it will just be sold on global markets. It is an erroneous argument because European production would take power away from OPEC, the cartel of Middle Eastern oil producers. Small adjustments in how much oil OPEC countries are prepared to pump onto global markets can have a large effect on prices; the more European and American production, the less influence OPEC has on prices.

Just look at what the shale gas industry has done for US energy security and affordability. When global gas prices surged after the Russian invasion of Ukraine in 2022, the US was not immune. Wholesale gas prices rose to just over $100 per megawatt hour, roughly twice the average price of the preceding few years. But it was affected a good deal less than Europe. Wholesale prices in Europe peaked at over $400 per megawatt hour as European countries desperately tried to fill their reserves before winter.[8] A European shale gas industry could have avoided much of that.

As with GM foods, Europe may not produce shale gas, but it certainly consumes it. In 2022, following the loss of Russian gas, 34 per cent of Europe's gas was imported in the form of Liquified Natural Gas (LNG), much of it shale gas from the US.[9] That represents a huge loss of economic opportunity for Europe, but not only that, it also undermines Europe's claims to be leading the world on cutting carbon emissions. Importing gas in the form of LNG rather than producing gas locally is increasing global emissions, because around 10 per cent of the energy in natural gas is lost in the liquification and regassification process.

There has never quite been an EU-wide ban on fracking; in this case it was left to member states to decide. Nor is it true that there was no European effort to exploit shale gas: a lot of exploratory work was done in Poland, with disappointing results. But the short story of European fracking speaks of a general attitude which permeates the EU: that of the precautionary principle, where new innovations are not allowed to be put into practice until they can be proven to be safe. But if something is not allowed to happen then that can never be the case. One has to wonder whether anything novel would ever be allowed to be unleashed on Europe were it not first possible to test it in the living laboratory of ideas that is the United States.

Yet, even when ideas have been tested in the United States, it is often still not enough for the EU, which is seeking things to regulate at an ever increasing pace. What it did with GM foods the EU is now in danger of repeating with the emerging technology of the moment, artificial intelligence (AI). The EU has great plans. It even has a target: it wants 75 per cent of small and medium enterprises (SMEs) to be using AI by 2030 – a decision that might perhaps be better left to the businesses themselves rather than the EU's planners. But already the EU looks like harming innovation through its new AI Act.

The act proposes a tiered structure of regulations, from light rules on everyday things such as spam filters to outright bans on some applications. Providers of online services will be forced to inform users when they are communicating with a chatbot. They will have to tell people when they are looking at deepfake images. Creators of chatbots will be obliged to keep records of what data their bots are building, supposedly so that the creators of that content can be compensated. Some of these regulations are sensible, especially where the use of deepfakes is concerned. Others are harmless but pointless – is anyone really fooled that the chatbot with whom they are engaging is a human? And some of these rules threaten to destroy innovation. While there is a genuine issue of intellectual property when a chatbot might be inclined to rip-off an author or an artist's work, it is hard to see how see how the mass compensation of 'content creators' is going to function in practice. A dataset used to create a large language model, for example, will use many millions of words from the internet, from a vast number of different documents. If everyone who put the words there is going to have to be paid, it will make AI impractical. There are also some demands that appear to have little to do with the issue of AI itself but have ulterior purposes, such as environmental aims. Creators of AI models, for example, will have to provide data on how much energy they are consuming. That has nothing to do with online safety but is just an environmental objective tacked on. It is the sort of pettifogging regulation that favours large businesses selling high volumes of products or services, but is injurious to smaller businesses.

The act seeks to outlaw all use of biometric surveillance such as facial recognition in public places, as well as 'predictive policing' – where someone's behaviour is analysed by AI to judge what they might be about to do next. True, there are many possible dystopian uses for AI – such as the 'Minority Report' scenario – but it took the intervention of police forces to point out that it actually might be useful to have cameras that are able to scan large areas for terror suspects, or which are able to pick out the faces of children who have been abducted. On this, a sensible compromise was eventually reached, where police and security agencies can apply for a court order to use AI biometric surveillance so long as it is limited to a short list of the most severe offences. The use of AI for 'social scoring' will be prohibited. We might not like the idea of a Chinese-style social credit system, but then again it is not hard to conceive how European credit agencies, with legitimate need to try to predict whether customers are going to be able to repay loans or not might be trapped in the legislation.

The act also seeks to ban the use of 'emotional recognition'

in public places, workplaces and in schools. True, it is not
hard to imagine how this might be misused – you wouldn't
want your employer to sound an alert when your facial expression indicates you are running low on enthusiasm. There
are plenty of applications of such technology which ought
to be banned. But again, an all-out ban seems to preclude
innovations that might turn out to have public support. It is
not hard to see where such technology might add to human
happiness – were it able, for example, to detect when someone
is about to embark on a suicide attempt.

While it is the big, dystopian uses for AI that capture all the
attention, it is the regulation of the humdrum side of AI which
is causing special concern among businesses in Europe. AI
relies on 'foundation models' which are then applied to a great
number of different uses – which could be anything from an
autocratic government trying to identify possible dissenters,
to a clothing company wanting to set up a system to predict
how many pairs of boxer shorts will need to be supplied to a
particular warehouse. Anyone who develops these generalised models in Europe will, in future, be subject to all kinds
of transparency rules, and will have to satisfy regulators that
they won't be able to be used for illegal purposes – which
seems somewhat difficult in the case of a generalised model.
True, we might not like the sound of governments using AI
to control the population, but if you have to jump through
regulatory hoops to build the foundation model then you are
making innovation difficult for the clothing company, too.
Indeed, you are likely to drive the developer of the foundation
model to an environment – say the US – where they will feel
the breath of regulators down their neck rather less. The scale
of the penalties laid down by the AI Act – ranging from 1.5
per cent to 7 per cent of global turnover – makes the EU look
an especially hazardous place to build an AI business.

The words of Commissioner Thierry Breton, the day after

the European Commission agreed the rules in December 2023, say a lot about the way the EU does things. The act, he said, is 'much more than a rulebook. It's a launchpad for EU start-ups and researchers to lead the global AI race.' The EU really does seem to see regulation as the great wellspring from which all wealth flows. You might argue that regulation of AI is needed to protect the public, that it helps to create a healthy commercial environment that is in everyone's best interests in the long run. But a launchpad for an enormous boom in creativity and enterprise?

That is not quite how European industry sees it. In June 2023, 150 European countries wrote to the European Commission to express their concern over the AI Act, warning that it threatened to 'jeopardise Europe's competitiveness and technological sovereignty'.[10] The signatories included some of Europe's largest companies, such as Airbus, Siemens, Renault and Heineken – whom I guess are looking to use AI in order to improve maintenance and distribution rather than as part of some sinister campaign to control the population. But it is the small businesses – the start-ups which you hope might grow into the big beasts of tomorrow – who face the biggest proportional compliance costs. The SMEs, whom the EU says it wants to embrace AI, are far from impressed. While you are trying to please the regulators, suggested Martin Ragan, CEO of cyber security company, Cequence, 'someone in the US can come up with the same idea, or copy it, get it into the market much faster and blow you out of the water. You could lose your entire business.'[11]

The EU isn't going to stop with AI. In January 2024, the European Commission proposed new regulations that would examine – and limit – foreign direct investment in many areas of technology, including quantum technology, cloud computing, robotics, drones, virtual reality and space surveillance. All member states would be obliged to report foreign investment in these areas and give the European Commission chance to object to it.[12] Some aspects, which are part of the EU's security strategy, might well be sensible – you wouldn't want Chinese companies buying up European defence companies, for example. But given the EU's record, it is not hard to guess where this is going – it will be used to try to suppress commercial threats to European vested interests.

Then there is the Digital Markets Act that came into force in 2023, which prevents online platforms tracking users for the purpose of advertising without their consent. It stops search engines advertising their own services with a higher ranking than services offered by third parties. It gives business users the right to access data generated through their use of online platforms. Clearly, some of these applications are creepy – I recoil from the idea of any organisation physically tracking me around the country. But dig a little deeper and you realise what the Digital Markets Act could exclude – and why it is not all in the consumer's interest. The reason we enjoy free social media sites, for example, is that our data is being used for advertising and marketing purposes – most of it harmless. Do consumers really want to give that up? Another interpretation is that EU regulators are jealous of US tech giants, which have built themselves up on the back of such a business model. The EU is quite happy for member states to use creepy technology to pursue motorists across borders for things such as minor traffic violations; indeed, it promotes it. Yet it comes down heavy on commercial organisations who just want to point us in the direction of a coffee shop. The fines for transgressions are eyewatering: up to 10 per cent of global turnover, or 20 per cent for repeated offences. The EU is very good at taking the consumer's side on anti-competitive practices by tech giants. But then some tech companies may wonder whether they want to take the risk of offering services to European users – just as they did after the General Data Protection Regulation.

Given the number of times that freedom from over-regulation was cited by the Brexit campaign, it would be easy to imagine that Britain had seized its new-found freedom and had rapidly deregulated. But this is very far from the case. In 2022, the government introduced a bill, the Retained EU Law (Revocation and Reform) Bill, that would have automatically removed 2,417 pieces of EU-derived legislation from the statute book by the end of 2023. It then found another 2,000 pieces of legislation that it intended to be repealed. The bill soon ran into opposition, however, including from many of the people it was supposed to help – some of the loudest opponents of the mass repeal were businesses who had got used to working with the legislation and rather liked it. Not for the first time, a government promising a 'bonfire of red tape' to help business discovered that pernickety rules and regulations tend to be quite popular among large businesses because, while they might make their lives a bit more difficult, they make life a lot more difficult for smaller competitors.

In the end, the list to be abolished was reduced to 587 regulations – with all the others remaining on the statute book indefinitely, or until they were specifically repealed. That still sounds like a lot of rules to be torn up – a 'significant removal of EU laws from our statute book' in the words of Business Secretary Kemi Badenoch.[13] So, did it herald a new dawn of light-touch regulation? Hardly. Most of the condemned laws were long-forgotten, redundant regulations, many of which had been initially passed to solve some temporary problems but had then lain on the statute book for want of a mechanism to remove them. Six of them, for example, had been passed to extend the maximum working hours that tractor drivers were allowed to complete in a single shift during the foot and mouth crisis. Not only had these regulations effectively expired along with foot and mouth but they were, in any case, a form of deregulation – their role was temporarily to relax a regulation which remains in place.

Other regulations which were snuffed out by the UK government in 2023 included several that had been passed to enact a protection scheme for salt marshes which had ended in 1999; a series of regulations regarding the safety of meat which had been superseded by newer legislation; and regulations to hand out penalties to businesses caught breaking a sanctions regime against Indonesia which had ended over twenty years earlier. It says a lot about the EU that hundreds of obsolete regulations were allowed to moulder on statute books for years after they ceased to be relevant. The EU is like the house of a hoarder who hasn't thrown anything away in fifty years, and where the kitchen drawers are stuffed with receipts for everything purchased in that time. But no, the UK has not so far acted to free itself from the EU's precautionary principle. On the contrary, it has continued to extend regulation in all manner of areas with homegrown laws, such as an act to force employers to offer employees more predictable terms and conditions, an Online Safety Act to force social media firms and other online services to remove harmful content from their platforms – the definition of 'harmful' being so vague that it could be used to justify virtually anything which upsets anyone anywhere, with the result it could seriously harm the right to free speech. There have been windfall taxes on oil and gas producers, a new infrastructure levy which piles yet more costs on housebuilders and a requirement for owners of holiday lets to seek planning permission, which threatens to drain some of the lifeblood of the tourism industry.

In employment law, the UK seems to be choosing to enact EU directives even when it doesn't need to. In July 2023, the UK parliament passed the Flexible Working Bill, which will oblige employers across Britain to consider requests from their workers to offer them working hours which fit their needs. Employees will be able to make two requests a year and employers must consult with them before they reject such requests. 'A happier workforce means increased productivity,' said a hopeful Kevin Hollinrake, the minister responsible for the legislation, as he thanked the opposition Labour MP who had campaigned for such a law. I say 'hopeful' because according to the Office of National Statistics (ONS) productivity in Britain's public services grew by a feeble 0.2 per cent between 1997 and 2019, in spite of a slew of employment regulations passed in the interim. It has since nosedived, failing to recover from the pandemic, so that by 2022 the average worker was actually producing less than they had been a quarter of a century earlier – even though considerable labour-saving technology has become available in the intervening years.[14]

Remarkably, the UK law mirrors the flexible working measures laid down in the EU Work-Life Balance Directive, which was passed in 2019 when Britain was already halfway out of the EU's door and its leaders were telling voters that the country was heading for a glorious, freer and less regulated future as an independent state. So, what was all that fuss and aggravation about then if, in leaving the EU, Britain just goes and does the same things anyway?

Employment law is one of the EU's greatest boasts. If you want job security and agreeable working conditions, Europe would seem like the ideal place to be. Since the social chapter of the Maastricht Treaty first began to constitute EU-wide employment law in the mid-1990s, there have been a bewildering set of directives aimed at improving the working lives of Europe's employees and protecting them from losing their jobs. There is a Transparent and Predictable Working Conditions Directive, which obliges employers to give employees good advance warning of their shifts and to give consideration to requests by staff for more predictable working hours. There is a Pay Transparency Directive, which imposes on employers the duty of producing audits of equal pay between men and women, and obliges them to consult workers' representatives about what to do if there is a gap. There is a Works Council Directive, which demands that companies consult with workers' representatives if they want to make workers redundant or close a plant altogether. An Acquired Rights Directive demands that where one company takes over another, the workers in the company which is being acquired continue to enjoy the same employment rights as they did previously, making it difficult for companies to reorganise after a takeover. The next initiative is a Platform Workers' Directive to lay down rights for anyone who works via a digital platform, such as taxi and delivery drivers. And, to cap it all, there is a Whistleblowers' Directive, which protects the employment rights of workers who report a company for breaking any EU regulation.

In addition to these, many member states have chosen to pass employment laws of their own. If you want to terminate an employee's contract of employment in the Netherlands, you must first ask permission from the director of the regional labour office. In France, it is a criminal offence to fail to inform, and to consult with, the workers' council before a company reorganisation. In Belgium, there is a 'right to disconnect' law, which limits how and when employers can contact their employees outside working hours. The Netherlands has drafted a 'work where you want' law, which would give workers the right to demand the ability to be able work from home – and employers the duty of listening to them, even if it is a nonsense request. It is not easy to weld an oil platform from your spare bedroom, and it would probably be better for airline passengers if their pilot was in the cockpit rather than at home.

The contrasts between European employment law and that in the US are stark. The US does have its rules. It had a national minimum wage since long before Britain introduced one – although it hasn't been increased from $7.25 (£5.70) since 2009. The US minimum wage isn't universal, either – waiters, or other jobs where staff can expect tips, can be paid as little as $2.13 an hour. Individual states do, though, have their own minimum wages. As in Europe, the US has federal and state laws to prohibit discrimination on the grounds of race, gender, religion and trade union membership. Companies in California with more than a hundred employees must produce statistics on pay broken down by race, ethnicity and gender. In New York, you can't refuse to hire someone purely on account of their physical size, which is probably just as well judging by the people you see going in and out of US fast food restaurants, and it is unlawful to use artificial intelligence to help you in making decisions over who to hire unless you have first conducted an audit into bias. Illinois grants employees the right to forty hours paid leave a year for personal matters. And so on.

Yet US workers have few rights to holidays, save in California, where employers must grant workers one day off a week, unless circumstances dictate otherwise. Where the biggest difference lies, though, is regarding rules relating to redundancy and reorganisation. Not for US firms the business of having to sit down with a workers' council to discuss whether that factory in Pittsburgh is really going to be necessary in future. Companies with more than a hundred employees must give sixty days' notice of a plant closing or of a mass reduction in staff. Otherwise, that is about it. In the US, firms can hire and fire as they see fit, so long as it is on economic grounds rather than because they don't like someone's face. Employment is 'at will'. There is no requirement for written contracts. If your employer decides that your job no longer fits with its business strategy, that is it – you are out of the door.

It is easy, from the European perspective, to portray US workplaces as a Dickensian nightmare – where jobs are ill paid and can be taken away at whim. European employment laws unquestionably do provide workers with a degree of certainty and security, and offer some protection against exploitation – although not to the extent that they have eradicated modern slavery, the existence of which continues to bubble to the surface. What good were fussy EU employment laws for the 400 Poles who were found in 2019 to have been exploited by a Polish gang in the West Midlands, and who were forced to work sorting rubbish or plucking turkeys for £20 a week while living in rat-infested houses? One man was stripped, doused in iodine and threatened that his kidneys would be cut out if he complained. Eight gangmasters were later jailed.[15]

Even where EU employment laws have saved jobs, though, it does not necessarily mean that those laws are working to the employees' overall advantage. The difference between European and US labour law can be summed up by what happened when the Covid-19 pandemic struck in 2020. Many US workers immediately found themselves thrown out of work. The unemployment rate quickly shot up from 3.5 per cent to 14.7 per cent, in April 2020. In the euro area, by contrast, unemployment never went higher than 8.6 per cent, which it reached in August 2020. Workers might not have been working, but furlough kept them on payrolls, helping to feed them and pay their mortgages. In the US, there was far less security against instant redundancy, however, the redundancies were quickly followed by an explosion in new job creation. By August 2020, the US unemployment figure had already fallen back below that of the euro area. By February 2022, it was down to 3.8 per cent and, by July 2023, it was down to 3.5 per cent – where it had started on the eve of the pandemic, in January 2020. In the euro area unemployment in July 2023 was still up at 6.5 per cent.[16]

The US has become an unparalleled job-creating machine. In the month of January 2024 alone, the Bureau of Labor Statistics reported that 353,000 jobs had been created. By that time, US unemployment had been below 4 per cent for twenty-four whole months – the first time that had happened since 1967.[17] Meanwhile, in many European countries, jobs remained elusive. In Spain, the unemployment rate was 11.6 per cent, and in Greece it was 10.8 per cent, Italy 7.6 per cent and France 7.4 per cent. Europe has become a continent in which, for those in work, life can be sweet, but where joining the ranks of the employed can be frustrating. It isn't just getting a job in the first place that is made more difficult by the reams of employment law; it is changing careers, too. The flipside of greater job security is a greater risk of being caught in a career that you find unfulfilling, and poorly paid.

Why is it so much harder to find a job in the eurozone than in the US? Because when it is easy to fire people, it is easy to hire them, too. Employers can effortlessly take on staff because they know, should the economic winds change, they will be able to discharge them equally quickly. Bosses are not going to be stuck in meetings with their workers' council while the creditors gather at the boardroom door. In the US, it is easier to take over other businesses, or to reorganise a company's operations. It is small wonder, then, that the US has become a far more dynamic economy with a growing gulf between its growth rate and that of Europe. Europe's burgeoning workplace legislation has coincided with a period of stagnating productivity and growth. Yet far too few people even want to consider whether there might be a causal connection between the two.

Britain is, at least, a little removed from the eurozone.

Relative to the rest of Europe, its labour market is freer. That is one reason, indeed, why it has become a magnet for migrants seeking to work their way to better lives. The free movement of labour – a cherished principle of the EU which eventually helped to prise Britain out of the bloc – tended to work more in one direction than the other: far more citizens of other EU countries took advantage of the freedom to come to look for work in Britain than Britons sought work elsewhere in the EU. Britain attracted workers from all over the EU, not just from Eastern Europe. While it was migrant workers from Eastern Europe who tended to grab the headlines, in the last quarter of 2019 (just before we left the EU) 1.03 million of the 2.44 million EU nationals working in Britain were from the fourteen countries of Western Europe, plus Scandinavia and Greece.[18] Some were drawn here by lousy employment opportunities in their home countries. On a trip to Rome before the Brexit vote, the waiter in a restaurant wanted to know where I was from. When I said England, he asked if I might help him find a job. There was little work in Rome, he complained, other than selling scoops of gelato.

On the subject of free movement of labour, it is worth going back for a minute to those 400 Poles trapped in the West Midlands and working in menial jobs for £20 a week. They are far from alone. The existence of multiple layers of employment regulations, on everything from homeworking to paternity leave to workers' councils, doesn't seem to have prevented Europe from developing a burgeoning industry in modern slavery. According to the campaigning group International Justice Mission, there are 2 million people in Europe who are working in conditions tantamount to slavery, 17,000 of them in the UK – all beneath the noses of the tribunals and agencies that are supposed to be turning Europe into a beacon for workers' rights.[19]

Indeed, the problem seems to be more acute in parts of the

highly regulated EU than it does in the lightly regulated US. According to the Global Slavery Index maintained by the charity Walkfree, Eastern Europe has become a haven for exploitative employers. In Poland, 5.5 in every 1,000 workers are employed in slave-like conditions. In Hungary, it is 6.6, Romania 7.5, Slovakia 7.7 and Bulgaria 8.5.[20] It compares poorly with regulation-light US, where 3.3 out of every 1,000 workers in the US is subject to enslaved working conditions. In the UK it is 1.8 per 1,000, France 2.1 and Germany 0.6. Italy is on a par with the US, with 3.3 workers per 1,000.

Free movement has helped bring modern slavery to Western European countries because it made it much easier for the slave-masters – who tend to be drawn from the same countries as their victims – to operate there. For years, the UK government of Tony Blair promoted the free movement of citizens from the EU's new Eastern European members, arguing that it was helping to boost the economy, without stopping to ask who was coming and in what conditions people were living and working. There was, for example, the case of 'Eva', a teenager from Lithuania, who, back in her home country, was offered a job as a nanny in Wales by a neighbour's friend. When she arrived in Wales, however, the true nature of the job became apparent. 'They brought someone to shave my legs,' she later said. 'And I'm thinking, if I'm going to be a nanny why do I need to shave my legs?' Next day, she was taken to the house where she was supposed to be working, and in place of some young charges to keep an eye on she found a room full of 'girls with stockings, high heels and sexy dresses'. She was made to work as a prostitute seven days a week until, as she put it, her back was black and blue all over. And she was just one of 150 children who were identified by a 2018 report by the Welsh government into sex trafficking.[21]

Twenty-nine Slovakians and Hungarians were found to be

working in a single car wash in Bristol. On arrival in Britain, their passports and other ID were taken from them and they were threatened with violence if they refused to work. Their captors were later jailed for sixteen and nine years respectively.[22] But it wasn't just employment law that seemed to go out of the window when Britain's labour market was opened up to Eastern Europeans; housing and sanitation laws seemed to be bypassed rather easily, too. Net migration to Britain from EU countries jumped from 15,000 in 2003 to 84,000 in 2004, then to 96,000 in 2005, before rising to peak at 282,400 in 2016.[23] If anyone wondered where these extra people were living, given low rates of housebuilding in Britain, accompanied by the high cost of housing, a clue was provided by the spy plane launched by Slough Borough Council in 2013. Thermal imaging equipment identified 6,000 suspicious back-garden sheds, many of them illegally built with basic or no sanitation and found to be crowded with migrant workers.[24] A similar exercise in the west London borough of Hounslow found a further 20,000 illegal and insanitary structures.[25] Migrant workers were also found to be living in makeshift shanty towns on waste ground in Peterborough, Northampton and other towns. The slum clearance programmes of half a century earlier had been reversed.

Britain, like all of Europe, imposes masses of pernickety regulations on employment and everything else; yet alongside them manages to exist a lawless underworld of sex trafficking, slavery and insanitary living conditions. In the fog of regulation which covers everything from bendy bananas to paternity leave, the things that really do need regulating seem to slip through the net.

3.

Not so Keen on Free Trade

Every time I enter a French supermarket I am met with the same puzzle: why, in the heart of a bloc that claims to champion global free trade and which has created a pan-European single market, is it so hard to find a bottle of wine that is not French? The EU may seek to weaken or dismantle national borders, but nationalism is alive and well in the supermarket aisles – whether it is a result of consumer demand or of producer pressure. French farmers, as has already been noted, have a reputation going back decades for getting a little uppity if they feel they are not getting their fair share of the country's food market – to the point of destroying lorry-loads of imported goods of which the disapprove. They are not doing their nation's consumers much of a favour; those who have crumbled and started to buy fruit and vegetables from Spain, Morocco and elsewhere have often found them to be half the price of French products.

In 2022, the polling company YouGov asked inhabitants of eighteen nations whether they agreed with the statement: 'When it comes to buying food I prefer to buy products that have been produced in my own country.' Italy turned out to have the most patriotic shoppers, with 74 per cent of the population answering 'Yes'. They didn't just want EU-produced tomatoes; they had to be grown in Italy. Next was Sweden, on 71 per cent. India (70 per cent) and Australia (69 per cent) came next, followed by France and Spain (both 67 per cent). Ironically, shoppers in Brexit Britain were far more eclectic in their shopping habits than almost anywhere else in Europe, with 54 per cent of them saying they preferred to buy home-grown food.[1]

While the EU boasts about its single market, one of its many agencies seems less enthused. The European Committee of the Regions, which represents local authorities across the EU, has started campaigning for more consumption of local food – in the name of shortening supply chains. The EU's own Farm to Fork Strategy 'seeks to reduce long-distance transportation of food' on the grounds that it will somehow aid 'sustainability' of the food system.[2] Under the strategy, European consumers are invited to measure their 'food miles' – or food kilometres – on the pretext that the distance an item of food has travelled is a proxy for the environmental-friendliness of its production. Yet, it is an extremely poor proxy. Grow food in a heated, local greenhouse and it can easily have a higher carbon footprint than food produced on the other side of the world and transported to Europe by ship. A Bangor University study found that even green beans flown in from Kenya had a lower carbon footprint than those grown in Britain because of the way they were produced.[3] Moreover, for people who live in densely populated urbanised regions it is simply not possible to satisfy their demand for food within their local area – which is why Singapore came bottom of the poll asking people if they would rather stick to local food. According to one estimate, only between 11 and 28 per cent of the world's population could feed themselves entirely on food grown within 100 km (62 miles) of where they live.[4]

Given that the EU seems a little reluctant even to promote the trade of food across national borders within Europe, it is little surprise that it is often less than enthusiastic about global trade. It has thirty-one free trade agreements (FTAs) fully in force and a further forty-five that have been provisionally applied.[5] It is, to be fair, involved in a lot more global trade than is the United States, which has a similar population. Imports to and exports from the EU are equivalent to 106 per cent of GDP; with the US the corresponding figure is just 25 per cent.[6] Yet the EU applies very high punitive tariffs to countries with which it doesn't have trade agreements, especially on agricultural goods. Schlep 100 kg of New Zealand lamb to the EU, for example, and it will cost you €171, plus 12.8 per cent of the value of the consignment. Beef costs even more to export to the EU: €303 per 100kg, plus 12.8 per cent.[7]

Britain's exporters avoid paying these tariffs because of the UK's free trade deal with the EU, negotiated at the dying gasp just before we left the EU's transitional arrangements at the end of 2020. But once we were out, we began to learn rather more about non-tariff barriers, of which the EU is a master. The EU's regulatory requirements impose their own onerous costs. Licensing, certificates, labelling requirements and physical checks are adding 2–5 per cent to the cost of UK plant-based goods exported to the EU, according to the Agriculture and Horticulture Development Board, and 5–8 per cent in the case of animal products. Those are, effectively, pretty hefty tariffs even if they do not officially go by that name.

The word 'pettiness' hardly does justice to the treatment of the lorry driver who arrived by ferry in the Netherlands, in January 2021, to find a customs officer eyeing up his sandwiches. Did they contain meat, he was asked? When he said they did, the officer then demanded he hand them over because they came under the EU's sanitary rules and he didn't have a veterinary certificate. Could he at least keep the bread, he asked? 'No, everything will be confiscated,' came the reply. 'Welcome to Brexit, sir, I'm sorry.'[8] Similar stories became common in the days after Brexit took effect as it became clear that the words 'free trade deal' didn't really mean free trade, just an absence of tariffs. There were still obscure fees to pay, certificates to obtain – even though the UK continued to have the same product standards as the EU. Bill Philpott of Suffolk, who ran a business designing personalised posters, was surprised to be contacted by a customer in the EU who was complaining about being charged €34 in brokerage and sales tax on top of the £80 cost of the poster. Anne Neill, who ran an online womenswear store found her EU customers being charged €100 on orders.[9] Many small-time exporters gave up serving customers in the EU; it simply wasn't worth their while. Larger firms were forced to set up subsidiaries so that they could dispatch goods to EU customers from within the EU.

A cauliflower, Mark Twain once remarked, is 'nothing but a cabbage with a college education'. But it is one with far less impressive paper qualifications than a cabbage exported from Britain to the EU – which will first need a 'certificate of conformity' under the EU's Specific Marketing Standards, as well as a phytosanitary certificate. To qualify for these, you will need to pay for an inspection, which will be charged a minimum of £127.60, or more if it takes an inspector over half an hour to inspect your cabbages, plus £33.56 if a sample needs to be sent off for laboratory analysis. Then the phytosanitary certificate itself costs £25.52. I don't know whether cabbages qualify for student loans.

Such cases have often been presented as a reason why it was foolish for Britain to leave the EU. Yet they are hardly a great advert for the EU. The EU poses as a noble project with high ideals but, in reality, it is a loose association of vested interests which see to it that the high ideals are manipulated in a way that suits them – in many cases this means making the lives of importers so miserable that they give up, and leave the EU market for French farmers. Do we really want to be inside a bloc that erects such high barriers for businesses even when they are supposedly operating within a free trade environment? Non-tariff barriers are especially burdensome for small-time businesses, which are easy to strangle at birth with excessive charges and bureaucracy.

Britain, when it left the EU, could have opted to go down a different route and cut out non-tariff barriers, or at least reduce them to the bare minimum. Imports of animal and vegetable produce to the UK from the EU were at least allowed three years' grace from the need for veterinary and phytosanitary certificates, though they were then imposed from 31 January 2024. Why, when we still have pretty much the same standards as the EU in food and drink? We need to 'level the burden, level the playing field', campaigned the British Poultry Council, so that importers from the EU are treated in the same way as exporters to the EU.[10] In other words, they're punishing us, so let's punish them. But in punishing EU exporters we are also punishing food producers from all around the world, as well as our own consumers. All we are doing is pushing up food prices. We could be going in a different direction, freeing up trade with all countries, but instead we have chosen to emulate the EU.

Brexit allowed us to do our own trade deals, but how is that going? A deal has been done with Australia, which will see trade barriers in agricultural goods lowered over a period of fifteen years. A deal with New Zealand is also underway. Britain has rolled over the trading arrangements it had with non-EU countries by virtue of its membership of the EU and has applied to join the Comprehensive and Progressive Agreement for Trans-Pacific Partnership (CPTPP), a trading bloc of eleven countries on the Pacific Rim. The last initiative raised eyebrows, but why should trading partners be confined within regional boundaries? In any case, it is a pretty long way from Malaysia to Mexico, or from Canada to New Zealand, and so Britain is not so much of a geographical anomaly within the group as it sounds. Yet these developments don't seem to have pleased Britain's own opponents to free trade – many of whom also happen to be Remainers. Those who campaigned against Britain's departure from the EU show a remarkable inconsistency in their attitude towards free trade. When there was a chance that Britain might drop out of the EU without any kind of trade deal, they presented it as a disaster which would impoverish Britain by forcing up prices for consumers and cutting off opportunities for UK exporters. Yet, when the government signed its trade deal with Australia and started discussions towards a deal with the US, the very same people saw this as a disaster, too. Our farmers and our food standards will be undermined, they bleated. It seems that, for some people, free trade is only a good thing – indeed, essential for our prosperity – when it is conducted with the EU. Engage in free trade with anyone else and it is a threat to our economy and health.

While the UK looks to expand trade, the EU is retreating. The success of Chinese car-makers in producing affordable electric cars – something which has eluded European manufacturers – led to the EU in 2024 to propose punitive tariffs of up to 38 per cent. This was in spite of car-maker Stellantis – the parent company of Peugeot-Citroen, Vauxhall and Fiat – saying it didn't want to be protected from Chinese competition, not least because it feared retaliation against its own imports and because it carries out some manufacturing of its own in China.[11] It was back in 1999 that the EU first began to negotiate with a group of South American countries – dominated by Brazil and Argentina – which form the Mercosur trading bloc. The name is a contraction of the Spanish for 'Southern Common Market'. It seemed simple enough: Europe produces a lot of cars and other consumer goods which it would like to sell to South America without paying the stiff tariffs – 35 per cent on cars – which currently apply to imports to Mercosur countries. South America, on the other hand, produces large quantities of agricultural goods which it would like to sell to Europe, again bypassing high tariffs. The deal has indeed been nicknamed 'cars for cows'.

It wasn't until 2019, however, that a deal was finally drawn up. But then EU individual member states, especially France, began to object. Europe couldn't possibly open itself up to cheaper food from South America. So, the EU started to introduce extra demands, notionally based on environmental concerns, fearing it would lead to more deforestation. France refused to support the deal while Jair Bolsonaro was Brazilian president, but when Lula da Silva returned to the presidency in 2023 promising to tackle the issue of deforestation – something on which he had a track record, slowing down the rate of deforestation dramatically during his previous stint as president – France still didn't want to play ball. Following the protests by French farmers in January 2024, the whole thing was kicked into touch. The EU's position seems to be that it wants free trade but only in one direction – it wants to export stuff to South America more freely. That is no basis for a free trade deal.

The environment is increasingly being used by the EU as a device with which to thwart free trade. In October 2023, it began to phase in its Carbon Border Adjustment Mechanism (CBAM) – a tax based on the carbon intensity of imports from outside the EU. Initially, it will apply only to a basket of raw materials: cement, iron, steel, aluminium, fertilisers, electricity and hydrogen. Notionally, it is designed to equalise the tax situation for imports versus domestically produced goods, so that the former do not have any advantage over the latter. Except that it seems to be skewed very much in favour of EU products. Energy UK – a trade body that represents the UK electricity generating industry – has warned that electricity exports from the UK to the EU via undersea cables will be taxed on the assumption that its generation has produced 463 grammes of CO_2 per kWh, a figure that is long out of date, given that the current mix of UK electricity generation emits around 80 grammes of CO_2 per kWh. The result will be that exports of low-carbon wind energy will in effect be taxed at a rate of 40 per cent, making it uneconomic to export power to the EU.[12]

However, this is just the beginning. The intention is to extend the CBAM to manufactured goods, every element of which would have to be assessed for the greenhouse gases emitted in their manufacture. There is a logic to it: given that European industry has to pay carbon levies, the CBAM is supposed to level the playing field. But the consequence is going to be a vast amount of bureaucracy in calculating the emissions, as well as taxes to be paid. Over the years, the EU has worked to eliminate tariffs, only to introduce green levies in their place.

Then there is the EU's ban on imports of palm oil, which is being phased in by 2030. Initially, the EU encouraged imports of palm oil, seeing it as a means by which to decarbonise road transport. But then two things started to happen: firstly, environmentalists began to object to biofuels in general – arguing that they were taking up too much agricultural land, thus pushing up food prices for the world's poor – and to palm oil imports in particular. Secondly, European farmers started to sniff the opportunities for getting into biofuels themselves.

Palm oil, 85 per cent of which comes from Malaysia and Indonesia, was getting in their way.

The environmentalists had a point: if the world is going to try to power vehicles from biofuels it is quickly going to gobble up a lot of arable land. But if you are going to grow biofuels it is far better that it be done using a crop with a very high energy density – like palm oil – rather than the less energy-dense crops like oilseed rape and maize used in the European biofuel industry. According to one estimate, rape seed requires ten times as much land to produce the same quantity of energy as does palm oil.[13] The EU biofuel industry is currently consuming 9.6 million hectares of land, roughly an area the size of Ireland. If this land was allowed to go fallow, according to the environmental pressure group Transport and Environment, it would absorb twice as much carbon dioxide as the biofuels would save in fossil fuel emissions.[14] Moreover, Malaysia and Indonesia have both set up sustainable palm oil certification schemes, to give the EU confidence that palm oil imports are not being grown on recently deforested land. Yet the EU is pushing away palm oil imports, while at the same time being happy to encourage Europe's biofuel industry. Given this, the environmental concerns over palm oil begin to look rather more like a non-tariff trade barrier – a means of protectionism dressed up as something else.

There's more than a whiff of protectionism, too, in the EU's push for a digital tax on things like social media platforms. Although this is currently in abeyance while the OECD investigates the idea, the proposals tabled by the EU in 2018 would levy a 3 per cent tax on digital services provided by companies that have a global revenue in excess of €750 million and EU revenues of €50 million. It is, in other words, pretty well dreamed up to target US tech giants. It is a symptom of the EU's envy of successful US companies – businesses that Europe has been quite unable to create itself.

The EU is not, of course, the only protectionist influence in the world. The US has hardly been exemplary in recent years. First, Donald Trump started a trade war with China and then Joe Biden passed his Inflation Reduction Act – a blatantly protectionist piece of legislation dressed up in green clothes, which showers US businesses and consumers with handouts so long as they buy American-made stuff. Most countries apply high tariffs to protect some industries, most often agriculture. But the EU makes grand claims to be a champion of free trade, and yet is left wanting. It is devious in its use of non-tariff barriers, which it disguises as environmental or health and safety rules. Its efforts to negotiate free trade deals have become very more much complicated and stuffed with ulterior motive. Rather than start small with things on which both sides can agree – the EU should surely have no problem, say, in agreeing to remove all tariffs on bananas as it does not produce significant quantities of them – it spends years, or decades in the case of South America, trying to come up with comprehensive trade and partnership agreements which attempt to bring the other side into the EU's regulatory orbit. It tries to insist that workers in other countries will have the same rights as European ones and that other countries should follow EU environmental law. As Hildegarde Muller, head of the German Automotive Industry Association, puts it: 'We make overly complex agreements and end up harming ourselves because we can't achieve anything in any of the common areas.'[15] While it might suit featherbedded, subsidised-to-the-eyeballs French farmers to have South American beef kept out of European markets, the result is that German car makers continue to have to pay 35 per cent tariffs on vehicles they export to the continent.

The EU has failed, too, to complete the deals with the US and China that it was negotiating in the mid-2010s. It has pulled back on a proposed deal with Mexico, and one with

Australia. The Mercosur is stuck in a quagmire. There is a golden opportunity for Britain to escape this retreat into protectionism and to stand out as a global champion of free trade – if it wants to.

4.

Malfunctioning Currency

New Year's Day, 1999, was a happy day, according to Willem Duisenberg, president of the European Central Bank. Eleven EU countries had just surrendered their own currencies and became part of the euro. 'Monetary Union was a unique and significant achievement,' declared Mr Duisenberg. 'It promises a credible and lasting environment of price stability for almost 300 million people', and will provide 'the foundation for sustainable economic growth, better employment prospects and improvements in the standard of living throughout the Euro area'.[1] Two years later, Greece abandoned the drachma and joined – in spite of objections that 'euro' sounded just a little too much like the Greek word for 'urine'. In 2002, came the physical manifestation of the euro: banknotes with their imaginary bridges. A further eight countries have since joined, taking the total to twenty – though seven countries have so far opted, like Britain did, to keep out of the single currency. Should the EU grow further, however, any new member will be expected to enter the eurozone, too.

But what of Mr Duisenberg's promise of eternal sunshine? Alas, it was not to be. The warnings were there from the beginning. In 2002, for example, Nobel economics laureate Milton Friedman warned of the dangers of subjecting very different economies to a single interest rate. Ireland and Greece, he noted, were experiencing very different economic effects, 'and if each had its own central bank they would be following very different monetary policies', but instead were forced to follow one – that laid down by the Frankfurt-based European Central Bank (ECB). 'I will be surprised if you do not have very serious problems arising in the next five years or so among the 12 countries in the Euro regime.'[2]

He wasn't wrong. Inevitably, the ECB tended to be influenced by economic conditions in the eurozone's largest economy, Germany, which in the early years was still in need of a bit of monetary stimulus as it pulled along the deadweight of the old East Germany. Interest rates, therefore, ended up being kept too low for perkier economies like Ireland, Spain and Greece. Low rates enticed individuals and governments to take on debt, and provoked in these countries what, until 2007, seemed like an economic miracle of over 4 per cent growth a year.

Then the music stopped. It wasn't just Greece: the financial crunch of 2008–9 affected all Western economies, leading to the deepest recession since the 1930s. While the US and Britain were able to recover from 2009 onwards, for Greece and other parts of the eurozone the worst was yet to come. It didn't help that for years Greece had been understating the size of its public debt. When that was restated, increasing debt by 10 per cent, global investors lost confidence, demanding far higher interest rates to lend money to the Greek government. In April 2010, Greek government bonds were relegated to junk status by several ratings agencies, forcing the country close to default. If Greece had still had its own currency, it could at least have followed a crude method of staving off government insolvency: printing money. But, as a member of the euro, that option was no longer available. The government was forced to look instead to the ECB, which agreed to a €110 billion bailout, but with strict conditions. Public spending was to be slashed; the pension age raised. Greece was forced, beyond its control, into austerity measures which caused riots on the streets and fuelled the rise of neo-fascist political parties. Again, if Greece had had a floating currency, it would have devalued, pushing up the price of imports but speeding the recovery of export industries. But, fixed in the straitjacket of the euro, that option was not available. A recession that might have been over in 2009 lasted until 2016.

In Ireland, membership of the euro fuelled a mad property boom that was already underway in 1998. Between 1991 and 2007, wages in Ireland doubled, yet house prices increased by 551 per cent in Dublin and 489 per cent elsewhere. Mortgage debt ballooned from €47.2 billion in 2002 to €139.8 billion in 2007. Many countries experienced a property boom during this period, but nothing like Ireland's. It wasn't just housing, but agricultural land, too. By 2007, the value of land in Ireland had reached €58,000 per hectare, by far the most expensive in Europe and nearly five times the average value in England – all the more remarkable given that much of it is unproductive bog.[3]

Many homeowners thought the boom was great; they thought they were getting richer. The government encouraged the boom, too, despite an increase in demand for social housing as people were priced out of the market. Speculative housing developments spread across the whole country, including in distant rural areas with few facilities and few jobs. The city of Dublin sprawled into the surrounding country, with people, unable to afford to live anywhere near their work, forced to make long commutes by car.

Then came the crunch. Credit dried up and prices crashed. Vast numbers of housing developments ended up abandoned, half-built. By 2010, there were 2,846 unfinished housing estates in Ireland, only 429 of which were still being worked on. By the time the market bottomed out, house prices had fallen by over 50 per cent and land prices by up to 98 per cent in some places. In 2010, with banks on the point of collapse, the ECB arranged an €85 billion bailout.

In Spain, in some ways, the boom sparked by joining the euro was even more pronounced. A dramatic fall in interest rates sparked a borrowing binge by private individuals and local municipalities alike. Great public works were unveiled, while speculative housing developers went into overdrive. Between 2000 and 2008, they put up 800,000 new homes a year – this for a country of 45 million people.[4] Many were bought by foreign buyers – especially from Britain and Germany – looking for a place in the sun. Then, as in Ireland, the crash came. Not only did prices collapse, but it turned out that many homes had been built illegally and were now worthless – with the national government ordering their demolition. As in Ireland, many estates were abandoned, unfinished. The collapse of the construction sector spilled over into a recession from which it took nine years for GDP to return to pre-crisis levels. At the nadir in 2013, the unemployment rate was 27 per cent, higher than anywhere in Europe. As in Greece, government bonds were downgraded and the ECB had to arrange a €100 billion bailout.

What marked out Spain from Greece and Ireland was that it was no minnow; this was the eurozone's fourth largest economy. Yet, even so, the need for monetary tightening between 2000 and 2007 did not seem to feature on the ECB's radar in distant Frankfurt. The same was true of Italy, the eurozone's third largest economy, which also suffered a sovereign debt crisis in 2011 – with high levels of borrowing exacerbated by a poor rate of tax collection. While Italy survived without an ECB bailout, the economic devastation that followed the boom years has been even more profound than in other eurozone countries. GDP has still not returned to the high of $2.41 trillion it reached in 2008. In 2022, output was $2.05 trillion.[5]

What has happened to prevent a repeat of the economic cataclysm that came after the prosperity of the early euro years? A bailout process has been formalised under the European Stabilisation Mechanism. A fiscal compact has attempted to encourage euro member states to behave and not over-borrow – with, in theory, penalties for those who transgress. It stipulates that governments should balance their budgets over the medium term, that they should not run a budget deficit of more than 3 per cent nor have accumulated debt exceeding 60 per cent of GDP. But the latter two requirements were already supposed to be conditions of joining the euro. How are eurozone countries coming along at sticking to the rules? In the second quarter of 2023, six out of twenty eurozone countries were listed by Eurostat – the European Union's statistics agency – as running a deficit of greater than 3 per cent of GDP. No figures, however, were given for Greece, Italy or Cyprus on the grounds that the information was 'confidential'. Hmm. As for accumulated debt, in 2022, twelve out of twenty eurozone member states were in breach of the 60 per cent threshold. Greece still has debt in excess of 150 per cent of GDP and Italy is very nearly at that level. Remarkably, it is the EU's non-eurozone countries that are the better fiscally behaved: six out of seven of those have debt lower than 60 per cent of GDP.[6]

Britain can hardly preach on financial responsibility; with debt of 101.2 per cent of GDP and a deficit of 9.5 per cent of GDP in the second quarter of 2023, it is one of the most fiscally incontinent countries of Europe. As with Greece, Italy, Spain, Portugal in 2011, the UK had its own run-in with global bond investors when, in September 2022, they lost faith in the ability of newly appointed Prime Minister Liz Truss to keep control of public finances: bond yields surged, forcing a rapid retreat, followed four weeks later by Truss's resignation. But at least Britain had full control of monetary policy, and the Bank of England was able to step in and buy £65 billion worth of government bonds, thus preventing the collapse of pension funds. But if Britain had been in the euro?

As for the eurozone, essentially nothing has changed. Very different eurozone economies remain trapped in the same monetary straitjacket. They all have to live with the same interest rate and they cannot devalue their currencies to help themselves out of a hole. Exactly the same could happen again – and probably will. Indeed, some believe that it very nearly did happen in the summer of 2022 – a few weeks before Britain's own mauling at the hands of bond investors. Interest rates rose sharply and it looked as if a loss of confidence in Italian government bonds might precipitate a repeat of the 2011 crisis.

The US, with 330 million people in fifty-one states spread across six time zones, copes happily with a single currency, so why can't the EU? But the individual states of the US are not analogous to the twenty member states of the eurozone. The US is a single nation, with a very strong federal government. The eurozone, by contrast, is made up of very different countries, each with their own fiscal policies, their own politics and their own contrasting attitudes. Some may see the EU as a superstate – but it isn't, and there is very considerable opposition to it ever becoming one. The 'ever closer union' of the Treaty of Rome is in retreat, with the rise of nationalist governments which are increasingly pushing back against control from Brussels. The euro might be very convenient if you are travelling and trading between different European countries; who wants to change to a different currency when they stop off in Luxembourg for lunch? It might ease trade, and eliminate the currency risk if you are transferring money from one country to another, say, to buy a property. But it has brought big risks, distorting economies and disempowering central banks.

The EU's elite can't admit that the euro is flawed because they have invested far too much faith in it. The single currency is – as Margaret Thatcher warned in 1990, when monetary union was still a pipe dream – not an economic project but a political one. It is about prestige, about asserting European unity, about trying to displace the dollar as the symbol of global economic might – and failing somewhat dismally.

5.

Faltering Transport

It is six in the morning and I'm standing on the platform at Banyuls-sur-Mer railway station on the Mediterranean coast of France. I have on my phone an itinerary of a journey I have just booked with SNCF, the French state railway company. It is going to take me to Narbonne, where I am told to change for the InterCity to Bordeaux, then change again onto a local train to take me up the Dordogne Valley, arriving around two in the afternoon. It's a long trek, but I have just walked the length of the Pyrenees, and I am in the mood for a long train journey, with nothing to do other than sit back, look out of the window and enjoy the French countryside.

But where is my train on the departure board? Nowhere to be seen. There is no apology, no explanation; my train, which was there in black and white on the SNCF website a few hours ago, and which is there, listed on my ticket, has simply failed to exist. I catch a later train, but now I have missed my connection in Narbonne and there is a two-hour wait for the next service. But is my ticket now still valid? The SNCF website suggests not, although I might be able to swap it for a new ticket. But the ticket office is closed, and the ticket machines offer no help. I take the train anyway and slump into a seat. There are castles and vineyards to look at, and rather a lot of time to enjoy them. Numerous times the train grinds to a halt, so that by the time I reach Bordeaux it is two hours late. The next train is running late, too. By the time I have reached the small village station where I have arranged to meet a friend, I am three hours behind schedule.

Three days later, I take three more trains and return to Britain. Again, two of them are delayed with no explanation. By the time I get home, I have taken six trains, four of which were delayed by more than half an hour and one of which was cancelled. The trip has cost me £600. It could have been worse, as it was when I took a night train down to the Alps, leaving at 23.40 from Paris Austerlitz. Or so it said on the ticket I had bought from SNCF. Except that when I got to the station – with nearly an hour to spare, so I thought – the departure time had been brought forward to 22.50, with no explanation and without the information being sent to me. Fortunately, I was able to run and catch the train, but without picking up my paper ticket from the machine. A peaked-capped guard decided I hadn't paid – in spite of the evidence I could show him – and charged me again. Not even a budget airline would do that: sell you a ticket for a plane which actually took off fifty minutes earlier than advertised. I got my money back eventually, but only after making a scene at the Gare de Lyon on the way home.

There are, of course, plenty of people who can report miserable experiences on Britain's trains. I have some of my own, though I can't ever remember being quite three hours late, and I certainly can't remember a rail company changing its timetable on a whim so as to throw off passengers who had bought tickets. But the point is that this wasn't the British rail system, which we moan about all the time – this was the French rail system, which we are supposed to look up to. While we travel about on rattling old nineteenth-century railways, the French have built long express lines capable of speeds of up to 200 mph – like HS2, except they actually exist. The trains look sleek and they belt past you at a speed that makes your car wobble from twenty feet away.

But just try travelling on them. Europe's most admired rail system can be remarkably quick if you are travelling from Paris to a distant corner of the country. But all the money has been sucked into the high-speed network. Elsewhere, services are sparse, with long gaps in the timetable. In 2021, 20 per cent of non-high-speed lines had ten trains or fewer per day (i.e. five or fewer in each direction). Or you may find that the line has been closed altogether: Docteur Beeching seems to be alive and well in France, with 155 further miles of line closed for good across the country since 2019. The French, like the Brits, subsidise their railways grandly: to the tune of 8 euro cents for every kilometre travelled by a passenger in 2021. The punctuality records read just like those on Britain's railways, too, though with less excuse given the less dense services on many French regional railways. In 2019 – before Covid had a chance to interrupt services – 8 per cent of trains in the Central-Val de Loire region were cancelled, and 10 per cent ran more than five minutes late.[1] Try to find an alternative form of public transport, though, and you will struggle. Bus services are rare outside the main cities. In 2022, my wife travelled to meet me in the small town of Amelie-les-Bains, where I was staying while walking the Haute Route of the Pyrenees. It was a lovely place to stop off – if you were travelling by foot. My wife's journey was a little more problematic. Her Ryanair flight from Stansted to Perpignan was fine, but what then? A train? The line is long since gone. A bus? Not today. A taxi? Even the taxi drivers, it turned out, only worked in the mornings. She ended up calling a taxi driver over from

Spain. Air travel, on the other hand, has been curtailed by a climate change law which has prohibited the provision of flights in cases where it is possible – at least theoretically – to complete the journey by rail in under two and a half hours. The effect has been to make travellers more dependent on the strike-prone railway system.

It could be worse for passengers, though. They could try to take the train in Germany. Once famed for the efficiency of its rail services, and admired for the high-speed network of lines constructed over the past three decades, the country's state-owned national rail company, Deutsche Bahn, has sunk into what the National Audit Office calls a 'permanent crisis'. In 2022, a third of long-distance trains were delayed. Lines have been closed for weeks on end, trains delayed for several hours in some cases and passengers left bewildered by excuses. In the words of the auditors, DB has become a 'bottomless pit', losing €71 million in the first six months of 2023 and accumulating €30 billion of debt.[2]

Rail services fail in the EU for the same reason as they fail in Britain. Railways are, by their very nature, expensive to build and run. When things go wrong, they go very wrong: when a train breaks down you can't just steer another round it as you can with road vehicles – the whole system breaks down. Signalling and overhead wiring brings complexities that do not exist on the roads. On top of that, it is painfully easy for a militant union to close down a whole rail system. A high-speed train is a marvel when everything is working; an over or underheated prison when, as is far from uncommon, passengers find themselves stranded for several hours. That happens as much on the EU's railways as it does in Britain. You want a tale of misery on a European rail system that isn't in Britain? Take your pick. In August 2020, passengers from Bordeaux took twenty-two hours to reach Paris after an electrical malfunction.[3] In Italy, strikes in July 2023 left passengers stranded in 37-degree heat for hours.[4] In Spain, on New Year's Day 2019, passengers spent nine hours trying to reach Madrid from Badajoz in freezing conditions when their train broke down and they were decanted onto another train, which itself broke down twice.[5] Strict rules on drivers' hours led to passengers being abandoned for hours in a small village station between Santander and Madrid when the driver walked off duty having reached the end of his six-hour shift.[6]

What Britain can claim, at least, is to have safer railways than most of Europe. Between 2015 and 2019, Britain suffered 2.1 fatalities per billion train kilometres, with only Finland and Ireland – which have relatively few services – having a better record. For France, the figure was 7.0, Germany 10.4 and Spain 12.4.[7] It is a similar story on the roads, with 26 deaths per million inhabitants in the UK in 2022, the same as in Denmark and bettered only by Norway (21) and Sweden (22). In Germany, the figure is 33 deaths per million inhabitants, Spain 37, France 48 and Italy 54.[8]

My first experience of French driving was aged eighteen when, after learning that the train I was hoping to catch from a remote rural station in the Auvergne was delayed by an hour and half, a family who were heading in the right direction kindly offered me a lift. I say kindly, but what followed was sheer terror. No, you can't overtake there, I heard myself saying, because you can't possibly see if something comes round . . . But we overtook anyway, lolling around the bend in a little tin can of a Citroën, which leaned away from the bend so far I thought I was going to scrape my ear along the ground. Then we did it again. By the time we arrived for frogs' legs at the little pension where I was staying (and they really were frogs' legs), I felt as jumpy as the animals themselves.

Things have changed a little for the better since the 1980s. France seemed to discover road safety after the Princess of

Wales was fatally injured in a Parisian underpass in 1997. Out went the traditional amnesty for motoring fines granted by an incoming president – anticipation of which led to an upwards blip in already horrendous accident figures. (The election of Jacques Chirac in 1995 was blamed for an extra 300 deaths on the road.)[9] In came speed cameras. French roads are now only twice as lethal, mile for mile, than British ones – rather than three times.

European cities now like to think of themselves as civilised places built for people rather than cars – so very different from car-bound America. Some of the expressways along the Seine have been closed to cars, even turned into seasonal beaches. Low emission zones have been set up to ban the dirtiest cars from the road. In 2024, Paris voted in a referendum – albeit with sparse participation – to subject sports utility vehicles to punitive parking fees. In contrast to traffic-choked London, European cities are supposed to be places of light, freely flowing traffic where most people choose to travel by cheap public transport. True, the Netherlands has its impressive cycle lanes, as does Sweden. Madrid has buried some of the big roads that used to choke its centre and reconnected its cultural heart with a large area of parkland. Yet you don't have to walk far to find yourself having to negotiate a hellhole of concrete overpasses and screeching traffic – in Madrid or most other European cities. Berlin has started to go back on pedestrianisation. The Périphérique continues to disconnect Paris from its suburbs.

London still claims the dubious crown of traffic jam capital of the world, at least in the Global Traffic Scorecard published by data from Inrix. The city's drivers apparently spend an average of 156 hours a year sitting in jams. But Paris is not far behind, in third place on 138 hours. Much smaller cities than London or Paris scarcely score any better: Dublin is 12th with an average of 114 hours a year spent in jams,

Rome 13th on 107, Brussels 17th on 98.[10] It is easy to admire free-flowing French autoroutes – or at least it was until the automated toll misread my car as an HGV and charged me nearly £50; French road tolls are becoming as tricky to negotiate as Britain's increasingly Byzantine network of congestion charges, low emission charges and bridge tolls, many of which demand online payment only. But the admiration for French roads ends when you come off the autoroute to find it choked with lorries which are avoiding those hefty tolls. The French road system works for motorists who want a rapid and largely congestion-free journey on the autoroute and who are prepared to pay heftily for the privilege; it works rather less well for the residents of towns and villages that have supposedly been bypassed by motorways yet, nevertheless, find themselves besieged by heavy traffic.

Germany can claim to have had the first extensive motorway network in the world – an achievement the country tends to downplay given that much of it was built under the Nazis, but has become a hellish one in places, its two-lane, narrow and twisty carriageways not designed with modern traffic in mind. The absence of any speed limit on many sections adds to the horror. The autobahnen continue to be a national cultural blind spot; even a government full of Greens can't bring itself to impose a blanket speed limit of the kind used in almost every other country. The right to drive at whatever speed you like is to many Germans what the right to bear arms is to many Americans – and with needless deaths the inevitable result. You don't have to travel for long on an autobahn to realise why the Germans hold the all-comers' record for the biggest pile-up in history, when 259 vehicles crashed on the A2 near Braunschweig in July 2009, apparently blinded when heavy rain gave way to bright sunshine.[11] The per kilometre death rate on motorways is twice as high in Germany as it is in Britain (although Belgian motorways drivers still manage to outkill even their German counterparts).[12] Still, the government dares not upset the powerful motorists' and car manufacturers' lobby, in spite of some evidence that the German public has come round to the idea of civilising the autobahnen. A poll in 2021 by the broadcaster ARD found that 60 per cent were in favour of a speed limit, with 38 per cent against – although they were asked in the context not of the carnage but of cutting carbon emissions.[13]

But surely EU countries are better at getting on and building infrastructure projects than we are in Britain, with our delayed, extravagant HS2 and non-appearing third runway at Heathrow? Not always, no. True, Britain has set new standards for spending wild amounts of money on public inquiries, reviews and redesigns before we even get down to putting spades in the ground – if we ever get that far. But Berlin Brandenburg Airport certainly gave us a run for our money. Originally conceived in 1990 to serve as the gateway to the capital of newly reunited Germany, construction began in 2008 with a planned opening date of 2011. That was later put back to May 2012, but weeks before the planned ceremony inspections revealed 120,000 defects, from doors that would not open, sagging roofs , dangerous cabling and many other things. Engineers hired to put everything right couldn't find the plans to help them; the drawings later turned up in a skip. At one point, complete demolition and rebuild was contemplated.

The airport finally opened in October 2020, when there was little to go wrong because hardly anyone was flying due to the Covid-19 pandemic. But as air traffic did start to recover, it rapidly became apparent that the new airport, designed for 27 million passengers a year, could not cope with the 35 million passengers who had used the two airports, Tegel and Schoenfeld, it was designed to replace. The project ended up costing €7 billion, three times its original estimate.[14] It wasn't just passengers who suffered from the fiasco but the memory of poor, blameless Willy Brandt, the former West German chancellor, in whose honour the airport was going to be named. Thankfully, he has since been reduced to a subtitle.

It isn't just Britain that is wracked with indecision, either. It is half a century since city authorities in Lisbon started talking about a new city airport. In 2010, they almost started building one, at Alcochete, across the Tagus River. Then it was dropped on the grounds of cost and a cheaper option of expanding a military base at nearby Montijo investigated. But this was then blocked on grounds that it would harm a habitat of migratory birds. In 2023, several other sites were put forward, with the latest having a planned opening date of 2035. Except there is now an environmental pressure group, Climaximo, blocking roads, protesting that Lisbon doesn't need any more airports. All sound familiar?

Lisbon's existing airport has managed to challenge Britain's airports for the honour of being declared the world's worst. Like Willy Brandt, I don't know what poor Humberto Delgado did to deserve having his name appended to what in recent years has regularly featured as the least favourite place to fly from in the annual survey compiled by AirHelp, a company that helps stranded passengers and others aggrieved by awful experiences with airports and airlines. Delgado founded the Portuguese national airline, TAP, before taking against the fascist regime that governed his country in the 1950s and 1960s and eventually being assassinated. A good guy, in other words. But his airport? Never have I come so close to missing a plane in spite of having arrived at the airport more than two hours in advance – so long did it take me to get through check-in and security. The good news is that in the 2023 survey, Humberto Delgado has climbed to being merely the world's fourth least-popular airport, with strike-bound Gatwick claiming the third-worst spot and

Malta the second worst. A regional airport in Indonesia came
out bottom, at 194th. In all, Europe had six of the ten worst
airports and none of the top ten.[15] Remarkably, many middle-
income countries seem better able to keep their passengers
happy than do European ones, with airports in Brazil and
South Africa taking top spots, along with Oman and Japan.

If you want an example of how to handle the construction
of an international airport, it isn't the EU to which you need
to look but China, which seems able to rollout international
airports at a rate of ten a year – not that they tend to ask
the local residents or take much notice of environmentalists, mind.

Nor has Europe's growing high-speed rail network been
built quite so painlessly as many make out. True, Britain's
HS2 – now severely truncated after costs ran out of control – has set new standards in how not to approach an
infrastructure project; estimations of its cost rising from £30
billion to over £100 billion before Rishi Sunak's government
started chopping bits off it. But the Lyon–Turin rail link must
run it a close second. A high-speed line was first proposed in
the 1990s to complement the existing line from the 1870s, and
to serve the environment by transferring travellers from air to
rail and freight from road to rail. The new line was to avoid
the twists and turns of the old route by diving through the
Alps at a much lower altitude – the price being that it would
require a far longer tunnel. At 36 miles it was to be longer
even than the Channel Tunnel. Engineering work began in
2002, yet it wasn't until 2016 that the tunnel-boring began, by
which time the estimated costs had reached €25 billion and
its opening date put back to 2032. By 2019, only 5 miles of
tunnel had been dug, and communities along the route had
had enough of the dust, spoil tips and general interference
with their lives.

To cap it all, the European Court of Auditors then began

to question the environmental claims made for the new line, bringing the whole project into question. The construction process, it calculated, would release 10 million tonnes of CO_2 by the time it was complete. Even if it was well used, it would take twenty-five years before the emissions saved exceeded the emissions from the construction work itself. If the line was not so well used, it would take fifty years.[16]

Belgium has had so many misfiring infrastructure projects that they spawned a popular TV series, *Le Journal des Travaux Inutiles* – the 'journal of useless public works' – in 1986. The programme started investigating unfinished bridges, motorways that came to a screeching halt in the middle of fields, extravagant motorway interchanges built to serve roads that were never built. You might imagine there would be enough examples to fill a couple of programmes, but no; the producers found so much material that it ran for twenty-six years, revealing metro stations that had never been used, a vast hospital that was only in use for a few months before being closed and a ring road that sent traffic lurching around a 180-degree bend, taking them back where they came from, because the road had never been completed. Many of these fiascos were the product of arguments between government departments or regional administrations. In one case, a long cable-stayed bridge was built over the Albert Canal at vast expense for a motorway that was never completed. The motorway seems to march up to the bridge but then, at the last minute, swerves around a corner and heads off in a different direction. The four-lane carriageway of the bridge itself connects only two village streets. Never in human history has so much concrete been poured for so little purpose. The boom in useless works must have made money for someone, and has entertained a generation of Belgian TV viewers, but sadly not the taxpayer.

Anything Belgium can do, however, Spain can do better.

What Belgium can't boast is an entire international airport sitting idle, its 2.5-mile runway gathering dust rather than welcoming the Airbus A380s that it was built to handle at a cost of €1 billion. Ciudad Real Airport, 100 miles south of Madrid, is another product of those boom years, following Spain's entry into the euro. Built to handle 2 million passengers a year, it finally opened in 2009 – after the usual fussing over animal habitats had held the project back years – to handle, er, a few flights to Majorca and, the following year, to Stansted. Then it went bust, leaving its ghost-like terminal and air-traffic-control tower as a faded memento of the good times. Yet you scratch your head wondering why a planeload of Airbus A380 passengers would ever have wanted to visit Ciudad Real in the first place – as the 'city' only has a population of 75,000. A high-speed train was supposed to whisk passengers to Madrid in under an hour – except that the proposed station on a nearby high-speed line was never built and the bridge linking the site to the terminal building stands dangling in the air.

The EU has been a great promoter of new road networks for its peripheral and emerging regions. From Poland to Bulgaria, new motorways have changed the face of Eastern Europe since the days of the Trabant. But, sometimes, I do ask myself, why are there quite so many roads in places where the traffic is so light? You can get a whiff of it by driving from Inverness to Kinlochewe in Wester Ross in the Northwest Highlands of Scotland. The A832 is a wonder of a road – the main wonder being just why is a village of only sixty souls, whose population could fit onto one double-decker bus, served by a road built to such a high standard, especially when the Scottish government is dragging its heels over improvements to the much busier A9, which travels the spine of Scotland? The boards beside the road give the answer: EU regional development funds. The EU has a thing about no part of

Europe being left behind – even when there really isn't much to be left behind.

Take out the road map of Portugal and it gets even more bizarre. Yes, that really is a pair of two- and three-lane motorways, the A1 and the A29, running a couple of miles apart, linking Porto with Esgueira, 30 miles to the south. In places they nearly touch each other. Then, a little to the south, we have the A1, A13 and the A17 all competing for traffic. No doubt the construction made someone rich – as well as the mysterious companies that seem to have developed a habit of sending out demands for toll payments on journeys apparently made on Portugal's labyrinthian motorway system several years earlier.

The maze of tolls and charges has become a serious impediment to navigating Europe's road network. Free movement? Not if you are venturing onto roads that are unfamiliar to you. Take a journey from Dublin to Paris, via London. The customs facilities as you pass out of and then back into the EU are the least of your worries. First, you might come across the Dublin ring road, the M50, which is subject to a €3.70 toll for a car. But how to pay? There are no toll booths, just an overhead sign giving you a web address and a telephone number that you are somehow supposed to take down while you are driving. Fail to pay by 8 p.m. the following day and you face a fine. Take the ferry to Liverpool, and you then might find yourself taking the Runcorn Bridge, where a similar toll system operates – with no opportunity to pay at the site; just an invitation to pay online under threat of another fine. Reach London and there is the Congestion Charge, London's Ultra Low Emissions Zone (ULEZ) and the Dartford Crossing – each with their own online payment system, which new visitors to the city are unlikely to know anything about. When you get to Paris, there is another snare waiting for you. Anyone driving in the city is required to display a Crit'Air sticker, which classifies their vehicle in one of six emission-based categories – with bans on certain categories on certain days. There is a €68 fine for failing to display the sticker. Somehow, motorists are expected intuitively to know about all these schemes, and how to pay. Given the EU's stated enthusiasm for free movement, you might think that it would insist that Europe's road-charging schemes be rationalised so that there is one, easy to understand system. But, no. It seems quite happy for each country to spring its own devious schemes on people trying to get about the continent. Perhaps there is an ulterior, protectionist motive in making it more difficult for other country's lorries to navigate your own road network?

The official-looking document that dropped onto my doormat in March 2019 came as something of a surprise – it was a speeding fine from a journey on a French autoroute six months earlier. As someone who is quite religious about speed limits, and who had never previously incurred a speeding fine anywhere, I was a little intrigued, but there it was. I had apparently been photographed at 98 km/h on a stretch of autoroute that was limited to 90 km/h. But, given I hadn't seen any signs to the contrary, surely this stretch of open road had been subject to the standard limit of 110 km/h? I went onto Google Street View to check. Sure enough, there on the slip road, where I joined the autoroute, was a warning of a 90 km/h limit, which appeared to refer to a short stretch of tunnel. But, apparently, it still applied on the open road several miles later. I paid my €40. I didn't feel quite as cheated as the Dutch lorry drivers who, in 2023, launched a legal action against the mayor of London after receiving numerous fines for failing to pay the charge for entering London's ULEZ – a restriction that is advertised only by small signs at the side of the road, telling you to pay online. One driver who delivered fresh flowers to London had racked up €400,000 worth of £180 fines. Brexit had not affected in the slightest the ability of Transport for London (TfL) to pursue haulage companies via debt collection agencies.

While motorways abound in the EU's peripheral regions, Europe's road network seems to struggle where there is a lot of traffic. Italy's crumbling infrastructure came to light as a result of the collapse of a 200-yard section of the Morandi Bridge in Genoa in August 2018, sending vehicles on the A10 autostrada plunging 150 feet into the Polcevera Valley and killing forty-three people. It soon became clear that engineers had known for years about corrosion in the pre-stressed steel cables that held up the road platform. Remedial works on the bridge, which was built in 1967, had been carried out in 1993. But, as one of the engineers who was involved at the time, Professor Janusz Rymsza of Warsaw's Road and Bridge Research Institute, had warned, the patch-up job failed to address an essential design flaw with the bridge. There was no inbuilt structural redundancy, which meant that if one cable failed then the entire bridge was doomed. Moreover, the single cables were coated in concrete and so were virtually impossible to inspect. Rymsza had suggested adding extra steel cables to the bridge but his idea had been rejected – on the grounds of aesthetics, he believed.[17]

The disaster brought the whole sorry story of Italian infrastructure to light. The country which first gave the world concrete – in the shape of the Pantheon, whose magnificent 142-foot high concrete dome is still standing after 2,000 years – lives, works and travels in shoddy structures which are on the point of collapse after a few decades. The Morandi Bridge wasn't the first to fail. A year earlier, a bridge in Fossano, in the northwest of the country, where the Alps meet the Mediterranean, had similarly fallen down. Also in 2017, an apartment block in Naples fell down, killing eight people. While in some cases the finger of blame can be pointed at faulty designs, the role of organised crime in Italy's crumbling infrastructure is slowly coming to light. Core samples taken from concrete used in bridges and tunnels in some parts of the country have revealed that the materials contain far too little cement – with the Mafia suspected of profiting from selling weak mixes passed off as the proper thing.[18]

You can't be sure of flying, driving or travelling around Europe by train, but what about staying at home and communicating with the rest of the world via the internet? Notionally, Europe has some of the highest rates of connection and broadband speeds anywhere in the world, with an average EU download speed of 61.5 Mbps (it is 66.8 in the UK and 69.8 in the US). But try telling that to the 5,000 people of Dagneux, a small town which lies a not-very-remote 15 miles from Lyon, France's second city. Just 4 per cent of homes and business enjoy download speeds of 100 Mbps and 13 per cent achieve 30 Mbps. Or try telling it to the 16,000 people of Grafschaft, 15 miles from Bonn, where only 29 per cent of broadband connections reach 100 Mbps.[19] European countries have connected their larger cities but left peripheral places in the dark. Remarkably, the EU country with the widest access to broadband is Romania.[20]

Send something by post instead? We moan about delayed and non-arriving letters in Britain – in 2023, Ofcom fined Royal Mail £5.6 million after only 73.7 per cent of first-class letters arrived the following day, compared with a target of 93 per cent. Among those fuming was Gordon Chalmers, himself a former postman, who missed a cancer referral appointment after the letter inviting him to hospital failed to arrive on time – he complained he hadn't received any post for a week.[21] But it is little different – worse, even – in many parts of Europe. In Denmark, deliveries have been reduced to once a week since 2018. In Italy, it has been three times a week since 2017. In Norway, Sweden and Belgium it is three days one week and two days the next.[22]

Europe is often resistant to electronic means of communication, with the EU forever threatening US tech giants with swingeing fines for various misdemeanours, but it doesn't seem to be very good at doing snail mail, either.

6.

Less than Radiant Cities

No one does urban decay better than the United States. From the abandoned streets of Detroit, where the odd, leaning clapperboard house has somehow managed to cling on amid the onslaught of weeds while its neighbours have vanished without trace, to the hissing steam pipes that every so often sear Manhattan with boiling effluent, the US has something of a reputation of allowing scenes of ruin to coexist with fantastic wealth. But surely Europe is different? Think of European cities and the first thing that springs to mind is glorious piazzas, precipitous stone walls of cathedrals, royal exchanges, palazzos, mansion blocks and all the other stuff which fills the tourist guide books.

In many ways, European city centres have improved over the past few decades. Tourist areas have been pedestrianised; handsome new public buildings erected. One of the great models for urban regeneration was Barcelona, which was reinvented as a cosmopolitan city and shown off to the world for the 1992 Olympics. It gave us such institutions as the angular glass-faced waterfront buildings and white tubular steel bridges which have become symbols of so many regeneration projects. Around the same time, a reunified Berlin also started to show itself off with new symbols and monuments.

But these are shows put on for us, which disguise and distract us from seeing the guts of those same cities. For the more adventurous visitor to Berlin there is an alternative itinerary provided by a website called abandonedberlin.com, which, with the motto 'if it's verboten, it's got to be fun', opens up an extraordinary world of dereliction, much of it formed of vast buildings on sprawling sites that haven't been touched for decades. There are such treasures as the Spreepark, a 75-acre former funfair filled with decomposing rollercoasters and the hulks of fallen concrete dinosaurs, opened by the German Democratic Republic in 1969, closed after reunification, opened again in 1991 and closed for a second time in 2001. Since then, what could be a gorgeous riverside park has been shut off from the public while city authorities dither over what to do with it – save for a 90-year-old woman who, in 2013, crept in for old times' sake, entered a car of the old Ferris wheel and had to be rescued when a gust of wind caught hold of it and turned it round, leaving her suspended in space. Then there's the delights of the Rüdersdorf chemical factory, built in 1899, which used to make bauxite for the Nazi war effort. There's also the Haus der Stastistik, a hated building where the Stasi kept their records on the East German population; the Olympic village of 1936, still abandoned nearly ninety years on; the Sporthotel Hohenschönhausen, where East German athletes were plied with performance-enhancing drugs – a nearby housing complex used to house refugees in the 1990s; the SS Bakery, where food was prepared for the occupants of Nazi concentration camps; and, out on the Oder river to the east, a power station that Albert Speer never quite finished before its two concrete chimneys were blasted by shells fired by advancing Soviet troops.

We might make allowances for the fact that Berlin was ever so slightly damaged during the latter stages of the Second World War, and then the communists spent forty years squeezing the life out of their half. But it is nearly thirty-five years since reunification, and still Germany's capital city is ridden with vast scenes of dereliction. We are as far from the days of communist Germany now as we were from Nazi Germany in 1980; by which time West Germany was well into its economic miracle, and huge reconstruction had transformed war-torn cities into smart metropolises. East Germany is taking longer to recover from communism than West Germany did from the Second World War. Moreover, not all of Berlin's dereliction can be blamed on the communist era; a lot of it comes down more recent inaction. There are plenty of abandoned sites in the old West Berlin, too, such as a vast former Tetra Pak factory, which was opened in 1980 and closed in 2013, before being left to rot – although it was briefly sized up as a possible home for refugees after Angela Merkel's government decided to open the borders to migrants in 2015.

Berlin has a history of division, but it is far from alone in European cities of having an elegant centre that stands some-what apart from its miserable outer regions. Let's pass over the Belgian city of Charleroi, whose appellation as the 'world's ugliest city' by a Dutch newspaper in 2008 sparked a tourist boom of visitors out to see whether it really could as bad as all that ('To me, it is more "exotique",' explained tour guide Nicolas Buissart, as he proudly showed off a rusting blast furnace just 550 yards from the city centre).[1] Excuses might be made for an industrial city fallen on hard times. But what of Paris when you wander from the elegant arrondissements of the city proper?

Aside from the Bois di Boulogne and the Bois de Vincennes, which straddle either side of the city of Paris, it is remarkable how much less green are that city's suburbs when compared

with London or any other British city. The banlieue are
densely packed places with the odd caged asphalt sports
pitch provided for physical exercise. Residents are packed
into beaten-about high-rise blocks, with communities set
apart by wide roads and aggressive traffic. The Boulevard
Périphérique – the grandest name for a mundane urban
motorway anywhere – divides Paris from its banlieue more effectively than the defensive wall and ramparts that it replaced.
At least you could fling fireballs and plague-ridden sheep over
a castle wall with a trebuchet; the eight lanes of tarmac that
make up the Périphérique, on the other hand, divide different worlds: a smart and fashionable, instantly recognisable
city centre and torn suburbs which brim with those regular
eruptions of anger that have turned them into bywords for
social unrest. As the architect Richard Rogers, who gave
Paris one of its most notable modern buildings in the Centre
Pompidou, commented, there are few cities 'where the heart
is so detached from its limbs'. The Paris banlieue can match
US cities for poisonous relations between police and disgrun-
tled ethnic populations. In October 2005, police called to
investigate a break-in at a building site in Clichy-sous-Bois,
in the northwest of the Paris metropolitan area, attempted to
interrogate a group of youths of North African descent, three
of whom ran off to hide in an electricity substation, where
two were electrocuted, throwing the neighbourhood into
darkness. There followed three weeks of rioting in cities across
France, in which two people were murdered, 9,000 cars were
set alight and several electricity substations attacked, causing
further blackouts.

In June 2023, similar unrest erupted when police shot a 17-
year-old youth who had twice disobeyed instructions to stop
his car after breaking several traffic laws and nearly collid-
ing with other road users in the western suburb of Nanterre.
Again, there followed three weeks of riots, which spread to

cities all over France, with over a thousand vehicles set alight, along with the town hall in a small town north of Paris. Riots have happened in Britain, too, of course – in 2011, there were several days of riots after a similar incident in which a suspect was shot dead in a car. In July and August 2024, several days of rioting followed the murder of three girls at a dance class in Southport, Lancashire, beginning with an attack on a mosque after a false rumour that the assailant was a Muslim. But rioting seems to be a way of life in some European cities. Madrid has erupted on several occasions during the past few years; over pardons granted to Catalan separatists and over farmers' protests. Rome rioted for several days over vaccine passports in 2021. The same year, there were several nights of rioting in Amsterdam and several other Dutch cities over curfews imposed during the Covid-19 pandemic. The German city of Stuttgart, too, saw rioting over Covid measures in 2020. The Nørrebro suburb of Copenhagen has twice erupted in rioting over attempts to clear a large squat.

America has riots, too, as do many other parts of the world. But it is remarkable how little Europe's interventionist social policies seem to prevent social unrest. They don't stop the breakdown in relations between community and police, or help migrant populations to assimilate. State support for industries, agriculture especially, merely seems to instil dependence, which then generates anger whenever that support seems to be under threat. Moreover, stagnating European economies are introducing new social tensions. High taxation is itself becoming an issue that is destabilising societies. The *Gilets jaunes* protests, beginning in 2018, instigated what has since become an increasingly common theme as European governments try to achieve net zero carbon emissions before the technology is really there to allow that: an uprising against taxes, levies, charges and bans, which are perceived to be falling more heavily on people of modest means than on the wealthy. The *Gilets jaunes* protests persisted for several weekends in November and December 2018, and then carried on throughout 2019 and into 2020, until stopped by Covid lockdowns. Once again, cars were burned and several lives were lost in battles with police, which involved tear gas and batons. And this time, the protests came to the very heart of Paris. Hotel bookings fell; tourists stayed away. French cities were advertising themselves to the world as hotbeds of social unrest. So long as wealth-creation in Europe is stuck in the doldrums, and people are consequently deprived of real-terms wage increases, the tensions are not going to lessen – and European cities are going to become increasingly fraught places.

Most European countries are assumed by many, by virtue of higher public spending, to enjoy superior social conditions compared with Britain. But where is the evidence? We often talk about Britain having a housing crisis, with younger people unable to afford a decent home to rent, let alone buy. According to the housing charity Shelter, there were 309,000 people in England who were homeless in December 2023, the vast majority of whom were in hostels or temporary accommodation. The number of people sleeping rough on any one night in England was put at 3,069, with 1,391 of them in London[2] – although the Greater London Authority has produced a much higher estimate of 4,389 people sleeping rough at some point between October and December 2023.[3]

But are things really any better elsewhere in Europe? Not according to the Federation of National Organisations Working with the Homeless, which credits Britain as one of only three countries in Europe where authorities are making progress over homelessness. In September 2023, it estimated that on any one night 895,000 people are homeless across Europe, with 262,645 in Germany and 209,074 in France. These figures, as in Britain, included people in temporary accommodation. As for those out on the streets on any one night, there were estimated to be 2,598 in Paris, 1,063 in Barcelona, 965 in Berlin and 719 in Brussels.[4] All of these, with the exception of Paris, are cities with far smaller populations than London.

As for Europeans who do have homes, in many cases those homes are highly inadequate: 14.8 per cent of European households are living with leaks, damp or mould; 17.4 per cent are living in overcrowded conditions; 7.5 per cent are unable to keep their homes at an adequate temperature; 1.7 per cent have no bath or shower; and 1.8 per cent no indoor toilet.[5] Don't be fooled by the new EU-funded roads which run across Romania and Bulgaria; housing in those countries is lagging a long way behind the prestigious public infrastructure projects: 45 per cent of Romanians live in overcrowded conditions, while 13 per cent of Bulgarians have no indoor toilet. Even in Western Europe, housing conditions can be pretty poor: 18 per cent of French households are deemed to be living in housing that is unfit for habitation in some way.[6] Eurostat keeps data on the proportion of people living in dwellings with a 'leaking roof, damp walls, floors or foundations, or with rot in window frames or floors'. Across the EU, 14.8 per cent live in this way, including 18.0 per cent in France, 19.7 per cent in Spain, 19.6 per cent in Italy, 25.2 per cent in Portugal and – topping the European league for crap housing – Cyprus on 39.2 per cent.

In 1990, just before reunification, I took the train back from Greece, where I had spent several days walking around Mount Athos, the monastic colony, and went to visit a friend near Stuttgart. I hadn't had a chance to wash for a week and looked forward to having a bath or a shower. Surely, every home in West Germany by then had a bathroom, or somewhere to wash that was better than a bucket? But apparently not. It took a trip to the local swimming pool to get clean – where I had a whistle blown at me for not swimming. But I only wanted a bath.

What about the high cost of housing in Britain? In December 2023, the average homebuyer was spending 18 per cent of household income on mortgage repayments, the average tenant in social housing was paying 26 per cent of household income on rent and the average tenant in the private sector paying 32 per cent of household income on rent.[7] But it is not much better in other countries. Greek households are spending an average of 34.2 per cent of their disposable income on housing costs, rising to 60 per cent among low-income households. In Denmark, it is 26.3 per cent and 56.5 per cent among low-income households. In the Netherlands, it is 23.9 per cent and 48.0 per cent; Sweden 22.1 per cent and 44.4 per cent; Germany 23.4 per cent and 43.8 per cent. Many European countries have exactly the same kind of housing problems as in Britain, but without having to cope with net migration of over 700,000, as Britain experienced in 2022. Moreover, in most European countries land is a lot more plentiful and cheaper. As Eastern Europe becomes wealthier, Europe's housing crisis is spreading there, too – with rents galloping upwards at a far higher rate than GDP. Between 2010 and 2022, rents in Estonia were up 210 per cent and in Lithuania, 144 per cent.[8]

In Paris, in early 2024, tenants were paying an average of €1,362 per month for a one bedroom flat. But that didn't seem to give them much security: there were numerous reports of tenants being told they had to vacate their homes for two weeks during the summer so that their landlords could let their properties out on Airbnb to visitors for the Olympics.[9] As in Britain, tenancies tend to be of only short duration – usually a year – and the landlord need only give three months' notice to ask a tenant to leave. Tenants do, at least, have the right to keep a pet in their Parisian apartment.

But, unfortunately, a lapdog isn't the only creature many find themselves sharing their home with. In 2023, Paris experienced one of its periodic explosions in the bedbug population. One in ten households reported suffering from the pests – in some cases disposing of their bedding and even the bed itself, and still having an infestation.[10] Bugs were reported in restaurants, theatres, metro trains. The deputy mayor of Paris demanded an investigation. A report by France's food and environment agency duly responded with a report blaming the infestation on the banning of the insecticide DDT – and a rise in tourists.[11] It couldn't possibly be a problem that had originated in France, obviously.

Contrary to popular perception, Britain is not an especially expensive country in which to buy a home, at least not by European standards. Look at house prices relative to local earnings: in Britain a 100-square-metre home costs the equivalent of ten years' earnings (based on 2016 prices). This is only just over the European average. Prices are higher relative to local earnings in the Netherlands, Switzerland, France, Cyprus, Luxembourg, Ireland and Croatia. If you want an affordable home, best head to the US where a 100-square-metre home is just 3.5 times the average salary.[12]

If young people in Britain struggle to see how they will ever afford to buy a home, they should be thankful they are not living in Germany where, even now, 50.5 per cent of households live in rented accommodation, never building up capital in their homes. Those renting spend an average of 27.8 per cent of their income on rent, heating excluded. Moreover, many will have had to install a kitchen at their own expense, because the majority of rented properties come without. Just over one in ten households are living in officially overcrowded conditions.[13]

The appalling Grenfell Tower fire of June 2017, in which seventy-two people died after flammable cladding caught light on a tower block in west London, was seized on by some Remainers as a way of attacking Britain's decision to leave the EU. 'Brexiteers call it useless red tape, but without it people die,' declared Polly Toynbee in the *Guardian*, a few days after the fire. Reckless, go-it-alone Britain, went the argument, is opting out of the safe, regulated EU way of doing things – ignoring the fact that the cladding had been installed while Britain was under EU regulation and that it was a failure of both Britain and the EU for not producing proper regulation on the safety of cladding. Moreover, the very same cladding had been fitted on buildings across the EU. In February 2024, a very similar fire in a block of apartments in Valencia killed eleven people.[14] Notwithstanding Grenfell, Britain actually has a good record of avoiding deaths in fires: in 2019, it had a rate of 0.38 deaths per 100,000 from fires and burns, the lowest in Europe after Spain (0.27), Netherlands (0.34) and Italy (0.35). In Germany, it was 0.43, France 0.54 and Belgium 0.66.[15] In this case, the well-insulated timber residential buildings of Scandinavia seem to have counted against those countries: Norway had a death rate of 0.64 and Denmark 0.76.

Are building standards really higher in the EU than in Britain? That's not how it might have seemed had you been in the Radisson Blu Hotel in Berlin in the early hours of 16 December 2022, when a 50-foot high cylindrical aquarium burst, washing 1,500 fish through the lobby and out, gasping, into the street, while showering the hotel with flying shards of glass. Fortunately, it happened shortly before 6 a.m., and only two people were injured.[16] Marseille, where Le Corbusier's 1950s concrete slab La Cité Radieuse was once heralded as the future of urban living, and which did so much to inspire post-war housing development across France and many other European countries, has since earned a dubious reputation for the safety of its housing. In 2018, two buildings in the Noailles area of the city collapsed, killing eight people. Three years earlier, the authorities had published a report claiming that there were 40,000 dangerous homes in the city, which is home to 100,000 people. Some residents said that they were taking sleeping pills to stop themselves lying awake worrying about cracks in their homes so wide that they let in the daylight.[17] In 2023, it happened again: another building collapsed after a gas explosion, killing eight people.[18]

Poor quality concrete has left Italy with a deadly legacy when it comes to apartment buildings, just as with its bridges. In November 1999, sixty-six people died after a block of flats collapsed in the southern city of Foggia,[19] with an investigation concluding that inappropriate materials had been used in the foundations. The country has seen several smaller collapses since.

It is easy to look with a disapproving eye on the Soviet-style housing projects of Eastern Europe and think how awful it was that any society should have packaged its residents in the equivalent of battery chicken cages. Yet the truth is that so many Western European countries spent the twentieth century putting up social housing that was little better. Britain certainly went mad in the 1960s for vast housing estates with 'streets in the sky', but other countries did it on a larger scale. The common perception of West Berlin was that of a showcase for Western, capitalist society; a place that dazzled compared with the drab East Berlin. So it was, if you went shopping, or to a car showroom. But, as far as housing was concerned, it is not easy to tell where the East ended and the West began, so similar were the huge concrete slabs of the housing estates on its fringes. Märkisches Viertel, built between 1963 and 1975, was supposed to be a model for social housing, yet, by 1968, an article in *Der Spiegel* had already appeared giving air to the desperation of those who resided there. 'I feel like I'm in a prison camp,' said one resident; 'I will die in this monotony,' said another. 'Every night when I come home I curse the day we moved into these barracks,' said a third – quite strong words when you realise but for an accident of a military pen they could have been living in the real prison of East Berlin, just half a mile away and easily visible from the upper storey windows.[20] The vastness of the estate amazes – it is on an entirely different scale to London's housing estates, with 37,000 people in residence, more than in many an English market town. There are two other estates in West Berlin on a similar scale.

As for the public realm, Londoners don't know how lucky they are, with 18 per cent of the city made up of publicly accessible green space.[21] The average for capital cities across 38 EU and EEA countries, according to the European Environment Agency, is just 7 per cent, with only Stockholm (19 per cent) enjoying more parks and gardens than London. In Ljubljana, Slovenia, it is just 1 per cent; in Lisbon, Bratislava and Zagreb just 2 per cent. In Europe's non-capital cities, the average is just 3 per cent.[22] Add on private gardens and London is 48–51 per cent green space. That is nearly twice that of Paris (26 per cent). In Athens, which of all cities could do with some green lungs owing to the fierce heat of its summers, it is just 17 per cent.

But how many of us really see these realities when we descend on European capitals for a weekend and spend our time between hotel, museums, art galleries and restaurants, never really pausing to think what it would be like to live in these places? It is holiday syndrome again: we see European cities through very different eyes than we see our own.

7.

Weak on Crime

Brexit Britain would become a 'safe haven' for criminals after Brexit. So warned the National Police Chiefs' Council in September 2019, when it still seemed that a no-deal Brexit might be a possibility. Not to be outdone, an unnamed 'government source' commented that 'the fear is that every paedophile, rapist and murderer who wants to come to Britain will be on the first ferry on November 1'.[1] (This was at a time when Britain's official departure date was 31 October 2019). It would have been quite a ferry ride, with even fewer survivors, one imagines, than the boat in Agatha Christie's *Death on the Nile*.

The reasoning was that a no-deal Brexit would mean Britain crashing out of Europol, police no longer being able to use the European Arrest Warrant and ceasing to have access to various databases. In the event, the no-deal Brexit never occurred. Although the EU might have wanted to punish Britain for voting to leave its grand project, common sense prevailed and both sides agreed to continue to share fingerprint, DNA and numberplate data, as well as to continue to surrender criminal suspects in both directions across the Channel. Those who predicted chaos and a tide of criminality failed to notice that the UK wasn't the only European country to be leaving Europol – Denmark had done so quietly in 2017, yet cooperation on fighting crime continued without the Danes being assailed by all the continent's criminals.

Cooperation over crime is, of course, a good thing. The days of East End gangsters sheltering from justice in their Spanish villas – as they did before we had an extradition treaty with that country – are thankfully over. But has the EU really helped to deliver a low-crime Europe? The existence of Europol and the European Arrest Warrant doesn't seem to have prevented Europe from becoming the fastest-growing criminal market in the world. According to the Global Organised Crime Index, maintained by the Swiss-based Global Initiative Against Transnational Organised Crime, Europe saw the fastest rise in criminality of any continent in 2022.[2] The European parliament estimated criminal revenues in the EU in 2019 to be €139 billion – equivalent to 1 per cent of the bloc's economy.

Organised crime has a long history in parts of Europe, needless to say. Looking back, it was probably a bad idea for me to leave it until Naples before I tried to get any Italian currency – this being 1989, the days of the lira. I emerged from the central station on an overnight train from France to find a square full of banks. But how to get in? Every bank had two sets of doors, between which sat a security guard, who, like a nightclub bouncer, looked would-be clients up and down before allowing them through the first door, let alone the second. I didn't pass muster, not with my leather suitcase. But there was one weak link: at one of the banks the security guard had gone for a pee, leaving the doors unlocked. I went in – only to provoke customers to scatter to the sides of the room. I only wanted enough money for a sandwich.

Southern Italy has a reputation as, what police are now apt to call, a 'crime hotspot' – a land of Godfathers and criminal associates who might disappear into the concrete supports of motorway bridges – far from all of it apocryphal. But it did, at least, used to be a land apart. It was more of a surprise when, in 2021, Dutch police, acting on some intelligence they had obtained by hacking into an online communications system, discovered a row of seven shipping containers in the woods on the country's border with Belgium, all soundproofed with thick layers of insulation. Six of them appeared to be makeshift cells, with facilities to suspend people vertically. They had handcuffs hanging from the ceiling and attached to the floor. In the seventh, was a dentist's chair with straps on the armrests and footrests, around which was scattered a rich arsenal of torture weapons, including scalpels, pliers and pruning shears. It was being used by a gang involved in the trafficking of cocaine from South America. On this occasion, at least, Europol did its job and eleven men were jailed for between one and nine years – to which the obvious reply is: was that all?[3]

Free movement, open borders under the Schengen Agreement, high levels of migration and the expansion of the EU into the countries of Eastern Europe with higher levels of crime have all created opportunities for organised gangs, the extent of which is only just becoming clear. According to Europol, 50 per cent of criminals active in Europe are non-EU nationals, and half of them come from the Western Balkans, non-EU countries of Eastern Europe and North Africa. Having entered the EU, they find it easy to transport people, goods and weapons across borders, bringing organised crime to areas that once had little connection with it. The single market has facilitated the growth in cybercrime, with much more business – and fraud – being conducted across borders. Much organised crime is hiding in plain sight: according to Europol, eight in ten criminal operations use seemingly legitimate business structures, and three fifths involve corruption of public officials.[4]

One area of crime that is aided by free movement is benefit fraud. Thanks to the insistence of the EU that migrant workers be allowed to claim benefits from the first day they arrive in another country, it greatly increased the number of people who could make claims in Britain – before, quite possibly, disappearing out of the country again. One Bulgarian gang succeeded in making industrial-scale benefit claims, involving faked and stolen identities, managing to steal £50 million in Universal Credit over a five-year period before being caught in 2021.[5] The UK benefits system has not helped itself by moving applications online – where claims are theoretically cheaper to process but which, with fewer face-to-face interviews, makes it easier for fraudsters to make bogus claims involving people who are either fictitious or who might not be living in Britain.

It is not easy comparing crime across countries and continents. What constitutes a crime in one place might not be a crime in another. Public attitudes vary enormously – a sexual assault in one country might be regarded as normal behaviour in another, or at least something not to be complained about. Major crime tends to swamp minor crime – if you live in a crime-ridden favela that is ruled by gangland overlords, you may be less inclined to report your stolen bicycle than if you live in a neighbourhood that is generally law abiding. And would your report make it into national crime statistics even if you did try to report it? Police are better at recording crimes in some countries than others.

But sifting through the various available data two things become fairly clear: that Europe is not the low-crime zone that matches many Europeans' perception of their continent as a haven of civilisation – even if its experience of crime is modest compared with the worst parts of the world. Secondly, the UK does not come out especially well among European countries, but then neither does it come out the worst.

One attempt to create a standardised international index for crime has been made by the website numeo.com, which uses crowdsourced data to build a picture of overall crime. Users are asked about their perception of crime in their neighbourhood as well as their actual experience of it, with the data used to build a crime index figure of between zero and 100, where zero means no crime at all. Out of 144 countries, the UK comes 66th on a score of 46.9, which makes it the fifth most crime-ridden country in Europe, behind France (38th on 54.6), Belgium (58th on 48.9), Sweden (59th on 48.1) and Italy (62nd on 47.3).[6] The most crime-free country in Europe is the Isle of Man (141st on 17.9). Slovenia was the best EU country, 134th on 27.2. Generally, European countries come out mid-table, with far higher experience of crime than Gulf states, such as the United Arab Emirates and Bahrain, as well as the wealthier Far Eastern states, such as Taiwan, Japan, Singapore and Hong Kong (which is included in the index on its own, distinct from China). When Europeans think of their continent as relatively safe, they tend to overlook these places and make comparisons instead with the world's most violent places – Venezuela, Papua New Guinea, Afghanistan, Haiti and South Africa took the five most crime-ridden slots.

Another way to try to compare crime across countries and continents is to look at homicide rates – on the basis that this, as the most serious of crimes, is the one most likely to be reported wherever in the world it is committed. On intentional homicides, according to the UN Office on

Drugs and Crime (UNODC), England and Wales had a rate of 1.0 per 100,000 in 2021 – putting it around mid-table among European countries, behind France (1.14 per 100,000), Sweden (1.08) and most Eastern European countries except Poland and the Czech Republic.[7] The UNODC figures also allow comparisons to be made over time. Generally, the world is becoming less murderous – a trend that has been in evidence since medieval times when what is now Italy has been estimated to have had a murder rate of 71 per 100,000, worse than modern-day Columbia (27.48) or South Africa (41.87). Most European countries have followed this trend, with the homicide rate in France halving in the past thirty years, from 2.4 per 100,000 in 1990 to 1.14 in 2021, and that in Italy falling by over 80 per cent, from 3.16 per 100,000 in 1990 to 0.51 in 2021.

Yet there are parts of Europe that have bucked the global trend and failed to become less violent. The existence of the European Convention on Human Rights, Europol and European Arrest Warrants have hardly disturbed the gangsterism deeply embedded in the social fabric of Corsica, which, with a murder rate of 3.4 per 100,000,[8] appears to have taken over from Sicily as Europe's murder capital. The outward serenity is part of the problem: the island conceals the code of omertà, the culture of silence which protects serious criminals from the official justice system. There are frequent assassinations but rather few murder trials – at least official ones; perpetrators are often bumped off in extrajudicial revenge. The island's separatists have taken over from the IRA and ETA as Europe's most violent nationalists. The French government is often accused of giving up on the place; not least after the prefect, sent from Paris, was assassinated in 1998. It is easy to admire the pristine coastline of this West Belfast-with-maquis-and-sunshine without realising that its preservation has been bought partly with violence.

The coast has been saved from unsightly development thanks not to a wise planning policy, which is debated, set into law and then judiciously enforced, but through an informal planning system which employs the threat of violence to keep developers well away. Those who have attempted to build villas there have often found themselves trampling on the feet of local gangs who jealously guard their territories – Corsica's version of zoning. At least the owner of a villa on the island's south coast and his six holiday companions were spared when masked gunmen arrived one evening, in the summer of 2012, and ordered them out before rigging the place with explosives and blowing it up.[9] In July 2022, an estate agent and owner of a holiday letting business was less lucky when he was executed while eating lunch at a restaurant in the southern port of Propriano. 'Do not trust the summer calm nor the translucent blue of the sea,' concluded the newspaper *Le Monde*. 'They reveal nothing of the deadly atmosphere which reigns here.'[10]

Armed violence has spread to parts of Europe that previously had few links to organised crime. The homicide rate in Sweden and Denmark – at 1.08 and 0.8 per 100,000 respectively – has not grown hugely in thirty years. But that raw figure doesn't do justice to the explosion in gang crime. Sweden provides a good case study in how not to handle the problem. Knife crime, according to the Swedish National Council for Crime Prevention, doubled between 2010 and 2022.[11] At the turn of the century, Sweden had one of the lowest rates of gun crime in Europe; two decades later, it was second behind Croatia.

For years, Swedish authorities declined to admit to that pattern behind the sudden rise in violent crime until, in 2021, it finally published statistics relating to origin of criminal suspects. It showed that migrants were two and a half times more likely to have become crime suspects compared with

Swedish citizens with two Swedish parents. But within that there was a very strong pattern: while migrants from East and South Asia were very unlikely to become criminal suspects (much less likely than Swedish nationals), those from South America, Central Asia and Africa were very much over-represented.[12] This reflected crime rates in the places from whence the migrants had come. Sweden, in other words, has imported violent crime from violent parts of the world, on the back of a laissez-faire migration policy, and without properly considering what was going on. I will look at the effect of this on Swedish politics in a subsequent chapter.

The Netherlands, too, is struggling to cope with criminality imported from elsewhere in the world. In February 2024, an Eritrean festival in the Hague erupted into rioting between two factions: one of which was reported to be supportive of the Dutch government and the other which seemed to think that it should itself be in charge of its own affairs. A coach was set alight, a conference centre stormed and running battles fought with the police. In the same month, dozens of explosions were reported across the Netherlands, as criminal gangs fought each other. A fortnight earlier, an explosion partially demolished a block of flats in Rotterdam, killing three people. Traces of a drug laboratory were found in the wreckage. Not only are Dutch police struggling with the crime wave, the criminal justice is coping even less well. In February 2024, it was reported that 1,800 criminals who should have been jailed were instead living in the community because of a shortage of staff in the prison service.[13]

The Netherlands are often held up as an example of how 'enlightened' liberal policies towards drugs can work. Rather than conduct what critics like to call a 'war on drugs', the Netherlands has long tolerated personal use of cannabis in Amsterdam cafes and employs policies that treat drug use as more of public health issue than a crime. While the production and sale of hard drugs remains a criminal offence in theory, along with the import and export of all drugs, the drug dealers' customers have little to fear. Thanks to the softness of the law, Amsterdam has been attracting drug users from around the world for years. But has it stopped the war? That is not quite how it seemed in an Amsterdam court in February 2024, when Ridouan Taghi and three colleagues from his Moroccan cocaine cartel received life sentences for a string of murders, including that of suspected informers and a TV journalist who was investigating the case. Thanks to the threats made towards potential witnesses, the trial – nicknamed the Marengo trial after the code name for the police operations that had led to it – had taken six years. So high was the risk of retribution, that the name of the judge had to be kept secret and their face obscured as the verdicts were delivered. A liberal drugs policy has pushed the patience of many in the Netherlands, including the mayor of Rotterdam, Ahmed Aboutaleb, who declared: 'Pleas to regulate or legalise drugs ignore the fact that entire groups or young people in our working-class neighbourhoods are confronted with this misery and are corrupted. The phenomenon of high-class users enjoying a line on a Friday night has heavy repercussions on working class neighbourhoods.'[14]

In spite of the lynchpins of the cocaine trial being in custody, industrial quantities of the drug continued to enter the Netherlands – the police seized €3.5 billion worth of it in 2022, almost certainly only a small proportion of the total. Saskia Belleman, a reporter for the newspaper *De Telegraaf*, summed up the laid-back attitude that had allowed to the Netherlands to become the hub of the European cocaine trade: 'Until Marengo we always thought as long as they kill each other that doesn't have such a huge impact on our society. But then they killed the brother of the crown witness. They killed the lawyer ... and they killed the most well-known journalist in

Holland.' The Netherlands, once a law-abiding backwater, is suddenly turning to Italian mafia experts for advice in how to handle organised crime.[15]

Don't let anyone say that cross-border cooperation on crime isn't leading to any wrongdoers being captured. As previously mentioned, the sharing of vehicle registration plate data has enabled the industrial-scale issuance of traffic fines for minor traffic misdemeanours and the failure to pay the Byzantine system of tolls increasingly deployed on European roads. Yet, at the same time, European agencies are struggling to tackle organised criminals, not least those who are abusing the asylum system in order to circumvent its border controls and establish their criminal networks in Europe. A large part of the problem is the fundamentalist application of human rights laws. In quick succession in 2023 and 2024, several convicted criminals from the Balkans were granted the right to stay in Britain in spite of rules that were supposed to see them deported upon reaching the end of their sentences. An Albanian, who had acted as a courier for a crime gang, carting thousands of pounds out of Britain on aircraft flights, successfully convinced an immigration tribunal that his right to a family life should prevent him losing his joint UK citizenship – this despite the National Crime Agency describing him as a leading and controlling figure in the gang and that he would continue to present a threat to the UK public when released from jail. The tribunal accepted that he should be allowed to stay in Britain with his Albanian wife and their two children.[16] Another – a cannabis farmer caught tending £500,000 worth of the crop – persuaded a court that he couldn't be returned to Serbia, where he was brought up, because he had forgotten how to speak Serbian and wouldn't survive there using his native Albanian tongue.[17] A second cannabis farmer was allowed to stay on account that he had a Filipino wife in Britain.[18]

Ironically, these cases came to light at a time when the UK government was trying to make it much harder for UK citizens to bring foreign spouses to the country – couples had just been told that, from April 2024, one of them would have to be earning at least £38,700 a year for them both to live in Britain – more than double the previous threshold of £18,600 a year. For some reason, the right to a family life does not apply to them – only to convicted criminals with clever lawyers, many of them funded by legal aid. So much for ending freedom of movement with Brexit – free movement seems still to apply so long as you are a convicted criminal.

The main villain in this case is not the EU; it is the European Convention on Human Rights, which is incorporated into UK law via the Human Rights Act. That the act would create perverse outcomes was foreseen by Lord McCluskey, former solicitor general for Scotland, who, in a debate on the legislation before it was passed in 1998, predicted that it would turn out to be 'a field day for crackpots, a pain in the neck for judges and legislators and a goldmine for lawyers'. The problem is that it has incorporated into UK law a series of vague principles which are open to a wide variation of interpretation, allowing laws passed by a democratic parliament to be overthrown by judges.

As well as incorporating the European Convention into domestic law, the UK remains under the jurisdiction of the European Court of Human Rights (ECHR). Not to be mistaken for an EU institution, the ECHR is a body of the Council of Europe, which has a far wider reach; its forty-seven members includes virtually every country in Europe (although not the Vatican City), plus Turkey, Armenia, Georgia and Azerbaijan. Until its expulsion following the Ukraine invasion of 2022, Russia was a member, as was Belarus. The fear of being tarred with the same brush as those countries perhaps explains why no other state has dared to table serious proposals to leave the ECHR. But many have adopted an alternative strategy: simply to ignore the ECHR's rulings. While a supranational court keeping national governments in check is a noble venture, the ECHR has undermined itself by venturing into too many areas that ought to be the realm of democratically elected governments. Its institutional overreach has led to long backlogs and an attitude towards it of general contempt.

For the first sixteen years of existence, the ECHR didn't deliver a single judgement against the UK. There was a good reason for this: the convention which it existed to enforce was made up of a few, very serious provisions that had been agreed by all signatory governments. A democracy like the UK had little trouble in complying. But, from the 1970s onwards, the ECHR started to evolve something called the 'living instrument doctrine' – a euphemism for making up the law as it goes along. UK courts, thanks to the Human Rights Act, have adopted the same approach. The lawyers who drafted the European Convention in 1950 would be horrified to learn, for example, how the right to a family life has evolved. The original text demanded that there should be no interference in this right, 'except such as in accordance with the law and is necessary in a democratic society in the interests of national security, public safety or the economic wellbeing of the country, for the prevention of disorder or crime, for the protection of health or morals, or for the protection of the rights and freedoms of others'. Find there the clause that demands foreign gangsters be allowed to remain in Britain because they have a Filipino wife in the country – and yet that is how the 'right to a family life' is now being exercised.

Similarly, the ECHR has decided – all by itself, with no democratic input – that the right to life does not extend to the unborn child and that the right to life prohibits the use of the death penalty. In 2013, the ECHR decided (again, all by itself) that prisoners must not be handed whole-life tariffs – they must have the chance of parole. It demanded that prisoners be granted the right to vote – a ruling which the UK has so far refused to implement – and that the full provisions of justice should apply to military operations in war zones, with the result that the British army had no right to detain Taliban fighters in Afghanistan. In the words of former UK Supreme Court judge Lord Sumption, this amounts to applying to a war zone 'regulations designed for policemen turning in pickpockets at European police stations'. Sumption has added his weight to those calling for Britain to withdraw from the ECHR, arguing that a UK bill of rights could return the concept of human rights a little closer to what was originally intended.[19]

Thanks to the ECHR and its living instrument doctrine, Europe has helped disarm itself against criminals and terrorists. It has also resulted in the UK suffering 216 judgements against it since 1975.[20] Yet, contrary to what some people like to imagine, Britain is not a cavalier nation when it comes to respecting judgements of the ECHR. On the contrary. In spite of public hostility to the ECHR on the part of some politicians and commentators, it has yielded to 96 per cent of judgements over the years. That makes it one of the most obedient children in the class, ahead of France (93 per cent of judgements enacted), Germany (88 per cent), Spain (75 per cent) and Italy (73 per cent), and even ahead of many countries with a goody-goody reputation like Denmark (82 per cent). Many countries are happy to sign up for the ECHR while, seemingly, having little intention of obeying its judgements. Malta has only enacted 54 per cent, Georgia 55 per cent. Azerbaijan has only bothered with 27 per cent of them, lower even than the 35 per cent that Russia saw fit to enact prior to its expulsion. By launching a power grab against elected governments – attempting to make the law as well as enforce it – the ECHR has invited contempt. It is, sadly, all too typical of the European way of doing things: to create supranational institutions with few democratic underpinnings, which over-reach and eventually fail. Of Europe's democratic deficit, more later.

8.

Food

With only a passing acknowledgement that we were in the middle of a pandemic, a leader in the *Guardian* newspaper declared – almost with glee – that some empty shelves in supermarkets in August 2021 were the result of Brexit. Leaving the EU, it suggested, had 'drained the labour pool', and 'without workers food rots before it can get to market. Without hauliers goods sit unshipped in depots.' This was 'all predictable and predicted', yet 'the pandemic functions as political camouflage for Brexit-related problems'.[1]

It happened again in February 2023, when tomatoes and other salad crops temporarily disappeared from shelves in UK supermarkets. While Asda placed a limit of three packs of tomatoes per customer (a meaningless restriction given that many shops had not a single pack), Britons living in France took to Twitter with delight to post photographs of shelves in their local supermarket burgeoning with tomatoes and other fruit and vegetables.[2]

Never mind the real reasons: high energy costs had led to tomato producers in the UK and the Netherlands to turn off their heated greenhouses, leading to supermarkets in Northern Europe trying to source more tomatoes from Spain and Morocco, which were themselves experiencing poor weather. The great salad shortage of 2023, in other words, was caused by a set of circumstances that, temporarily, caught suppliers unawares but which was resolved within a couple of weeks. In a historical context, supermarkets would still have seemed extremely well stocked – travel back in time to a 1970s supermarket and you would find a paucity of fresh green vegetables every single winter – your choice might be between wrinkled carrots and frozen or canned vegetables. Yet the narrative that has been established in many minds is that Britain has somehow returned to something akin to post-war rationing, while EU consumers enjoy a cornucopia of fresh food – and that it is all down to Brexit.

There is nothing that inspires many Britons to play up the virtues of the near Continent more than food. In the past half century, European food has captured our imagination and, for some, transformed our diets. We did have a bottle of olive oil in the house when I was a child in the 1970s, but it wasn't in the kitchen; it was in the bathroom cabinet – for softening the wax in your ears. Our national inferiority complex is there to be seen in our restaurant menus, which are just about the only context in Britain where you will see the widespread use of foreign languages, often untranslated at that. We may have moved on during our forty-six years in the EU, from greasy fish and chips and overcooked mutton to a diet dominated by oven-ready pizzas and microwaveable chicken tikka masala, but France, Italy, Spain, in the popular imagination, are still countries where people sit down every evening to home-cooked food, or go out to eat at family-run restaurants, with recipes handed down the generations. We stuff our faces, in other words; while other Europeans experience high culture whenever they sit down to dine.

Like so much else, the reality fails to live up to the fantasy – and not just because of the way that some restaurants in Southern Europe seem to have adopted the wheeze of trying to solve their countries' debt crisis by landing extortionate bills on the heads of customers who don't take the precaution of asking the prices beforehand. Among the delights reported in recent years were a €125 bill for six prawns at a restaurant in Lanzarote,[3] a €830 bill for six calamari on the Greek island of Mykonos,[4] and a €1,100 bill for three steaks, fried fish and mineral water in Venice[5] (the latter of which did at least result in the restaurant being fined and the three students who had been ripped off invited back for a free stay in the city by a hotel worried at the damage to the city's reputation).

I struggled to recognise the France of gastronomical excellence the day I found myself in Southern Corsica with a craving for some fruit. It was a hot day, I had walked a long way – and I just wanted a peach. I would have given anything for a peach. The roadside sign looked promising enough. There was a village shop up ahead, it said, selling '*products de terroir*'. It wasn't open because the owner took a siesta for most of the afternoon, but it did say it would reopen at half past five for a brief evening window of shopping. I went back. But where was the local produce which I had expected to be tumbling off burgeoning shelves? Unlike Asda during the great fruit shortage, there was a tray of tomatoes – huge ones at that. There were a few potatoes, too, though they were pebble-sized. But some fruit? Some salad? There was absolutely nothing else fresh – just packs of biscuits, tins of sardines and empty shelves, which, had they been in Britain, would have been taken as a sign of the evils of Brexit. That is the problem with an ethos of promoting only local food – if you are in a locality that doesn't have much in the way of agricultural potential, like the steep wooded hills which come right down to the sea over much of Corsica – there isn't a lot to promote.

Later on, I went out to find some dinner. There was a posh restaurant, where it would have cost £100 a head to eat. Other than that, there was a pizza restaurant – and another pizza restaurant. That is the reality of France – no longer the gastronomic paradise of the English imagination, where the working day is punctuated by two-hour lunches washed down with fine wine, but a country that is gulping down fast food as much as anywhere in the world. The family-run restaurants that once sat in the former of village squares are mostly long gone. In their place – if there is anything at all – you might find a pizza joint; the very same standardised fast food you will find all over Britain. In 2023, according to data company CHD Expert-Datassential, there were 52,500 fast-food restaurants in France, up from 13,000 two decades earlier. In Amiens, in northern France, nearly one in six businesses is now a fast-food outlet, which must give Great Yarmouth a run for its money.[6] But then, is it any wonder the French have been tempted into fast-food joints when the alternative takes up so much time? When you have waited ninety minutes to be served a pretty ordinary crêpe in one of the remaining traditional restaurants in Brittany, the concept of 'slow food' does pale a bit.

As for the shops, they are little different from Britain, either. On one of my first visits to France – a school trip in the 1970s – my teacher was adamant. If we didn't get to the market in Boulogne in time for her to buy her cherries, there would be trouble. It was the same for many Britons: France was imagined as a country of overflowing market stalls where you could eat so much more adventurously than you could in prepackaged Britain. At the time, the closest I had come to a fresh peach was a slimy one tinned in syrup. Vegetables tended to consist of peas and diced carrots out a frozen Birds Eye packet. France, by contrast, was the land of fresh produce straight from the fields and orchards. In the mid-1980s, I remember marvelling at the sight of a girl on a French train sink an entire bagful of fresh apricots – a fruit I had previously encountered only in a jam pot. But here was the real thing.

But those images of France and Britain are a long way out of date. The opportunities to eat well in Britain have improved immeasurably. Our supermarkets – notwithstanding the occasional encounter with an empty shelf – boast at least as good a range of fresh food and vegetables as those in France. There are, as in Britain, a few rarified towns where Brits have their holiday homes, and they can be found queueing up to buy their artisanal charcuterie. But, elsewhere, the markets have mostly been replaced by vast supermarkets lined up on the strung-out commercial boulevards leading out of the large towns. The next time I went back to Boulogne, in the late 1980s, it wasn't the apricots that caught my eye but a street of *hypermarchés* doing a rapid trade flogging cut-price booze to English day trippers.

Do Britons really have an inferior diet to other Europeans? Not according to a US/Canadian study of dietary quality in 185 countries between 1990 and 2018, using the Global Dietary Database. The study looked at intake of sugars, fats, salt, vitamins and so on and condensed it into a single figure, the Alternative Healthy Eating Index (AHEI), for each country. It showed Britain on a par for Western Europe, with a diet of middling quality. Some Southern European countries, notably Italy, Greece and parts of the Balkans, came out higher. France, Germany, Spain, Benelux and the Netherlands had very similar diets to Britain, while Scandinavia had slightly inferior diets. Globally, the US and most of South American scored worse than Britain, while India, Indonesia, Australia and much of Africa came out better.[7] A study by the OECD of thirty countries found that 33 per cent of Britons succeed in eating five portions of fruit and vegetables a day – higher than any other country except Ireland, which is on a par. In

France, the figure was 20 per cent and in Germany just 11 per cent.[8] We fool ourselves into thinking poorly of the British diet by comparing the nice restaurant where we ate on holiday with the takeaways which line our local high street, yet the truth is we eat just as well, or badly, as our neighbours. It is just that we turn a blind eye to the fast-food outlets in France and elsewhere.

Brexit wasn't just going to make food scarce; it was going to make it expensive, too. Here is former Deputy Prime Minister Nick Clegg, for example, prophesising in October 2016 – after Marmite briefly disappeared from Tesco shelves over a dispute between retailer and supplier: 'It's clear that Marmite was just the tip of the iceberg. A hard Brexit will lead us off a cliff edge towards higher food prices, with a triple whammy of punishing tariffs, customs checks and workforce shortages.'[9]

Even when Britain negotiated a trade deal with the EU, the doom-laden claims continued. In April 2022, the London School of Economics' Centre for Economic Performance decided it had come up with an answer: Brexit had added 6 per cent to the cost of food in Britain, equivalent to £210 a year on average bills.[10] Never mind the pandemic, which had disrupted supply chains all over the world; never mind the surge in energy costs that had followed the Ukraine invasion; it was Brexit wot had pushed up food prices.

But is it really the case that Britons are paying through the nose just to fill their tummies, while other Europeans have an ample supply of good, nutritious, affordable food? Not according to World Bank figures. On the contrary – and notwithstanding Brexit – Britain is one of the most affordable places on earth to eat, and to eat well. The website looks at the cost of a basket of food in each country and adjusts it for local wages, to produce an index for the daily cost per person of a nutritionally adequate diet. In Britain, in 2021, it came to $1.53. No country in Western Europe came out cheaper:

in France it was $1.87, Germany $2.22, Spain $1.75 and Italy $2.23. In the US, by the way, it was $2.21.[11]

But let's not just look at a nutritionally adequate diet; what about a 'healthy' one? To afford a more-than-adequate, well-balanced diet in Britain will set you back $1.95 a day. In France it comes to $3.25, Germany $3.08, Spain $2.88 and Italy $3.18 (against $3.50 in the US). In other words, when it comes to the price of healthy food, the gap between Britain and other European countries is even greater. This is not to say, of course, that everyone in Britain does eat healthily – but there is greater opportunity to do so in Britain than just about anywhere, even if we do suffer an occasional dearth of tomatoes.

Why is it cheaper to eat in Britain than elsewhere in the EU? Partly because most food is VAT free in Britain, unlike in other countries, and partly because we have a more competitive supply chain. As befits a strong trading nation, our supermarkets shop around more for the best and cheapest goods, from wherever they may be in the world. This might not always help UK farmers, who frequently complain of low margins, or even of being forced to take a loss thanks to hard negotiating by supermarkets. But it does favour the consumer.

Scouring the world for the best- and keenest-priced food, however, is against the ethos of the EU. The bloc's food and agriculture policies are based on the conceit that food is part of Europe's high culture, and that European producers must not be undermined by those from elsewhere in the world. The EU also claims that its Common Agricultural Policy promotes food security. 'Thanks to this common policy,' the European Council claimed in 2023, 'EU citizens are at no risk of food shortages. The CAP supports farmers to ensure continuity of production.' Except that it does no such thing. That might have been a reasonable thing to claim up until 2003, when CAP subsides were based on food actually produced. But since the reforms of that year – which were designed to eradicate the butter mountains and wine lakes produced by the old system – most CAP subsidies have been simple payments based on land ownership. Money has been doled out not to produce anything but merely to keep land 'in agricultural condition'. In Britain, prior to Brexit, this led to the ridiculous sights of wealthy landowners receiving subsidies for their children's pony paddocks.

Far from ensuring continuity of food production, a lot of CAP payments seem to be disappearing into the pockets of fraudsters. In the space of seven years, Sicily received €5 billion in CAP payments, some of which was eagerly claimed by the Mafia. In one case, land supposed to be used for breeding buffalo was in fact used by the US navy for hosting satellite communications. Another claim concerned 500 parcels of land that the claimant claimed to have leased for farming – yet closer inspection revealed that seventy-seven of the landowners mentioned were dead. Mafiosi had submitted one claim in the name of a child whose father had been approached under the veiled threat of violence.[12]

It isn't just Sicily. An investigation in the Netherlands found that 231 claims for CAP payments were made on land that wasn't used for farming and didn't actually belong to the claimant. Much of it was owned by the country's forestry commission, which had no idea of the claims made on the land.[13] In Bulgaria, most CAP payments seem to be ending up in the hands of just a hundred individuals, while money supposedly for the development of tourist accommodation is being used to build lavish holiday homes for the landowners themselves. A Green MEP who serves on the European Parliament's Budgetary Control Committee complained that the European Commission 'seems to be turning a blind eye to the rampant abuse of taxpayers' money, and member states are doing little to address systematic issues'.[14]

At the same time as funding systematic fraud committed by European farmers, or people claiming to be farmers, the EU protects its agricultural interests by placing high tariffs on many food imports. The average tariff on food imported into the EU – under the World Trade Organisation's 'Most Favoured Nation' rules these tariffs apply to any country with which the EU does not have a formal trade deal – is 22 per cent. But on some products it is much higher: 56 per cent on beef, for example, and 70 per cent on whole milk.[15] The EU is also a master at non-tariff barriers, such as quotas and outright bans, justified on somewhat flimsy grounds. For example, while the tariff on poultry imports is relatively low – 14 per cent – the EU bans imports of US chicken that has been washed in a chlorine solution. While notionally a safety measure, it makes no sense given that Europeans quite happily eat salads that have been washed in a chlorine solution. They drink water, too, that has been chlorinated. The chlorination process is simply an extra safety measure to protect against infections such as salmonella. But, of course, banning chlorine-washed chicken does have the effect of keeping keenly priced US chicken out of European markets.

Given the fuss that the EU has made over chlorinated chicken, you might assume that it had an impeccable record on food safety itself. But not so. My first brush with French food standards was at a celebratory meal after successfully completing a charity hitch-hike to Paris as a student. Foolishly, I chose the shellfish – and spent a gruesome return journey leaning over the side of the Dieppe to Newhaven ferry, as well as the next two days in bed. Things don't seem to have been getting a whole lot better of late. In 2022, cases of food poisoning across the EU increased by 49.4 per cent compared with the year before. The number of people hospitalised increased by 11.5 per cent and the number of deaths by 106.5 per cent. There were 137,107 cases of campylobacter, including 10,551 hospitalisations. Of a sample of 2,774 ready-to-eat foods tested for the bacterium, 0.11 per cent tested positive; of 25,601 non-ready-to-eat foods – such as raw meat – 11.1 per cent were infected.[16]

As for salmonella, 65,208 people fell ill, 11,287 were hospitalised and 81 died. The pathogen was present in 5.1 per cent of broiler chickens and 3.3 per cent of turkeys tested. And these are just the cases we know about – notification of cases of salmonella is voluntary in France, Spain and the Netherlands. Listeria killed 286 Europeans, E. coli a further 28. The latter was found to be present in a shocking 1.1 per cent of ready-to-eat foods. So, no, Europe has no right to preach over US food safety standards. To decry American chlorine-washed chicken as a threat to human health while your own food producers are serving up E. coli and salmonella is nothing more than food nationalism – protectionist policy in disguise. If the EU really wanted to stamp out food poisoning it would ensure that its own chicken was washed in chlorine – as well as making sure that all milk and cheese was pasteurised. But that would never do because cheese in France is seen as high culture. 'How can you govern a country with 246 varieties of cheese?' Charles de Gaulle is reputed to have said. It might at least be a start if reporting common pathogens was made mandatory in France – as it is in most EU member states – and diners were not forced to play bacterial roulette every time they tucked into a treasured delicacy.

The EU was quick to weaponise biosecurity in its efforts to try to make sure that the UK suffered from Brexit. From day one following Britain's departure from the EU, UK food producers have had to obtain veterinary certificates, plant passports and all manner of other pettifogging bureaucratic measures – even though standards remained the same on either side of the Channel and UK authorities allowed three years' grace. But those who think it was all plain sailing

exporting food to the EU prior to Brexit have very short memories. In the first three months of 2016 – shortly before the
Brexit vote – UK lamb exports to France suddenly plunged
by 7 per cent. Given that France then accounted for half of
UK lamb exports, it had a serious impact on UK farmers.
Why did it happen? Because French lamb producers had
staged a campaign to keep out foreign competition, emptying
lorries and clearing supermarket shelves of imported meat.
Some supermarkets had given into the bullying tactics and
ceased to stock UK-produced lamb.[17] This was a recurrent
problem stretching back to 1990, when French farmers scattered nails on motorways and set up roadblocks made of hay
and burning tyres to prevent lorries delivering their loads of
imported meat. One lorry was set alight, killing 219 lambs.
Other animals were poisoned or doused with insecticide to
prevent their being allowed into the human food chain.[18] So
much for respect for the single market. We forget, now the
EU is idolised by many in Britain as a champion of open
markets and free trade, just how many vested interests were
out to frustrate the single market – even when we were fully
paid-up members of the EU.

The effect of all this formal and informal protectionism
is to keep food prices for European consumers higher than
they need be, as well as restricting choice. This is not to say
that Britain, following Brexit, has made full advantage of
leaving the EU. Many of the prohibitive tariffs on meat and
dairy products have been retained, or merely tinkered with –
imports of beef to the UK, for example, are now subject to
tariffs of 12 per cent plus £147 per 100 kg, instead of 12.8 per
cent plus £147.95 per 100 kg as they were while we were in
the EU. Big deal. The UK government can now set whatever
tariffs it likes; it could, if it wanted to, unilaterally remove all
tariffs on imported food – something that would not help
UK farmers but would see consumers enjoying even cheaper

food in the shops. The government has at least signalled its intention to move towards freer trade in food products. It has removed tariffs on 2,000 goods where they were considered unnecessary because Britain had no relevant producers to protect, and a further 500 goods which were previously liable for 'nuisance tariffs' of 2 per cent or less. It has also simplified tariffs for processed foods.[19] The UK has made some progress in negotiating free trade deals which are less protectionist over agricultural goods, such as a deal with Australia which will see tariffs on imported meat phased out over fifteen years.

While Britain seeks new export markets for agriculture, one European country seems determined to shrink its own hugely successful agriculture sector. In the latter stage of the Second World War, Amsterdam and the populous centre of the Netherlands nearly starved as the advancing Allied troops cut off the capital from the food-producing regions that surrounded it. A lesson was learned, and post-war food security became a cornerstone of national policy. It was so fantastically successful that by the twenty-first century the Netherlands had become the second largest food exporter in the world – remarkable given that it is also one of the world's most densely populated countries. In 2022, it exported €122.3 billion worth of agricultural goods. While some of this was imported goods re-exported after processing, €79.8 billion worth was produced in the Netherlands. What's more, Dutch agriculture is very well diversified. Huge greenhouses produce fresh fruit and vegetables all year round. Fresh flowers remain a large part of the rural economy, but the country still finds room to farm large quantities of livestock, from cattle to pigs to poultry. In 2022, exports included €11.9 billion worth of dairy products and €11 billion worth of meat.[20] What's more, Dutch farmers have achieved this on far less subsidy than most of their counterparts in other European countries. In 2020, just over 10 per cent of farm income in the Netherlands came from CAP subsidies, lower than in any other EU country. In France, the biggest consumer of EU subsidies, it was a third and in Slovakia and Estonia over 70 per cent.[21]

What could possibly go wrong? EU environmental regulations, that's what. In 2019, the government announced that in order to prevent nitrogen emissions breaching allowable levels in the country's nature reserves the agriculture sector would have to be shrunk. Farmers would be offered incentives to give up their farms: 3,000 of them would be offered a total of €1.5 billion to sell up and retire. Livestock numbers would be reduced by a third. As for the farmers, they weren't too impressed. They descended on the Hague in 2,000 tractors, causing hundreds of miles of tailbacks, and deposited straw on the doorsteps of government buildings. Within months, a political party, the Farmer-Citizen Movement – or BBB – had emerged from virtually nowhere. By 2023, it had emerged as the largest party in regional elections.

The attempt to shrink the Dutch agriculture sector was all too typical of the European way of doing things. An inflexible EU directive had gone out, without democratic legitimacy, which was then enacted by a national government that saw no need to consult the people because it felt it didn't have choice – a directive is a directive, after all. Couldn't there be other ways to reduce nitrogen emissions, without having to close down a large chunk of one of the country's most successful industries? It turns out that Dutch farmers had already reduced nitrogen emissions by two thirds since 1990 through cleaner practices, such as better controlled application of fertilisers and more careful handling of cattle manure and urine.[22] But no, rather than find some positive way of solving the problem, the government decided to hit a target by a means that will make the country poorer and Europe more reliant on food produced elsewhere.

The CAP isn't working for consumers, but then it isn't

working for farmers, either. The Dutch farmer protests have since spread to Germany, where, in January 2024, 30,000 tractors converged on the centre of Berlin, their drivers protesting about a plan to cut fuel subsidies, and to France, where, in the same month, farmers blocked an autoroute near Toulouse, held up lorries from Spain and emptied 20,000 litres of Spanish wine onto the tarmac. A government building in Carcassone was bombed. Tractors then converged on Paris, blocking several motorways into the city, with farmers' leaders threatening to starve the capital into submission. In a re-run of their old, established tactics, they set light to lorries, or used fork-lifts to tip them on their side – including those bringing in produce from neighbouring Belgium and Germany. French farmers were moaning not just about their usual gripe – overseas competition – but about EU red tape, which they claimed was strangling French agriculture. Given that EU red tape was practically invented to benefit French farmers, and protect them from competition, that might seem just a little rich.

But then they did have a point about excessive bureaucracy. An insight is provided by environmental journalist Emmanuelle Ducros, who has described farming in France as 'like reading Kafka on a tractor'. The reason, he wrote, why Moroccan tomatoes cost €2.50 a kilo and French ones €4.50, and why Thai chicken costs €5 a kilo and French chicken €11, is a bizarrely pedantic set of regulations which lay down such things as the required size of every trapdoor on chicken cages. There are fourteen regulations regarding hedge-cutting and many more specifying exactly on what day you must plough and harrow your fields. Worse, many sets of different regulations laid down by different agencies at local, regional, national and EU level contradict each other; in order to please one agency you might have to do something that earns you a fine from another.[23]

The EU often gives the impression of being run by a cartel of German car-makers and French farmers. Yet, even with a trading environment which is heavily designed around their needs, it seems that officiousness is now rendering French farmers unable to compete. They are struggling to maintain their country's image as a cornucopia of fresh and exotic produce. It was not just bad luck that made it hard for me to find a fresh peach on my trip to Corsica. Fruit and vegetable growing in France has withered in the past two decades. In 2000, French farmers produced 463,000 tonnes of peaches and nectarines; by 2020, it was down to 180,000 tonnes. Pears – one of the very symbols of Normandy – are down from 243,000 tonnes to 86,000 tonnes. Cherries – bless the soul of my primary school teacher – fell from 67,000 tonnes in 2000 to 36,000 tonnes in 2020. Tomatoes? Down from 840,000 tonnes to 643,000 tonnes. Lettuce? Down from 509,000 tonnes to 354,000 tonnes.[24]

You get the idea. But it gets even worse. Horreur of hor-reurs, the same has happened to wine production – the very lifeblood of French civilisation – down from 59.7 million hec-tolitres in 2000 to 46.9 million hectolitres in 2020. If you have noticed fewer French wines in UK supermarkets in recent years, you are not mistaken: UK imports are down from 2.4 million to 1.8 million hectolitres. Personally, it is rare that I reach for a bottle of French wine any more. If I am buying white wine, I tend to go for something New Zealand, mostly because it tastes good but also partly in admiration that the country's wine producers can produce it without subsidy, ship it halfway round the world, pay tariffs and still compete on price with a bottle of Chateau la Plonque.

In 2023, came the ultimate humiliation for the French wine industry: the government announced that it would spend €160 million buying up surplus wine – to turn it into industrial alcohol for use in pharmaceuticals. Even with reduced production, winemakers were struggling to shift their product. Government-sponsored studies claiming that red wine – and French red wine in particular – could protect you against heart disease have begun to lose their effect. But rather than accept the offer to sell their surplus wine to the government with grace, one winemaker in Bordeaux moaned that the plan didn't go nearly far enough – not when he had a twenty-four-month backlog of wine in his cellar. What he really wanted was for the government to pay farmers to grub up 15,000 hectares' (37,000 acres) worth of vineyards at a rate of €10,000 per hectare.[25] And that was just in the Bordeaux region. In other words, an industry built on subsidies from French – and other EU – taxpayers was now demanding €150 million for winemakers to exit the industry. There may be far fewer fruits growing in French orchards than there used to be, but there is still a very generous crop of magic money trees.

It isn't just France. Bart Dochy, a farmer from Ledegem, across the border in Belgium, has explained the byzantine regulations he must now navigate in his day-to-day business. Any delivery of fertiliser to his farm has to be registered with the authorities within seven days. He then has to register exactly how much has been applied to every parcel of land, down to the last kilo. If he is late in registering this information, or if he makes a small error, he can be fined hundreds of euros. It is no use trying to cheat, either: the EU has started to deploy drones and satellites to spy on what is going on in the fields. There are further rules laying down exactly when certain crops must be planted – rules that ignore the reality of having to work around the weather. A farmer, he says, is engaged in constant 'conflict between government and nature'. A crop may have to be planted by 1 September, for example, but 'if the last week of August is unbelievably rainy you will not be able to sow this properly but you are nevertheless obliged to sow, otherwise you may be faced with a fine'.[26]

In Germany, Jan and Annika Pape, who run a dairy farm with 280 cows in Lower Saxony, complain of having to spend 70 per cent of their time in the office rather than on the land or in the cowshed. On top of that, in 2023, the government announced that farmers were to lose the tax advantages on diesel fuel used on farms – they will in future have to pay the full whack, even though their tractors rarely venture onto the publicly maintained roads that fuel tax is funding (except perhaps when they are off to Berlin and Brussels to complain about bureaucracy). A report by DZ Bank estimates that at the current rate of decline Germany will only have 100,000 of its 256,000 farms left by 2040.[27]

In Denmark, Gill Andersen, who has farmed in Jutland for thirty-two years, is contemplating selling her land to the government in order for it to be turned into a raised bog, just as her neighbour's farm already has been. The government has put aside 200 million krone (£23 million) a year to do as the Dutch government is – buying up farms to take them out of production. In Denmark, the impetus was a study by Aarhus University which claimed that rewetting land and turning it back into bog could help remove 1.4 million tonnes of carbon dioxide from the air every year – around as much as is spewed out by Copenhagen. That might help Denmark reach its target of reducing territorial carbon emissions by 70 per cent, relative to 1990 levels, by 2030,[28] but it won't help the country feed itself or help to maintain a healthy agricultural sector. Nor, if it means the country ends up importing more food, will it necessarily mean a reduction in global carbon emissions.

As for Britain, membership of the EU – or European Economic Community as it then was – did not at first prevent farmers from increasing food production. A national food security policy – inspired by the privations caused by the German bombing of food convoys across the Atlantic during the Second World War – was allowed to continue for the first decade of UK membership. In 1973, the year Britain joined the EEC, the country's food production to supply ratio (a measure of self-sufficiency in food) stood at 62.1 per cent. Eleven years later, it peaked at 78.1 per cent, before European efforts to reduce surpluses began to demand land be taken out of production. Farmers were paid to set aside agricultural land and, from 2003 onwards, subsidies were decoupled from food production. By 2022, the food production to supply ratio was down to 60.5 per cent.[29] So, no, EU membership did not, overall, boost agriculture in the UK, even if it did make it a little easier for farmers to export to European markets. Now Britain is outside the CAP it has a chance to construct a more effective policy on food and farming.

9.

Environment

The thirteen officials and quangocrats who wrote to the then environment secretary, Liz Truss, in January 2016, were of one mind: vote for Brexit and the hedgehogs will get it. It was only thanks to EU membership that our beaches and rivers were clean, and that our flora and fauna were in reasonable health. 'Brexit would halt or reverse four decades of progress,' moaned Baroness Young, former Chair of the Environment Agency.[1]

Brexit would return Britain to being the 'dirty man of Europe', according to Stephen Tindale, a former leader of Greenpeace. Craig Bennett of Friends of the Earth predicted, 'We could probably kiss goodbye to laws that protect our most precious wildlife sites. It's only legally-binding EU renewable energy targets that give us any hope that clean energy has much of a future in the UK.'[2]

Come the Brexit vote, and the prophesies grew even grimmer, with numerous malign bugs and triffid-like plants set to seize advantage of our decision to leave the EU. 'The number of native invaders setting foot in the UK is set to

grow,' warned Camilla Morrison-Bell of the Wildlife and
Countryside Coalition in March 2018, showing the kind
of hysteria about outsiders that many Remainers accused
the Brexit campaign of showing towards human migrants.
These invaders were going to 'wreak havoc in our rivers,
seas and countryside' as well as fell our buildings and infrastructure.[3] Free movement had suddenly become a curse
and a nightmare when it involved creatures with more than
two legs.

Yet, come Brexit, and the critics had to admit that, actually,
Britain hadn't turned into poisoned hellhole of Stygian pools
and mounds of smouldering ash. It is true that UK rivers
had a very bad winter in 2023/24 owing to sewage overflows,
but this is not due to deregulation – of which more later. 'So
far the UK has not used its new-found sovereignty to diverge
significantly from the EU's rulebook,' concluded a 2022 report
by Brexit and Environment, a network of academics that has
set itself the task of reviewing the effect of Brexit on the natural world. It even declared its approval of the government's
Environment Land Management Scheme, which 'rewards
farmers for meeting sustainability targets rather than the
amount of land farmed'. This, it said, is 'hardly the bonfire of
red tape that the then Prime Minister Boris Johnson promised'.[4] As for renewable energy, no, it wasn't only the EU that
was driving it. Growth in the wind industry carried on after
the Brexit vote to make Britain the world's largest investor in
offshore wind.

But why should it come as a surprise that a post-Brexit
UK government hasn't trashed the environment, given that
much of the EU's environment law had been inspired by the
UK in the first place? On many things, from air pollution to
welfare of farm animals, the UK has long led Europe, with
the EU only catching up with UK rules years later. In some
cases, UK environmental laws had been watered down by

weaker EU ones. The Common Agricultural and Common Fisheries Policies often prevented stronger regulations being put in place.

One of the big fears of Remain campaigners was that Britain would relax EU legislation on water quality. It is true that Britain's rivers and coasts have often been defiled by sewage discharges – a hangover from a fatal decision in the nineteenth century to combine surface drainage with foul sewers – with the result that emergency overflows during heavy rain contain sewage as well as rainwater. This problem has become worse thanks to a trend towards wetter winters, and will require billions of pounds of investment to put right. UK water companies have so far shown depressingly little interest in resolving the issue, often preferring to pay fines rather than invest in the separation of foul and surface drainage. But, if we are going to damn Britain for its sewage discharges, are things really much better in other European countries? Not if you live on the Mar Menor, a natural tidal lagoon near Murcia in southern Spain, once known as the Crystal Sea but now branded the 'green soup' owing to pollution from sewage, nitrates and phosphates. A lack of action has driven local carp and seahorses to the brink of extinction.[5]

A wet winter and consequent rise in sewage discharges marred the University Boat Race in 2024. Several rowers were reported to have fallen ill after high levels of E. coli were detected in the Thames. But were things any different across the Channel? In spite of spending £1.2 billion cleaning up the Seine for the Paris Olympics, the triathlon had to be postponed and even then, several swimmers fell ill and one had to be treated in hospital.

The existence of high theoretical standards doesn't necessarily mean they are observed in practice. In France, ANES, the Agency for Food, Environmental and Occupational

Health and Safety, warned in 2023 that a third of the country's drinking water has excessive levels of a pesticide called chlorothalonil – and that was four years after the chemical was supposedly banned.[6] Another study found drinking water supplied to a fifth of the population was contaminated by pesticides.[7] In Italy, 39 per cent of seawater samples taken from around the coast in 2018 were found to be heavily contaminated. Unbelievably, Venice still does not have a proper sewage treatment system, with buildings still discharging raw sewage into the canals – not just as a result of emergency discharges during times of heavy rainfall but as a matter of course. In addition, the Venice Lagoon is home to 2,000 abandoned boats which have been deliberately dumped there by their owners after the past sixty years, leaking oil and other chemicals into the water.[8] The city has constructed a long-delayed flood protection system to shut off the lagoon from the Adriatic, but without doing a lot to cope with the sewage and other discharges that the city relies on being dispersed by the exchange of water with the open sea. And Venice is one of Italy's great showcases to the world, so what, one wonders, is going on elsewhere?

The EU drafted its Water Framework Directive in 2000, with the aim of having all European waters reach an acceptable standard by 2015. Yet the deadline has since been put back to 2027, not least thanks to lobbying from Germany, 92 per cent of whose rivers, according to the German branch of Friends of the Earth, remain polluted to an unacceptable degree.[9] There are no longer directly comparable statistics, but how was Britain doing before it left the organisation as a result of Brexit? Better than most of its neighbours. The quality of European rivers, lakes and streams is assessed by the European Environment Agency and its report for 2018 shows that many of Britain's rivers are ecologically degraded – something it shared with all of northern Europe and southern Sweden. When it came to chemical pollution of surface waters, however, Britain was one of the cleanest countries in Europe, with nearly 100 per cent of water bodies in good condition. By contrast, Germany, Austria and Sweden had zero bodies of water in good condition, and Belgium had near zero. High levels of mercury were a factor many cases.[10] Britain's performance on keeping chemicals out of rivers is all the more remarkable given that it is one of the most densely populated countries in Europe, and it is thanks to legislation which, in many cases, pre-dates Britain's membership of the EU. So why would Britain need to rely on the EU to continue progress at cleaning up rivers?

Drinking water? Quality of drinking water is measured by the Environmental Performance Index (EPI) maintained by Yale University, which condenses forty performance indicators into a single figure between 0 and 100. In 2022, the UK came out top, with a score of 100. While European countries generally did well when compared with the rest of the world, some Western European countries scored surprisingly badly, with Germany 11th on a score of 98.6, Italy 13th on 97.8, Spain 16th on 94.8 and France 17th on 93.8.[11]

It is a similar story with air quality. In the European Environment Agency's 2018 assessment, Britain was the eighth cleanest out of thirty-nine countries (the agency has some members beyond the EU) when it came to a form of particulate pollution known as PM10 (particles no more than 10 microns in diameter). On PM2.5s (particles less than 2.5 microns across) it was twelfth. For ozone pollution it was third cleanest, for benzene eleventh. Only on nitrogen oxide did it score poorly, being thirty-first out of thirty-nine, but still ahead of Germany, which has similar densities of road traffic. As for air pollution, the figures have to be read in conjunction with the knowledge that Britain is one of the most densely populated countries in Europe, behind only Belgium and the Netherlands. Yet it still manages to have some of the cleanest air, thanks to Clean Air Acts that started off life in the 1950s, two decades before Britain's EU membership.[12]

There is room for further improvement. But, no, not by any stretch of the imagination can Britain be labelled the 'dirty man of Europe'. As European countries go, it is freshly showered and smelling of aftershave. A better candidate for the title is Germany, which, in spite of being the cradle of green politics and having a governing coalition that involves the Green Party, has some of the most polluted rivers and lowest quality air. Germany might like to boast of ambitious targets – it pledges to eliminate net carbon emissions by 2045, five years earlier than Britain. But, in practice, it has reopened coal mines and coal power stations as the folly of its reliance on Russian gas has become apparent. There are frequent tales of environmental degradation. A report in 2018 found that 55 per cent of German waters were suffering from eutrophication – where an excess of nutrients has spilled off the land and fed the growth of algal blooms in the sea. Even Germany's efforts to switch to green energy have left their mark, with the German Environment Agency saying that the construction of offshore windfarms has damaged ocean habitats.[13] In 2022, eleven tonnes of dead fish were pulled out of the Oder River, which forms the border between Germany and Poland, with authorities on either side unable to identify what had killed them.[14]

When it is blocking the development of fracking and GM foods, Europe might like to assert that it has higher environmental standards than the US, but it is hard to stand that assertion up against the reality. The EU has higher standards than the US on air quality? Not when it came to the diesel emissions scandal, it didn't. It was a European company, Volkswagen, which put 'cheat' devices into the software that governed its diesel engines, so that they could detect when they were being subjected to an official test and go automatically into a low-performance, low-emissions mode. Once out on the open road they emitted up to forty times as much nitrogen dioxide as during the test.[15] And it was a US regulator that caught out the company: the US Environmental Protection Agency and West Virginia University, which conducted a series of emissions tests involving real-world driving. The scandal, exposed in 2015, cost Volkswagen billions of dollars in fines and compensation to motorists.

Where were the effective regulations to prevent, for example, Brittany's coast being infested by the toxic algae which had affected the area's beaches since the 1970s? The green slime is not just unsightly; it is lethal. When it rots, it emits hydrogen sulphide gas which can overcome humans and animals in seconds – among them a 50-year-old jogger who died on a beach near St Brieuc in 2016.[16] Three years later, an 18-year-old oyster farmer and a 70-year-old holidaymaker succumbed in the same way on the same stretch of coast. Effluent from pig farms is blamed for providing the nutrients which feeds the algae.[17] The main problem is run-off of nitrogen from farmland – caused by excessive application of fertilisers as well as by poorly managed effluent from livestock farms. There are ways to cut the pollution through better farming practices, yet environmental authorities in Brittany complain that their efforts to persuade farmers to adopt more friendly practices have so far proved in vain. The EU's Common Agricultural Policy, they say, simply doesn't incentivise farmers to look after the environment, and they recommend that, in future, aid should be tied to the adoption of methods which result in very low run-off of nitrogen.[18] That is what Britain's new system of agricultural subsidies does: it rewards more environmentally friendly farming practices. But Britain had to the leave the EU in order be able to create such a system.

The EU claims high standards on recycling, too. In 2021, according to the European Environment Agency, 49.6 per cent of municipal waste in Europe was collected for recycling, up from 27.3 per cent in 2000. Germany, on 67.8 per cent, is top of the class, not just in Europe but across the world, followed by Austria (62.5 per cent) and Slovenia (60.8 per cent).[19] It isn't just about cutting waste, according to the European parliament; it is about creating a 'circular economy', which will 'increase competitiveness, stimulate innovation, boost economic growth and create 700,000 jobs in the EU alone by 2030'.[20]

But something seems to have gone missing in this noble scheme to move on from the days when waste was simply tipped in the nearest hole in the ground, covered up and forgotten about: the small matter of what actually happens to the waste after it is collected for recycling. For many years, much of Europe's waste was exported to China for recycling – until that country began to tire of being sent shipments of contaminated waste. China started to turn away imports of European waste in 2017, and banned them altogether in 2021. Where did our waste go then, after being carefully sorted into all those colour-coded wheelie bins and other containers (seven different receptacles in the case of some English councils)? An investigation by Greenpeace into waste tips in Malaysia shed some light. The group found a rubbish dump near the town of Jenjarom, 10-foot high and covering three acres – and full of packaging from dishwasher tablets, yogurt pots and crisp packets, all with branding from UK and other European supermarkets. Similar scenes were found at two other waste sites, where locals were complaining about pungent smells as the plastic was burned or melted, often under cover of darkness. Between January and August 2018, 88,000 tonnes of plastic was exported to Malaysia from the UK alone. But it wasn't really being recycled; just shipped halfway around the world to be dumped in a developing country instead. As with its carbon emissions, 'clean' Europe is simply offshoring its waste while claiming to be setting the world an example of how to treat the environment.[21] It gets worse. According to an estimate by the charity Ocean Conservancy in 2016, 60 per cent of all the rubbish in the oceans gets there via just five countries: China, Indonesia, the Philippines, Thailand and Vietnam.[22] Two of them – China and Indonesia – were at the time among the top ten destinations for EU waste. Since then, EU exports of waste have increased, from 25.7 million tonnes in 2015 to 32.1 million tonnes in 2022.[23]

In 2023, the EU finally took action and announced that it would ban export of plastic waste to countries outside the OECD from 2026. But don't hold your hopes that this will mean the end of European rubbish polluting other countries, and the oceans. It just so happens that Turkey, which now receives nearly half of all EU waste exports, is an OECD country. And guess what? An investigation in 2021 revealed similar scenes in Turkey as those reported in Malaysia – packaging waste bearing European brand-names found dumped and burned by the side of the road near the southern city of Adana.[24] Turkey, too, has now taken matters into its own hands and banned the import of most plastic waste. It looks as if the EU, finally, will have to start taking responsibility for its own waste – either by recycling, incinerating it or finding some other way of disposing it. What it won't be doing in future is shipping it to be dumped elsewhere in the world.

It is true that Britain has an impoverished natural environment compared with pre-medieval times, and that it is lacking some of the fauna that are still clinging on, or even reviving, in some parts of mainland Europe. You will not bump into a bear or a pack of wolves in the English country-side. But then neither will you do so in the Pyrenees, if many of the local landowners have their way. '*Mort au ours*,' read the slogan daubed on the road as I drove up towards the moun-tains south of Lourdes. Bears had recently been reintroduced but had not endeared themselves to many of the locals. The creatures didn't receive a much warmer reception in Austria after efforts to reintroduce them from 1989 onwards. While the population is believed to have reached thirty-five at one stage, all were gone by 2012, victims of poaching and pres-sures on their habitat.[25]

Britain is, however, one of seven European countries where tree cover grew between 2000 and 2020 (by 81.6 kilohec-tares), against the downward trend elsewhere.[26] Compared with much of mainland Europe, Britain has been far better at preserving its rural landscapes – when you take into ac-count the obvious limiting factor, population density. Spain has a population density just one third that of the United Kingdom, but you wouldn't think so if you took a trip along its Mediterranean coast. From Gibraltar to the French border is 800 miles of urban sprawl, with concrete villas broken up only by Benidorm-like protrusions of tower blocks. There are just a few open stretches left and, even there, motorways tend to hug the cliff line. It was a Spanish architect, Arturo Soria y Mata, who conceived the idea of a 'linear city', which he proposed might run from Madrid to Berlin. A few miles, in Madrid, were actually built. But the Costas really have become the linear city of which he dreamt – though perhaps not in the way he imagined.

The shame is that a national law exists in Spain to stop coastal sprawl. Under the Ley de Costas, passed in 1988, there is, theoretically, a 100-metre band along Spain's coast on which no new development is allowed. Yet, in many cases, it has been ignored – or enforcement has only been attempted belatedly, after homes had been built, sold and occupied by unsuspecting buyers. It is not just on the coast that this has happened, but in rural places inland. The result is despoiled landscapes – and innocent homebuyers caught in the crossfire between different public agencies. In some cases, the local government had given permission for properties to be built in places where, under national law, they were not supposed to go. The regional government would then catch up, or there would be a change of local government – and unsuspecting villa owners would find themselves facing the bulldozers.

Leonard and Helen Prior had been looking for a peaceful retirement in the sun, and, in 2002, thought they had found it in a €110,000 plot of land near the town of Vera, Almeria. The land came with planning permission from the local town council. They built a home, spending a further €375,000, and settled there in 2003. Three years later, they received a telephone call telling them to come down to the town hall, where they were presented with a letter telling them that planning permission for their home had been revoked on the grounds that it was in a rural area where no development was supposed to be allowed. They had fifteen days to demolish it.

They tried to challenge the decision in the courts but, while the case was still being determined, the town council sent in the bulldozers and took down the house in half an hour, leaving only the garage and swimming pool. Leonard, who had a heart condition, unsurprisingly collapsed as he watched. As a result of their case and many others like it, the European parliament started to investigate and address the obvious: that in a civilised country citizens should not find themselves thrown out of their homes nor have their property stolen from them as a result of power struggles between competing public authorities. The law was eventually changed so that properties built with official authorisation, but which had later been condemned as a result of contravening national law, were granted a stay of execution and regularised. Astonishingly, there turned out to be 327,000 of them in Andalucia alone – that is the equivalent of an entire city the size of Birmingham, which would have faced demolition as a result of bungling and bickering officialdom. Fortunes had been made by developers in the building boom that followed Spain's entry into the euro – while many of their customers face having their life savings obliterated. The Priors eventually received compensation in 2018, a whole decade after their home had been demolished – but only €220,000 of it; far less than they had spent on their building project.[27]

While not on the scale of Spain, there are signs of chaotic planning and feeble conservation laws across much of Europe. Many countries seem to have little interest in – or struggle with – enforcing rights of way. I am used to relying on Ordnance Survey maps to tell me where I can walk, but the Italian equivalent was of little use when trying to find my way to the Tuscan town of San Gimignano. What were marked on the map as minor roads or pathways had in many cases been blocked off by gates or wires as property owners had sought to expand their little empires. Their land grabs appeared to have attracted little interest from any public authority. As in Spain, illegally built homes have become an endemic problem in Italy. According to the Italian bureau of statistics, ISTAT, 19.7 per cent of homes built in the decade leading up to 2015 were constructed illegally. A further report showed a huge difference between north and south, with 6.7 per cent of homes in the north of the country illegally built and 47.3 per cent in the south.[28] Far from addressing the problem, illegal developments have been encouraged through regular amnesties.

My first impression of Greece, on a train journey through the country in the late 1980s, was mile upon mile of half-built houses, their skeletons of concrete and terracotta blocks rising from the maquis. Greece is supposed to have planning laws that protect rural areas, not without good reason. Land management is an essential defence against wildfires. Therefore, large areas have been designated as protected forest where no building is supposed to be allowed. Property developers, however, see it otherwise – and with few seemingly deterred from building whatever they want, wherever they want. As in Italy, they are often rewarded with amnesties for illegally built homes. As Ioannis Glinavos, a professor of law well versed in its practice in Greece, has put it: 'Greece, in spite of being a European Union member and a developed economy, exhibits many of the cultural traits found in less developed nations.'[29] The result are fire disasters in the making.

This leaves the issue of carbon emissions, which has come to dominate so much debate on the environment, and in which Europe likes to claim a lead. If you feared that Brexit would harm efforts to reduce emissions and so tackle climate change, your fears would surely have been dissipated in June 2019 when Britain became the first large country to commit itself to a legally binding target to reach net zero emissions by 2050. Other European countries followed soon after. Leave aside for the moment whether setting inflexible carbon reduction targets is a wise thing to do, Britain clearly does not need the EU in order to make its own commitments on cutting emissions.

Future targets are one thing, but what about past records? How does Britain compare with other countries? In 2022, UK per capita emissions were 4.7 tonnes. Nine out of 27 EU member states had lower per capita emissions, but the reduction in UK emissions has happened especially fast. In 2010, most UK electricity was still produced by coal; in 2022, it was down to a 1.7 per cent share, with most electricity coming from gas (38.4 per cent), wind (24.7 per cent) and nuclear (14.7 per cent). As a result of the transformation as much as anything else, total UK per capita emissions in 2022 were only a shade over those of France (4.6 tonnes) and were lower than in Denmark (4.9 tonnes), which is considered to be a world leader in renewable energy. They were also lower than in non-EU Norway (7.5 tonnes), which enjoys the gift of huge hydroelectric potential.

Britain is no laggard, then, when it comes to cutting carbon emissions or setting future targets – it is going faster than the rest of Europe. But all this rather presupposes that a hard and fast commitment to achieve net zero emissions by any particular date is a sensible policy. On the contrary, as I have argued in another book,[30] it is a massive hostage to fortune which threatens to devastate industry, impose huge costs on people of very limited means and is all too likely, in many cases, to result in emissions being offshored rather than actually cut. In this, Britain and the rest of Europe are joined in fatal lockstep.

As of 2024, twenty-seven countries around the world have made some sort of legal commitment towards achieving net zero carbon emissions. Fourteen of them are in Europe, including the countries that have set themselves the most stringent dates: 2045 in the case of Germany and Sweden, and 2035 in the case of Finland.[31] It all sounds terribly virtuous and progressive, yet Europe's net zero ambitions are collapsing as soon as they collide with reality. The EU's proposed ban on internal combustion car engines by 2035 has already been watered down, not least thanks to pressure from the German car industry. Engines will still be allowed in cars from that date so long as they are capable of being run on synthetic fuels. Given that you can make synthetic fuels – at high cost – to any recipe you like, it effectively means the whole ban has gone.

Germany's attempt to ban fossil fuel boilers in houses has already come a cropper. Under a law drafted in early 2023, homeowners would have been forbidden from fitting traditional oil and gas boilers from 1 January 2024; any new heating system, whether in an old or new house, would have been required to run on 65 per cent renewable energy. As the public began to digest the implications – the only real alternative, electric heat pumps, are far more expensive to buy than oil or gas boilers and they do not work so well in older homes with less insulation – it sparked mass popular opposition to what began to be called the 'Heat Hammer'. Some homeowners had been quoted prices of 25,000 to 30,000 euros. One landlord fitted heat pumps to seventy homes only to find that they could not be connected to the electricity grid.[32] There were too few engineers to fit the number of heat pumps that would be required. The coalition government threatened to break apart. The law had been proposed by the Green Party but was opposed by the Free Democrats, leaving the Social Democrats of Chancellor Olaf Scholz caught in the middle. It didn't help that the new law also sought to ban heat pumps that use fluorine-based refrigerants – which precluded many heat pumps on the market and, according to their manufacturers, would have been in contravention of the rules of the single market.

Eventually, a compromise was reached. The poor and elderly were exempted from the ban, as were any property owners whose local councils have not yet produced plans for district heating schemes – where multiple properties can be heated from a single heat pump system. But the whole debacle typifies the way that the project to decarbonise Europe is going. It starts with grand ambitions, and claims to be setting an example to the world. Then proposals are tabled, which have been dreamed up by a think tank or by academics with little idea of how people live and work. Targets are set, which simply assume that new technologies will magically arrive just in time. Considerations other than cutting carbon emissions are put aside: that food needs to be grown, that people need to keep their homes warm, and that they need to get about – and that most households are already quite financially stretched. Then the whole thing collapses as the implications of cost and practicality become clear to the wider population.

Europe's grandstanding over the climate will have limited impact on global emissions, in any case. Trouble is that its net zero targets refer only to territorial emissions – those physically spewed out within the countries themselves. They exclude aviation, shipping and, even more significantly, emissions made elsewhere in the world in the cause of making things and growing food for a country's residents. As a result, countries that have set a legally binding target for eliminating net territorial emissions have given themselves a perverse incentive to close down heavy industry and import stuff instead. They haven't really cut their emissions – they have merely offshored them, along with jobs and wealth.

The foolishness of it is there to be seen in the closure of the two blast furnaces at Port Talbot in South Wales, in January 2024 – facilities that are intended to be replaced with an electric arc furnace in a few years' time. The closure will reduce Britain's carbon emissions by 1.5 per cent in one go, but will do nothing to cut emissions globally because it will mean having to import steel instead – most likely from China, where electricity supplies are far more carbon-intense than in Wales. The electric arc furnace that will replace the blast furnaces is described as making 'green' steel but it won't be doing the same job. Steel-making is a two-part process. An electric arc furnace can only do the second part – turning pig iron or scrap metal into steel. As for the first bit – extracting iron from iron ore – that will, in future, have to be done abroad. Emissions are being offshored, helping Britain to creep towards its net zero target – but at the cost of 2,500 jobs.

Equally silly is the insistence of the EU, and the UK government, on counting the burning of wood pellets harvested from North American forests as a form of zero carbon energy. Actually, burning wood to generate electricity emits more greenhouse gases than does burning coal – 117 kg of carbon dioxide equivalent per gigajoule of energy produced compared with 103 kg for coal and 67 kg for gas.[33] But the EU and the UK count it as zero carbon energy on the basis that the trees being cut down in North American forests have only recently been grown and will be replaced by more trees. There are two obvious faults with this. Firstly, it ignores the emissions that come from harvesting the trees as well as manufacturing and transporting the pellets. Secondly, while it takes minutes to burn a tree's worth of pellets in a power station boiler, it will take many decades to grow the replacement tree. The planet would be better off if we tipped the wood pellets out in weighted bags in the middle of the Atlantic and let them sink to the anaerobic depths, where they would lock in the carbon they had absorbed while growing – and then burned gas in our power stations instead. But that wouldn't then allow Europe to claim it was eliminating carbon emissions. Europe's false carbon accounting is doing nothing to cut global carbon emissions, though it is helping to decimate American forests.

If you look at consumption-based carbon emissions – those based on where products are consumed rather than made – it tells quite a different story. UK emissions in 2022 were 4.7 tonnes per capita (territorial) and 7.6 tonnes (consumption based). In Germany, the corresponding figures were 8.0

tonnes and 10.0 tonnes. Look at China and it is the other way around: its consumption-based emissions, at 7.2 tonnes per capita, are lower than its territorial emissions (8.0 tonnes). This is because it makes increasing amounts of stuff for the rest of the world, including over half of global steel production. India, too, has lower consumption-based emissions (1.7 tonnes per capita) than it does territorial emissions (2.0 tonnes).

Like the steel industry, the European chemicals industry is also facing oblivion. No one knows that better than Sir Jim Ratcliffe, chairman and founder of chemicals group Ineos, which employs 26,000 people across twenty-nine countries. Europe, he wrote in an open letter to European Commission President Ursula von der Leyen in February 2024, used to have the largest chemicals industry in the world, but no new large facilities have been built on the continent in the past twenty years. In another twenty years, he predicted, the chemicals industry will be pretty well finished in Europe – taking with it the 20 million jobs and £1 trillion in revenues that it still accounts for in Europe

Why? It is too hard to get regulatory approval, for one thing. Ineos was in the process of building a €4 billion 'cracking' plant for the production of plastics in Antwerp. It should have been the cleanest such plant in the world, thanks in part to it using the hydrogen produced as a by-product of the process as a fuel. But a group of fourteen environmental pressure groups took the Flemish authorities to court, calling the plant a 'carbon bomb' which would contravene EU carbon reduction targets. In July 2023, the Flemish Council for Permit Disputes cancelled the permits that had been issued by the province of Antwerp and the Regional government of Flanders just months earlier.[34] The decision, it said, was made on the grounds that no environmental assessment had been made of the effect of nitrogen dioxide emissions on a nearby nature reserve – emissions which, according to Ratcliffe, would be lower over the course of a year than those emitted by a single family barbecue.[35] The permit was later reinstated, though the project remained under a cloud as environmental groups continued to lobby against it.

Then there are the carbon taxes. In 2024, Ineos was paying €150 million a year in carbon taxes, but by 2030 – thanks to the carbon border tax on imports of raw materials – it would be paying £2 billion. If, that is, it hadn't closed its European plants by then. Already, Ineos was paying four times as much for its electricity in Europe as in the US and five times as much for its gas. 'Instead of using the stick,' Ratcliffe said of the US, 'they are using the carrot of putting $500 billion of government aid to encourage technologies that will improve the carbon footprint of America.'[36]

Ratcliffe was speaking at a conference in Antwerp attended by a number of companies concerned at how Europe is strangling investment through excessive, complicated and expensive compliance, as well as excessive environmental taxes. Also warning about what she called the 'deindustrialisation of the European economy' was Karen McKee, president of ExxonMobil's Product Solutions division. which had been planning to invest $20 billion in carbon capture and storage and other decarbonisation projects but was now doubtful: 'When we make investments we've got very long time horizons in mind. I would say that recent developments in Europe have not installed confidence in long-term predictable policies.' It is not just operating the industrial plant itself that involved tortuous bureaucracy, she said, but obtaining finance in the first place. If the company's investment was withdrawn from Europe, she asserted, it would simply go elsewhere. In other words, it is not just a case of Europe trying to clean up industry and reduce emissions – it is becoming increasingly difficult to build a plant even when its very purpose is to reduce carbon emissions.

Europe leads the world when it comes to setting net zero targets, but it is falling a long way behind when it comes to making money out of green energy. In February 2024, Orsted, the sometime Danish national oil and gas producer turned wind energy company, shed 800 jobs and cancelled its dividend after losing 22.5 billion krone (£2.5 billion) in the second quarter of 2023. In the space of a few months in late 2023 and early 2024, eight European solar energy firms either went bust or fell into economic trouble as Chinese producers undercut them – not least thanks to the high cost of energy in Europe.[37] According to the International Renewable Energy Agency (IRENA), of the 13.7 million jobs in renewable energy in 2023, 5.55 million were in China and just 1.8 million in Europe.[38]

Nothing sums up better the European approach to the environment and business than the words of Martin Porter, executive chair of the Cambridge Institute for Sustainability Leadership, who complained that Ineos and ExxonMobil needed to show 'new thinking beyond complaining about red tape'. And what might that new thinking be? According to his organisation's website, it is an 'impact-led institute' which 'activates leadership globally to transform economies for people, nature and climate' and aims to 'rewire economic, social and environmental systems' by creating 'safe spaces to challenge and support those with the power to act'. On the one hand, we have real industries being driven from Europe by overbearing climate and environmental policies which have made their lives a misery, and even dissuaded business making investments in clean technology. And, on the other hand, we have Europe's boom industry of academic-activists spewing out platitudes on the climate while failing to listen to problems of those who want to invest. European governments – not least Britain – like to talk about 'green jobs'. But this is what we get: endless regulatory jobs rather than productive ones.

It is a good thing, obviously, to demand high environmental standards of industrial plant, as everything else. But
Europe's regulators – taking their cue from environmental
pressure groups – have gone far beyond simply demanding
high standards. They are pushing away industries by making
it impossible for them for them to operate in Europe at all.
That might not matter if Europe had found a way to do without fossil fuels, plastics, fertilisers and all the other products
of the global chemicals industry, but, of course, it hasn't. In
future, they will have to be imported from elsewhere, with
Europe forced to try to make its living by other means – an
increasingly difficult task as industry after industry is driven
from its shores. Nor, even, are Europe's regulators especially
successful in cleaning up the continent – as its air and rivers
attest.

10.

Not so Nice and Liberal

The conceit that Brexit was a symptom of innate racist and xenophobic attitudes in British society has been advanced ever since referendum day. By this narrative, Britain is a uniquely nasty country where people obsess about immigration – while the rest of Europe has learned to rub along with each other in a diverse, enlightened fashion.

The Brexit vote, asserted the *Guardian*, had unleashed a 'frenzy of hatred' and 'celebratory racism' – a theory it supported with a few anecdotes about locals in Great Yarmouth mouthing 'Bye-bye' to a group of Kosovans working in a car wash, a group of young men complaining about 'bloody immigrants' holding them up in a passport queue, and the firebombing of a halal shop in Walsall for which no evidence of racist motive, or identity of perpetrator, was produced (there are 320,000 cases of arson and criminal damage in England and Wales every year). It also cited the graffiti on the doors of the Hammersmith Polish and Cultural Association, which horrified locals and led to supporters of the Polish community turning out to leave flowers and messages of support.

The graffiti read 'Fuck you OMP'. The letters OMP, it later turned out, stood for a Polish think-tank which had favoured Brexit – suggesting that the words may have been written by someone within the Polish community who was angry at the Leave result and wanted to express their anger at those who had campaigned for it.[1]

In the last week of July 2016, it was widely reported at the time, and for many months thereafter, there had been a 58 per cent surge in hate crimes compared with the same week in 2015.[2] The blame for these incidents was placed firmly on the Leave campaign. 'Over the past few months, the men who are now shaping Britain's future outside the EU effectively ditched public decency, and decided it was okay to be racist,' wrote *Guardian* columnist Aditya Chakrabortty the week following the Brexit referendum, with just a passing admission that some low-paid voters might have been motivated to vote for less migration not out of innate racism, but out of a straightforward fear of its impact on wages. 'The unspeakable became not only speakable, but commonplace.'[3]

The 'Brexit is racist' brigade were still at it years later, only now Brexit had been elevated to a fully fascist exercise. 'When the 2016 Brexit referendum unleashed a nasty tide of xenophobia, racism and bigotry in the UK, in a way that I had never imagined possible in the country I had adopted because of its gentleness, openness, fairness and progressiveness, I began to understand the reality of what my parents had warned me about in my childhood,' a Dutch resident of the UK, Emmy van Deuzen, told the *Independent* in 2021; the thing her parents warning her about being the rise of fascism in the 1930s.[4]

Numerous academic studies picked up on the theme. The European Commission Against Racism and Intolerance – an offshoot of the Council of Europe, a not-altogether-disinterested body when it comes to Brexit – concluded that Britain had experienced an 'increase in xenophobic sentiment' and blamed it on 'considerable intolerant political discourse focussing on immigration'. As evidence, it cited an increase in the number of reports of hate incidents reported to the police.[5] Actually, recorded hate crimes in England and Wales have risen steadily since they were first published in 2012–13, with no explosion in 2016. The '58 per cent rise in hate crime following the referendum', quoted ad nauseum since the Brexit vote, even though it referred only to a single week's statistics, vanishes when you look at the annual figures.[6]

But there is a good reason why hate crimes have risen steeply over the past decade, and which has nothing to do with Brexit: police have only recently been instructed to record as 'hate crimes' offences that would previously have gone down simply as acts of violence or public disorder. Moreover, the definition of a hate crime used by the police – as anything which is perceived by its victim to be a hate crime – does somewhat boost the records. As the Home Office puts it: 'It is uncertain to what degree the increase in police recorded hate crime is a genuine rise, or due to continued recording improvements and more victims having the confidence to report these crimes to the police.'

A study by Goldsmiths College in 2017, claimed that people who are xenophobic, who express a belief in the greatness of their country (which it describes as 'collective narcissism') or who are 'right wing authoritarians' were more likely to vote Brexit. Needless to say, the study was eagerly picked up by frustrated Remainers who tended not to dwell on the details. It was based on an online questionnaire completed by just 280 people, 194 of whom voted remain – a strange lop-sidedness given that only 48 per cent of the UK electorate had voted that way. How did it define people as being 'right wing authoritarians'? It categorised them according to their answers to questions such as whether they agreed with the statement 'obedience and respect for authority are the most important virtues children should learn'. So, unless you think that children should be free and welcome to spit in the faces of their parents and teachers you are, apparently, a nasty right-wing authoritarian – and probably an unspeakable Brexit voter to boot.[7]

It goes without saying that all incidents of racist violence are deplorable and deserve to be tackled with the full force of the law. Little better is the less overt, everyday racism which discriminates silently, or with maybe just a few muttered words between friends and neighbours. Britain has its racists and xenophobes, of course, of both types. But is it really such a racist hellhole, and has it really been launched into a frenzy of hate since it voted to leave the EU?

There is a very big hole in the theory that Britain is an illiberal outlier among civilised European nations, whose disdain for foreigners and imperial sense of entitlement has poisoned relations between communities. If you really do think Britain is racist, xenophobic, hostile to migrants, you should like even less what is going on in most other EU countries.

Racist incidents are to be found all across Europe. There was, for example, the murder of nine people of various nationalities and ethnicities, from Afghan to Turks, in a Shisha bar in Hanau, near Frankfurt, on 9 February 2020. It emerged that their killer, 43-year-old Tobias Rathjen, had published a racist manifesto online, calling for the extermination of migrants. In Paris, in December 2022, a 69-year-old man walked into a Kurdish Cultural Centre and opened fire, killing three and injuring three more. In the same month a Nigerian street vendor was beaten to death in the town of Civitanova Marche on Italy's Adriatic Coast. In Mazarrón, in the Spanish region of Murcia, in March 2021, a Moroccan who had been living in the country for twenty years was shot dead by a former soldier.

Isolated acts of violence do not necessarily make for a racist country. There has never been a society that does not have its violent criminals, inspired by perverse ideologies. What makes the difference is whether racism is encouraged or discouraged by the prevailing attitudes. It is hard to compare the incidence of racist violence across countries because there is no internationally agreed definition of a racist or hate incident. Britain, indeed, is something of a pioneer in collecting this sort of data – which, as explained above, has resulted in a rising rate of reported crime. To get an idea of what is really going on, and to compare it across different countries, we need to look for surveys that are carried out under the same rules everywhere, preferably ones which have been carried out in many countries repeatedly over a long period. The World Values Survey, conducted by King's College London, seeks to analyse racist attitudes through a questionnaire filled in by 3,000 Britons and similar numbers of people in twenty-three other countries. Asked whether they would mind having a neighbour of a different race to their own, only 2 per cent of Britons say they would – a proportion which has fallen steadily from 10 per cent in 1981, Brexit notwithstanding. Only Sweden and Brazil, on 1 per cent, came out less racist on this measure. In Germany it was 3 per cent, France 4 per cent, Poland 7 per cent, Italy 12 per cent and Spain 13 per cent.[8] Would we mind living next door to immigrants/foreign workers? In the UK, 5 per cent say they would, just a little higher than Sweden (3 per cent) and Germany (4 per cent) but rather lower than France (10 per cent), Spain (13 per cent) or Italy (18 per cent).

How do European countries compare in the eyes of victims of racism? In 2016 and again in 2022, the European Union Agency for Fundamental Rights polled citizens of African descent in thirteen member states, asking them if they had thought themselves victims of discrimination during the preceding five years. In 2016, the UK came comfortably at the bottom of the table, with 23 per cent of respondents saying they had been discriminated against. In the next lowest country, Portugal, it was 33 per cent. The average across the thirteen countries was 39 per cent, while Italy was on 49 per cent, Austria 51 per cent, Germany 52 per cent, Denmark 55 per cent, Finland 60 per cent and Luxembourg (which perhaps doesn't have the largest African population in the world) 69 per cent. The UK, thanks to its leaving the EU, was not part of the 2023 survey, but the situation seemed to have deteriorated in an awful lot of countries that hadn't voted to leave. In Germany, the proportion reporting discrimination rose to 76 per cent and in Austria it rose to 72 per cent. The EU average had climbed to 45 per cent.[9] It was a similar story with those reporting racist harassment, with Britain (21 per cent) at the bottom of the 2016 survey along with Malta (20 per cent) and Portugal (23 per cent). In France it was 32 per cent, Denmark 41 per cent, Germany 48 per cent, Ireland 51 per cent and Finland 63 per cent. The EU average was 30 per cent.

Islamophobia? You will find far more of it elsewhere in the EU than in the UK. It is France which bans the burqa in public places, Muslim headscarves from public buildings and burqinis from public swimming pool. The northern Italian port of Monfalcone has banned prayers at the one Islamic centre in the city, and it isn't alone in trying to suppress Muslim places of worship. Italy has an estimated Muslim population of between 2 and 3 million, yet only five openly advertised mosques have managed to become established over the entire country.[10]

Antisemitism? A survey of 16,000 Jewish people across twelve European countries by the European Union Agency for Fundamental Rights in 2018 revealed shockingly high levels of antisemitism, but the UK was a long way down the list. In Britain, 18 per cent of respondents reported that family members had been subject to verbal insults and harassment over the past twelve months, compared with 28 per cent in Belgium, 27 per cent in Germany and 24 per cent in the Netherlands. In the UK, 60 per cent of Jewish people sometimes felt the need to avoid wearing and carrying any item which could identify them as Jewish, compared with 92 per cent in France, 81 per cent in Denmark, 78 per cent in Sweden and 75 per cent in Germany.[11]

Was Brexit racist? The migration that Brexit promised to control was mostly from Eastern Europe – where populations are overwhelmingly white. You might possibly call it xenophobic to seek to exclude Poles and Romanians from Britain, but the charge of racism is difficult to maintain. But, then again, people do have perfectly legitimate concerns about high levels of migration which have nothing to do with either racism or xenophobia. The sudden increase in population which accompanied the admission of Eastern European states into the EU in January 2004 put pressure on housing, public services and on wages. Moreover, the effects were very different according to who you were and where you lived. For well-off Londoners, high migration meant cheaper housekeepers and plumbers. If you were a housekeeper or plumber who was already living in Britain, on the other hand, increased migration meant downward pressure on wages. The effects varied geographically, too. Some parts of Britain saw few extra migrants; others, like Boston, Lincolnshire, saw a dramatic transformation. At the time of the 2001 census, Boston's migrant population was tiny, with 249 Germans the largest group. By 2011, more than one in ten people in the district were migrants, with Poles especially strongly represented. Four in ten babies born at the town's hospital were to mothers who had themselves been born abroad, while at one primary school 60 per cent of children were from migrant families.[12]

Following the Brexit vote, it became standard practice for the frustrated Remain lobby to try to make out that low-income Britons who had voted for Brexit had not known what was good for them. They hadn't realised that migration was helping to boost the economy, and that we would all end up poorer if we sought to reduce it. It was a baseless insult to the low paid. In 2022, I got speaking to a British lorry driver who had voted for Brexit. Did he regret it, as many Remainers believed he ought to have done? Not a bit of it. For years, he said, he hadn't had a pay rise. Then, suddenly, he had four pay rises over the course of a single year. Foreign competition for work had fallen away (a result of the Covid-19 pandemic as well as Brexit) and he suddenly found himself with more negotiating power. Whatever the effect on the UK economy as whole, Brexit had worked for him. He hadn't voted emotionally for reasons of xenophobia or some lost sense of national pride, but out of his own economic interest.

There is a good case for encouraging migration, as we shall later see: Europe's rapidly declining birth rate. Nevertheless, the effect of migration on wages, housing, public services is, needless to say, an issue that tends to excite passions in many European countries, even if it has not, as yet, inspired any other country to leave the EU. Polling by the organisation Eurobarometer between 2015–17 found that the UK public were more sceptical about free movement than in any other country – 63 per cent were in favour and 27 per cent against. But other Western European countries were not far behind. Austria, too, had 27 per cent against. In Denmark, it was 25 per cent, while in Italy and Belgium, 20 per cent were opposed.[13]

In spite of championing free movement during Brexit negotiations, many EU leaders have been quick to try to find ways of blocking migrant labour from elsewhere in the EU as soon as it starts to interfere with the interests of native workers. One of the first initiatives of Emmanuel Macron on becoming French president in 2017 was to try to clamp down on 'posted workers' – employees of Eastern European companies who had been sent to work in France but who were still being paid according to pay and employment policies in their home countries.[14]

Long before Brexit, British ski instructors in the French Alps were finding themselves banned from the slopes, even though their qualifications were supposed to give them the right to teach clients in any EU country. In 2014, Simon Butler and his staff in the resort of Megève were arrested, held in a police cell for thirty-six hours and charged with 'illegal teaching', a dramatic escalation of a battle that had been going on for at least a decade as local ski instructors attempted to corner the market for themselves.[15] The authorities insisted that only instructors with French qualifications should be allowed to teach. Ironically, the case was eventually settled in his favour three months after Brexit, in May 2020; he was able to carry on teaching on the basis that he was already settled and established in France before the UK left the EU. But it was a case that demonstrated the gulf between the ideals of the single market and how it works in practice.

When not trying to block migrant workers, European countries have been caught out exploiting them. In 2021, Amnesty International was moved to campaign on behalf of Eastern Europeans working in the care sector in Austria. Over the past couple of decades, Austrian care workers have been granted all kinds of employment rights regarding minimum rates of pay, maximum working hours and so on. Yet Eastern European workers seem to fall outside the rules. Austria has a minimum wage, which was supposed to guarantee an income of €17,484 for a full-time worker in 2021, however, Slovaks working full time were only receiving an average of €10,080. Employers were getting around it by putting 98 per cent of them on self-employment contracts which applied to few Austrian workers. Slovakian workers were also denied sickness benefits until they had been ill for forty-two consecutive days – by which time they would most likely have returned home, if they hadn't died.[16]

A 2017 study found that migrants employed as domestic workers were being exploited across the EU (Britain included). Some had to sleep on the floor, others had to share a bed with the children they looked after. One in the Netherlands had had only one day off in five months.[17] A follow-up study of migrant workers in other sectors across eight Western European countries, found cases of abuse. A farm worker in Portugal reported working 200 hours a month in return for wages of €400, or sometimes €200. Agricultural workers in the Netherlands reported not being paid at all: their employers would subtract every cent for food, accommodation and spurious 'commission' payments. In Germany, workers in the hospitality sector reported having to sleep outdoors in a park. In Poland, a catering worker had to feed sixty people all by herself, with no help. In the Netherlands, workers were made to handle chlorine chemicals that melted the skimpy overalls they were given; they weren't even given face masks.[18]

Britain is far from immune from cases of exploitation of migrant workers, but neither did it come out any worse than other EU countries in these studies. The EU's high-mindedness on free movement obscures the reality. It flung open borders without thinking of the consequences. Free movement encouraged exploitation, with employers finding it rather easier to exploit migrant workers who might have lacked language skills, as well as knowledge of employment law and where to seek help. Yet, for years, these problems went unacknowledged by those in Britain who championed EU free movement and who interpreted any criticism of the policy as a xenophobic attack on the migrants themselves.

As well as regular migration there is the issue of irregular migration: those arriving in European countries from outside the EU with the intention of claiming asylum here – or otherwise – only to simply disappear into the ether and live illegally. It would be hard for anyone to present the EU's handling of irregular migration as a success. In the ten years prior to 2022, over 3.8 million irregular migrants arrived in the EU.[19] But the EU and its member states have never managed to come up with a workable system for how to handle them. The EU has blown hot and cold over rescue operations. In 2015, it launched a system of air and sea patrols called Operation Sophia – but then, in 2019, pulled the sea patrols as member states failed to agree to which countries the migrants should be sent.

Notionally, there is a Common European Asylum System governed by the Dublin Regulation, originally signed between twelve members of the EU in 1990. There is a perfectly good logic behind the Dublin Regulation: it demands that asylum seekers make their applications in the first safe country in which they arrive. This is supposed to stop applicants travelling around and making multiple applications – although it doesn't seem to manage this. There were 881,220 first-time applications in 2022, but a further 74,800 were made by people who had presumably failed in a previous application.[20]

The EU's common asylum system is supposed to spread applications and resettlements around the bloc, so the burden is shared. But it fails miserably in practice. The number of asylum applications varies enormously from country to country. In 2022, Cyprus handled 21,590 applications – one for every fifty-eight residents. Hungary, by contrast, handled just forty-five applications – one for every 215,000 residents. There is a big difference between Western European countries, too. Also in 2022, Germany received 217,735 applications – one for every 386 residents. Denmark managed to keep applications down to 4,475, one for every 1,320 residents.

This might not matter so much if the EU was succeeding in rapidly resettling successful applicants from countries with too many applications to those with few, but it is failing spectacularly. The proportion of refugees who are resettled from one EU state to another after a successful application is tiny – it reached just 20 in every 1,000 applications in 2019, before collapsing to 8.5 during the pandemic year of 2020.[21]

Success rates for asylum applications vary enormously from country to country – thereby encouraging asylum seekers to shop around. Across the EU, close to 50 per cent of applications are successful, yet the success rate varies between over 95 per cent in Estonia to fewer than 5 per cent in Cyprus – it is hardly any wonder that Cyprus is motivated to reject so many applications when it has so many relative to its population. Among larger countries, the Netherlands accepted over 85 per cent of applications and Germany 65 per cent. France accepted fewer than 30 per cent of applications.[22] Is 'racist and xenophobic' Britain particularly harsh on asylum applications? On the contrary. In the UK, 67 per cent of applications for asylum made in 2023 resulted in the grant of refugee status or alternative forms of leave to stay in the country.[23] This disparity between French and British acceptance rates goes some way to explaining why so many asylum applicants are moved to make dangerous Channel crossings on small boats despite already being in a safe country.

Poorly controlled migration, unsurprisingly, has fuelled the rise of anti-immigration parties in Europe. Indeed, they have prospered far more in the EU than they have in supposedly xenophobic Britain. Many have taken their opposition to migration far further than has any British party – to the point, in a few cases, of outright neo-Nazism.

If you want to look for widespread support for far right

parties you won't find it in Britain. The last to gain any kind of foothold in a UK election was the British National Party (BNP), which won 6.2 per cent of the popular vote in the European parliamentary elections in 2009 and followed it up with 1.9 per cent in the following year's general election, before imploding. UKIP, which successfully campaigned for the Brexit referendum in spite of only briefly attaining representation in the House of Commons, has been damned by some as being a racist and xenophobic party, but it is hard to find evidence for that charge. Its policy at the time of the 2016 referendum was to reduce net migration to around 50,000 skilled migrants a year, but did not suggest picking on the basis of their race, religion or nationality.[24] In any case, UKIP has also since imploded. As for the latest upstart right-leaning party in Britain, Reform (formerly the Brexit Party), the BBC was moved to apologise for calling it 'far right' in a news bulletin in March 2024.[25] Britain may have a ragbag of far-right protesters, who erupted onto the streets in the summer of 2024, in one case attacking a mosque and in another a centre housing asylum seekers. Those spontaneous attacks by mobs were, of course, deplorable and deeply worrying. But at present Britain simply does not have a far-right party, or even organised movement, that emits so much as a bleep on the political radar.

You will find far-right parties, however, winning significant votes and seats in most EU countries. Look at the Netherlands, where the general election of November 2023 saw the PVV – or Freedom Party – winning the largest share of the vote, at 23.5 per cent. In its campaigning for that poll, the party dropped its previous demands for a ban on the Koran, Islamic schools and mosques, although still pushed for a ban on Islamic headscarves in public buildings. It also opposed all grants of asylum.

Leader Geert Wilders has a record of saying numerous

things that no UK politician would dare say – even if they wanted to. In 2016, he was convicted of insulting a racial group and inciting discrimination after encouraging the crowd at a political rally to chant that they wanted fewer Moroccans. The conviction for inciting discrimination was later overturned, but the other upheld.[26] It is hard to conceive, at least at present, that a politician could have won an election in Britain after such a history.

For those who saw Brexit as a racist and xenophobic exercise, the antithesis was provided by Angela Merkel's *Willkommenskultur*. In September 2015, a two-year-old Syrian boy, Alan Kurdi, was found washed up, drowned on a Turkish beach, the victim of a failed migrant crossing to Greece. The photographs of his body led to a public outcry, which inspired the then German leader to open the doors and tell migrants that if they could get to Germany, the country would look after them. Over the next couple of years, 1.2 million migrants arrived. They were still arriving long after public opinion towards the new arrivals had begun to sour. *Willkommenskultur* began to die on New Year's Eve 2015, when a crowd of around a thousand men congregated at Cologne railway station, seemingly with the purpose of assaulting women. There were over 1,200 reports of criminal behaviour, including more than 500 sexual assaults. The assailants were described by the city's chief of police as being mostly of 'Arab or North African appearance'.[27] As much as government ministers appealed to the public not to connect it with migration, rather a lot of Germans saw it otherwise – believing that the country had been a bit naive to extend an open welcome to migrants without asking why they were coming or investigating whether they had criminal pasts. As the manager of a refugee centre in Cologne put it: '*Willkommenskultur* was contradicted in that many people who had previously broadly supported it were suddenly fearful. A lot of support was lost, right up to the refugee homes, where many people had been helping us to advance social work and integration.'[28]

The pushback began with the government passing new laws to make it easier to deport migrants who had acquired criminal convictions in Germany – although that would make little difference in the case of the Cologne incident, as only two men were convicted of sexual assault, the police blaming poor quality film for failing to catch more assailants. Olaf Scholz, who replaced Merkel as chancellor in 2021, has pursued a very different policy – a policy that is very much in line with UK government efforts to reduce illegal migration. Laws have been passed to speed up the deportation of failed asylum seekers. The government has said it will look into the offshore processing of asylum claims. Contrary to how the Schengen Agreement is supposed to work, guards have been placed on the country's borders to halt people smuggling. In September 2024, Germany went the whole hog and reintroduced border checks on all its borders – which, under the terms of the Schengen Agreement, members are allowed to do in an emergency for a period of up to six months. Neighbouring countries were outraged, with Poland's Prime Minister Donald Tusk calling it 'unacceptable'. Free movement, after all, was a high-minded principle on which Tusk himself had refused to compromise during Brexit negotiations six years earlier. 'We are limiting irregular migration to Germany,' Scholz has declared. 'Too many people are coming.' By the end of 2023, government policy had turned to investigating the practicalities of a scheme to send asylum seekers to Rwanda for processing – the same destination as a very similar scheme that was proposed in Britain.

The collapse of *Willkommenskultur* brought something else in its wake: a huge boost for Alternative for Deutschland (AfD), which takes a far harsher line on migrants and migration than has any mainstream UK political party – including UKIP in its prime. AfD won its first mayoralty in June 2023, in the town of Sonneberg, Thuringia. It followed it up in the state elections in October 2023 by taking second place in Hesse and third in Bavaria. It began 2023 polling in fourth place on 14 per cent of the vote; it ended the year on 22 per cent, overtaking the Greens and Social Democrats to be the second most popular party in the country. In the European parliament elections in June 2024 it came second place, beating the Social Democrat party of chancellor Olaf Scholz and his two coalition partners – this in spite of the AfD's lead candidate declaring, mid-campaign, that SS officers hadn't all been criminals and that some were 'simple farmers' who had had no choice but to join Heinrich Himmler's force. AfD, which began as a Eurosceptic party but has since evolved into a pro-EU, anti-immigration party, stood in 2017 on a manifesto that declared: 'the ever-increasing number of Muslims in the country are viewed as a danger to our state, our society and our values'. Imams, it proposed, would have to seek permission from the government in order to preach, and they would only be allowed to preach in German.[29] AfD has a moderate wing and a far-right wing; the former can sound reasonable, the latter has been accused of using neo-Nazi language, and of antisemitism. In 2017, the party's leader in Thuringia, Björn Höcke, declared that the time had come to end commemoration of the Holocaust: 'These stupid politics of coming to grips with the past cripple us – we need nothing other than a 180 degree reversal on the politics of remembrance.'[30]

But AfD is not the most extreme party in Germany. The neo-Nazi National Democratic Party (NPD) has been going since 1964; it is often called 'far right' although a lot of its policies draw on socialism. It fed upon disaffected citizens of the old East Germany after reunification, but has declined in recent years, renaming itself Die Heimat (the Homeland) in 2023. Even further out on the fringe is the openly neo-Nazi

Third Path, which has policies of encouraging families to breed in order 'to prevent an imminent extinction of the German people' and pursues the 'peaceful restoration of Greater Germany with its original frontiers' – i.e. pre-First World War. In October 2021, fifty members of the movement were intercepted while trying to act as unofficial border guards to prevent migrants entering Germany from Poland.[31]

In France, the National Rally – formerly National Front – has come a long way since it was founded by Jean Marie Le Pen in 1972. Under the leadership of his daughter, Marine Le Pen, it underwent what she calls 'de-demonisation'. No longer is it so easy to dismiss it as racist or antisemitic. Nor is the term 'far right' appropriate given its belief in a big state. Nevertheless, it still pursues policies that would be pushing the Overton window of debate in Britain (a term which means the breadth of views considered acceptable in political discourse at any one time). In her 2022 run at the presidency, which ended with her winning 41.4 per cent of the vote in the second-round run-off, Marine Le Pen advocated banning women from wearing headscarves in public – something which would have perplexed my grandmothers' generation, many of whom wouldn't leave for the Co-op without one. This kind of policy is widespread in mainstream politics in France. Le Pen proposed, too, a ban on the slaughter of farm animals without stunning – i.e. halal and kosher meat – as well as to give French nationals a priority in social housing, which would appear to conflict with the EU's rules on free movement.

The moderation of National Rally policies by Marine Le Pen saw her being outflanked in the 2022 election by Éric Zemmour, a columnist and broadcaster who declared that Islam as practised was incompatible with French values.[32] He also proposed banning the first name 'Mohammed' from being given to babies born in France – along with most

foreign names, even Kevin.[33] Zemmour had been convicted
of hate speech for saying of unaccompanied child migrants
in general (when discussing the case of a particular Pakistani
youth who had committed a knife attack): 'they have nothing
to do here. They are thieves, they are murderers, they are
rapists, that's all they are. They must be sent back and they
must not even come.'[34] In the subsequent election Zemmour
came fourth in the first round, with 7 per cent of the vote.
As for the National Rally, it went on to win the European
elections in June 2024, becoming the largest single party in
the whole parliament.

France's fiery politics are accompanied some pretty rancid
community relations in many French cities. Britain, of course,
has had riots of its own, most recently a week of disturbance
in the summer of 2024. But, as already noted, the banlieues
of Paris and other French cities erupt on a far more regular
basis. For six days in June 2023, rioting afflicted the suburbs
of northern Paris, spreading to Roubaix, Marseille and other
cities, as migrant communities went to war with the police.
Two people died, several hundred police officers were injured
and public buildings, including the town hall in Gonesse, near
Charles de Gaulle airport, were firebombed.

It is the same all over Europe: liberal migration policies are
giving way as the realities of mass migration start to turn the
public against them. At the time of the Brexit referendum,
Sweden was still held up as an example of how a wealthy
country could and should extend a welcome to migrants from
poorer parts of the world. No country took in more asylum
seekers, per capita, during the moral panic that followed the
death of the Syrian boy on the Turkish beach in 2015. But attitudes began to sour quickly after a sharp rise in violent crime.
In 2017, gangland shootings took forty-one lives, four times
the toll of six years earlier. Then the hand grenade attacks
began – hundreds of them – beginning in the southern city

of Malmo before spreading to Stockholm. Among the victims was a 63-year-old cyclist who had stopped to pick up an object that had been lying in his path on a cycleway in southern Stockholm – and which exploded as he picked it up.[35]

Sweden is no longer a beacon of liberal attitudes towards migration. Since 2022, the largest party in the country's ruling coalition has been the Swedish Democrats, a party with far-right roots which, although it has moderated its position from its early days in the 1980s, continues to push for much greater restrictions on migration as well as more limitations on benefits for non-Swedish citizens.

Sweden is now following a model closer to that of Denmark. Denmark does have an anti-immigration party, the Danish People's Party, which operates along similar lines as the Swedish Democrats. But it doesn't do quite so well in elections, perhaps because it is not needed – as its ideas on migration have been enthusiastically adopted by the left of centre Social Democrat government, under Prime Minister Mette Frederiksen. Denmark now follows one of the least accommodating migration policies in Europe. Under a 2015 law, the state makes a distinction between political refugees – dissidents who have fled to the country in order to escape dictatorships – and refugees of war. The Danish government seeks to repatriate the latter at the earliest possible opportunity, as soon as hostilities have started to ease. In 2021, Denmark created an outcry by starting to withdraw the residency rights of Syrian refugees on the grounds that it believed the area around Damascus was now safe enough for people to return. Frederikson's target is to reduce the arrival of asylum seekers by irregular means to zero – with Denmark only taking refugees via the UN's resettlement scheme.[36] It is a policy that would cause outrage if it were proposed in Britain.

Italy? Georgia Meloni, leader of the Brothers of Italy, a party with neo-fascist roots, has been prime minister since

2022. Although it no longer dips its toes in such waters, it was elected on a mandate to put a stop to the arrival of migrant boats. Meloni promised a naval blockade, and said her government would repatriate the migrants arriving on Italy's shores and then sink the boats that had brought them to the country (many of which are operated by charities).[37] Her efforts have not proved, initially, a success. In 2023, 153,400 migrants had arrived in Italy by mid-December, up from 98,600 in the same period the previous year, and Meloni was trying to reassure her supporters that it would take time to come up with a long-lasting solution.

Spain? The Vox Party rose from nothing in 2013 to take 15 per cent of the national vote in the November 2019 general election on the back of promises to put an end to illegal migration – although it slipped back to 12 per cent in 2023. Portugal? Chega – whose name translates as 'enough' – was formed in 2019, promising to slash immigration, as well as to chemically castrate paedophiles. By 2022, it was already taking 7 per cent of the vote. The conviction of its leader, Andre Ventura, in 2020, for discrimination against Roma people, has done nothing to reduce support.

There is a lazy tendency to call all parties that focus on migration as 'far right' – a term which in many cases is inappropriate given that they are economically to the left. The rising political creed across Europe combines social conservativism with left-of-centre, redistributive economic and taxation policies, and a particular dislike of the global elite. But there are parties active in some European countries which can reasonably be described as hard right or neo-Nazi.

Europe's most overtly neo-Nazi party was Greece's Golden Dawn, which in 2012 peaked at 7 per cent of the popular vote and won 21 out of 300 seats in the Greek parliament. This was soon after the sovereign debt crisis. The party, which held torchlit processions through Athens and whose symbol bore a striking resemblance to a swastika, had skinhead thugs who would hunt down migrants in Athens, culminating in the killing of a Pakistani man and, in 2013, the murder of a Greek rapper who had opposed the party. Just a little contrary to the spirit of free movement, a New Dawn spokesman once proposed to place landmines around the country's borders.[38] Where those borders should be, however, was a matter never quite resolved as the party also flirted at times with reviving the Megali Idea – recreating the Byzantine Empire by annexing parts of modern Turkey, Istanbul included. Golden Dawn was banned in 2020, but it is not the end of anti-immigration politics in Greece. The Popular Orthodox Rally, or LAOS, has proposed to end all immigration from outside the EU. Several of its former members have since ended up as members of a New Democracy government.[39]

Hungary's Jobbik party has at times put forward even more disturbing ideas. In 2013, one of its MPs proposed that all Jews living in Hungary should be registered and evaluated for the potential danger it claimed they might pose to Hungary.[40] Party members have protested against the housing of Roma families in their districts. The party has not been in government, though after elections in 2018 it did become the second largest party in parliament.

Many of its policies, however, have been adopted by the ruling party Fidesz, which began as a party of the centre-left but has gradually moved towards an anti-immigration stance. In the same week in 2016 that the European Commission Against Racism and Intolerance published its report into Britain, Hungary held a referendum of its own. Not on EU membership – which has strong support in Hungary – but on whether to accept 1,200 refugees that the EU wanted to house in the country. The result? Ninety-eight per cent were opposed, including the president, Viktor Orbán, who declared that immigrants 'are not just banging on the doors, they're breaking the doors down on top us'. Far from embracing free movement, as the EU demands of its member states, Hungary had already started to build a Trumpian-style border fence to prevent the passage of migrants passing up through the Balkans. Hungary went on to make it a criminal offence for lawyers and activists to aid and abet migrants making asylum applications, with the result that applications in Hungary have been reduced to near zero. The EU threatened to withhold funds from the country, to which Orbán responded by blocking an aid package to Ukraine. But the EU has never quite directed the ire at Hungary as it did at Britain during the Brexit negotiations.

The existence of Poland's Law and Justice government between 2015 and 2023 presented another challenge to the idea that an open, liberal EU is rising above a xenophobic, inward-looking Britain. The government, which opposed gay marriage and abortion in most cases, found itself sanctioned by the EU, accused of undermining the legal system. But anyone offended by the Law and Justice Party needed to take a slightly deeper look at Polish politics. The party, which grew out of the Solidarity movement, combined social conservatism with left-wing economic policy. Meanwhile, there have been several minor parties that have been keeping the neo-Nazi flame alight. At a march on Polish Independence Day in 2017, some held banners declaring 'Europe will be white'.[41] The defeat of Law and Justice in the 2023 general election was heralded by many on the liberal-left as marking the return of Poland to European civilisation. 'We are witnessing Poland's democratic rebirth,' declared Stéphane Séjourné, whose own Renew Party was to become part of the new coalition government led by Donald Tusk. Not so fast. On the day that parliament was reconvened in December 2023 under the new government, an MP from the Confederation party, Grzegorz Braun, took a fire extinguisher to candles which had been lit to celebrate the Jewish holiday Hanukkah, calling them 'satanic'.[42]

No one should really be surprised about the existence of extremist politics in the EU. The EU may be presented by its fans as a haven of civilisation and culture, but many of its member states have, within living memory, been dictatorships – either fascist ones or communist ones. Britain is almost unique in Europe in having been a democracy continuously throughout the twentieth century. Unlike many EU member states, it has not experienced state-sponsored murder in recent times. Although we might not care for our politicians very much, we trust them not to throw us in jail for opposing them. We may look across the Channel and sometimes admire EU nations for seemingly being well run. But the political tensions that lie beneath are in most cases much greater than in Britain. Yes, in one sense, we are an island which is drifting away from the EU, but not in a bad sense. It is us who have the greater defences against extremist politics.

Should the EU be praised for promoting peace in Europe? Perhaps, at least in its early days. But its failure to deal with migration, and the contempt that it has shown voters, has helped radicalise parties across Europe. It is all too much for Alistair Campbell, chief spin doctor in Tony Blair's government, who has spent the past few years campaigning against a Brexit vote, trying to reverse the referendum result and then, once Britain had left, trying to reverse Brexit itself – but now seems to be changing his mind. 'Here we are, talking about could Britain get back into the European Union?' he said in a debate in February 2024. 'There is an argument to be made about whether it is developing into an EU that we'd want to be in.'[43] When even Alistair Campbell is questioning whether the EU is such a good thing, you really do have to wonder whether the game is up for the Rejoin movement.

Will you get a better welcome in European cities and

resorts as a tourist rather than as a migrant? Not always. Even if you have come only for a few days, during which you will pour money into the pockets of local businesses, Europe is becoming an increasingly hostile place. Never mind that Spain earned €155 billion from tourism in 2019 – 12.4 per cent of GDP[44] – it won't save you from waking up in your Barcelona hotel room to chants of 'Go home'. An anti-tourism campaign has resulted in tourists being pelted with eggs and smoke flares being let off in a restaurant. In August 2017, protesters believed to be from Arran, a youth group connected to the Catalan independence campaign, encircled a bus, slashed its tyres and sprayed 'Tourism kills neighbourhoods' on its windscreen. The group has also posted videos on Twitter showing tyres of tourist bicycles being slashed.[45] 'If it is tourist season why can't we shoot them?' reads one piece of graffiti in the city, 'Tourist, you are the terrorist', reads another. So much for the spirit of free movement.

Anti-tourist protests have spread to the Canary Islands, where, in 2024, thousands protested in Gran Canaria and Tenerife against what they saw as the environmental and economic ill effects of tourism. 'My misery, your paradise', read one slogan found daubed on a sea wall. Another informed visitors: 'Average salary in Canary Islands 1,200€'.[46] How the protester thought that local salaries would rise if tourists and the jobs which support them disappeared was not explained. True, mass tourism hasn't done a lot aesthetically or environmentally for places like the Canaries, but tourists have become a convenient scapegoat for the economic stagnation which has afflicted Spain ever since the crash of 2008–9.

There have been anti-tourist marches in Venice and Amsterdam, too. In the Croatian town of Hvar, the authorities have tried to turn tourists away by threatening them with eyewatering fines for what might seem rather minor demeanours, such as €700 for eating, drinking or sleeping in public – or €600 for wearing a swimsuit away from the beach. Trumping that, in 2022, the Spanish city of Vigo announced fines of €750 for urinating in the sea – just a bit rich considering that some of Spain's inland waters have been contaminated by discharges of raw sewage, without much in the way of fines for the water companies who have put it there.[47]

Beachgoers at Eraclea, near Venice, are threatened with a €250 fine for building sandcastles.[48] Anyone loitering to take photographs in parts of Portofino can be met with a €300 fine, while sitting on the Spanish Steps in Rome comes with a penalty of €300. How painful now to remember *Roman Holiday*, the 1953 film starring Audrey Hepburn and Gregory Peck, which did so much to promote Italy as a fun and carefree place.

The EU an open, welcoming haven of civilised values in contrast to xenophobic, narrow-minded Britain? That's what the rearguard Remain lobby like to try to tell us. But it does not survive scrutiny. Britain remains one of the most open and liberal countries in a Europe where community relations are becoming increasingly fraught. The EU is being torn apart by its failure to contain migration and an increasingly sour attitude towards the tourists on which, as other industries decline, it is becoming increasingly reliant.

11.

Struggling Healthcare

The NHS, depending on your point of view, is either 'the envy of the world' or a national embarrassment, which is killing Britons by the thousand through long waiting lists and indifferent care. The Late Lord Lawson, Chancellor of the Exchequer in Margaret Thatcher's government in the 1980s, once called the NHS 'the closest the British have to a religion'. If so, its pews are steadily emptying, thanks to scandals such as that at Mid Staffordshire Foundation NHS Trust as well as poor survival rates for cancer and other diseases. The fault, again depending on people's point of view, tends to be attributed to either government measliness or organisational failure.

But, however good or bad the NHS was to begin with, Remain campaigners prior to the 2016 referendum were agreed: Brexit was going to present the health service with a crisis too far. According to the Economist Intelligence Unit, it would mean NHS spending being £135 per head lower than it would be if Britain voted to remain. The Labour Party went further in forecasting a post-Brexit economic slump, which would lead to the NHS budget having to be slashed by £10.5 billion, with every hospital in England losing 1,000 nurses and 155 doctors.[1] EU doctors and nurses, it was confidently predicted, would turn tails and run – a fear which, to judge by the headlines, was quickly realised. 'Almost 10,000 EU health workers have quit NHS since Brexit vote,' reported the *Guardian* in September 2017.[2] Moreover, there had been a '90 per cent drop' in nurses registering to work in the NHS.[3]

None of these claims turned out to be quite what they seemed. While it might have technically been true that 9,832 NHS workers of EU nationalities left their jobs in the year leading up to June 2017, it somewhat ignored the other side of the ledger. Over the same period, 13,013 EU nationals joined the NHS.[4] For an organisation the size of the NHS it is perfectly normal to have a large turnover of staff. While there was a sharp drop in EU nurses registering to work in Britain – from 10,178 in the year to September 2016 to 1,107 in the following twelve months (registering is not the same thing as taking up a job) – this had rather more to do with a change in policy made in January 2016, five months before the referendum, when overseas nurses were suddenly obliged to achieve a grade seven in an English language test – a requirement that some nurses failed even when English was their first language. The rules were relaxed in November 2017, whereupon there was a rise in the number of overseas nurses coming to Britain. Seven years on, the fears that Brexit would lead to a haemorrhaging of staff has turned out to be an unfounded scare story. In June 2016, there were 58,702 NHS staff of other EU nationalities working in the NHS. By June 2023, it had climbed to 74,142. While the NHS doesn't capture the nationality of all staff (it says that it is capturing more data on this than it was in 2016), clearly there has been no collapse in the number of EU workers in the NHS, still less a fall in NHS staff generally. On the contrary, an organisation frequently cited as one of the world's largest employers, after the Chinese army and Indian railways, has continued to pile on the personnel. In June 2016, the NHS had 110,084 doctors, 317,428 nurses and 147,276 scientific, therapeutic and technical staff; by June 2023 the corresponding figures were 142,805 doctors, 372,605 nurses and 185,030 scientific staff.[5] There are always claims that the NHS is short of staff, yet, plainly, the NHS workforce has succeeded in expanding substantially – in spite of Brexit and supposed government 'austerity'.

As for the NHS budget, it has climbed in real terms (at 2022–23 prices) from £144.1 billion in 2016–17 to £181.7 billion in 2022–23.[6] That is an extra £720 million a week – more than twice the extra £350 million a week that the infamous slogan on the 'Vote Leave' bus claimed would be spent on the NHS if Britain left the EU. That is still quoted now as an example of the Leave campaign's 'lies' and 'deceit'. True, the £350 million figure was a gross figure, which didn't take into account Britain's rebate. But no one can say that a UK government has been unable to redirect money from the EU to the NHS – that is the one claim which has turned out to be realised. Even now, though, there are think-tanks trying to claim that Brexit has decimated the NHS workforce. According to the Nuffield Trust in 2022, the NHS has 4,285 fewer EU doctors than there would have been had we not voted to leave the EU – a claim it based on the assertion that the increase in EU doctors coming to Britain since 2016 has not been as steep as it was prior to 2016. It furnished its claim with graphs bearing imaginary lines showing how it thinks the number of EU doctors would have increased without Brexit. There is one problem with this: the slowdown in recruitment of doctors from the EU began in 2014, two years before the referendum.[7]

It is hard to see that the NHS has been really damaged by Brexit, but is it any good anyway? The UK, it is often asserted in that ever-so-original term, is the 'sick man of Europe'. We are fatter, unhealthier, more likely to die from cancer, heart disease and just about everything else. NHS waiting lists are longer. We have patients languishing in hospital corridors for hours on end. Our pets get swifter treatment than we do.

Some of this is fair comment, although don't assume it is a lot different elsewhere in Europe. In the winter of 2022/23, while the NHS was in the depths of its usual seasonal crisis, fed by the annual peak in viral infections and still reeling from the hangover from the pandemic, things were running far from smoothly in hospitals across the Channel. 'We are more than full – patients are overflowing into the corridors,' reported Pascal Bilbault, who was running the A&E department at Strasbourg University Hospital.[8] In the small town of Adenau in northern Germany, a stroke patient had to be driven to a hospital in Mainz, ninety miles away, and an injured child flown to Luxembourg for want of a bed in the town's hospital. One patient in desperate pain reported having to wait three hours for an ambulance. And life for patients in Adenau was about to get worse: the hospital was due to close altogether in 2023.[9]

In Spain, La Paz Hospital was trying in vain to find room for 110 patients admitted every day in January 2023, while A&E doctors were threatening to go on strike over what they saw as the collapse of the public health system.[10] The pressures in European healthcare systems long predate Covid. In the Netherlands, all of the country's eighty paediatric wards were full in December 2019, with sick children having to be transferred to Belgian hospitals. According to a paediatrician at Sophia Hospital in Rotterdam, it was the result of a 'national bed deficit in intensive care' which had been afflicting the Netherlands for years.[11]

This is the reality for countries with an ageing population, where demands for healthcare are ever increasing – they are all feeling the strain. But let's look beyond the anecdotal evidence and focus on one of the ways in which Britain, in particular, is often asserted to be failing: cancer survival rates. On the face of it, these do look quite damning. In Britain, 81.1 per cent of patients are still alive five years after a diagnosis of breast cancer. In Germany, it is 85.3 per cent, France 86.9 per cent, the US 88.8 per cent and Japan 84.7 per cent. As for colon cancer, the five-year survival rates are: UK 53.8 per cent; Germany 64.6 per cent; France 59.8 per cent; US 64.7 per cent; Japan 69.4 per cent. For lung cancer it is: UK 9.6 per cent; Germany 16.2 per cent; France 13.6 per cent; US 18.7 per cent; Japan 30.1 per cent. And for stomach cancer it is 18.5 per cent; Germany 31.6 per cent; France 27.7 per cent; US 29.1 per cent; Japan 54.0 per cent/[12]

In other words, in almost every cancer Britain seems to be doing worse than any other G7 country. These statistics almost certainly do tell us something about genuine failures in the NHS, but they are not the whole story. There is another remarkable thing about the UK: significantly fewer of us seem to have cancer compared with many developed countries. In Britain, 6.2 per cent of the population are living with cancer. In France, it is 8 per cent, Germany 9.1 per cent, US 5.5 per cent and Japan 20.8 per cent. Moreover, when you look at an alternative metric, disability-adjusted life years (DALYs) lost to cancer – which totals up the number of years of life lost to cancer, as well as taking into consideration the number of years spent living with a disability as a result of the disease – Britain doesn't come out looking especially bad. In the UK, in 2019, the UK lost 3,302 DALYs per 100,000 people to cancer. In Germany, it was 3,221, and in France, 3,310. In the US, it was 3,229. Japan, though, does look significantly better than any of these countries, with 2,503 DALYs per 100,000 people lost to cancer in 2019.[13] Britain slightly surpasses Belgium and the Netherlands but is behind Spain, Italy and Sweden. If you want to find developed countries that do have a significantly lower toll from cancer in terms of life-years lost, you have to look to East Asia – not just Japan but also South Korea (2,647 DALYs lost in 2019) or Singapore (2,101).

Put all this together and you start to wonder: are other EU countries flattering their cancer survival rates through different diagnostic practices? There are several possible explanations. For one thing, there is the possibility that healthcare systems are using different definitions of cancer. A database established by the International Agency for Research on Cancer had to exclude non-melanoma skin cancer because of the widely varying rates of diagnosis; with some countries more enthusiastic about diagnosing it than others. There seems to be something quite odd going on with prostate cancer, too, with the proportion of cancers made up by prostate cancer varying from 0.6 per cent in South Korea to 42.6 per cent in Martinique (a Caribbean island which is part of France)[14] – which makes you question whether some countries are diagnosing the extremely common condition of an enlarged prostate as a form of cancer.

Or are some countries diagnosing large numbers of cancers at an earlier stage but not actually treating them that much better than in Britain? Diagnose a cancer earlier and it ought to be easier to treat, with a better outcome, but not necessarily if the treatment doesn't work. If the treatment isn't effective and you die at the same time you would have died had it not been diagnosed early, you may still contribute to a better cancer survival rate, because that is defined as the percentage of people still alive five years after diagnosis.

A University of Hong Kong study tried a different metric: Proxy Relative Survival Rates, which take into account age-standardised mortality rates as well as incidence from cancer. On this comparison, Australia comes out as the country with the best cancer treatment in the world, followed by Iceland,

Norway, Switzerland, South Korea, USA and Israel. The UK came out a fairly lowly 26th, but the study didn't flatter EU health systems. The top EU member state was Finland in 8th place. Germany was 15th, France 16th, Italy 18th, Netherlands 22nd and Spain 24th.[15]

The case of Germany is especially intriguing, considering that the country has established a reputation for its private cancer clinics, which attract many patients from Britain in search of a cure after complaining they have been failed by the NHS. Yet Germans seem to lose just as many life-years to the disease as do Britons. There are rather too many stories of cancer patients who have been persuaded to pay for extremely expensive treatment in German clinics – after their own country's health systems had failed to cure them – but ending up dying anyway. Such a case was that of the US actress Farrah Fawcett, who was given chemotherapy in Los Angeles after being diagnosed with bowel cancer in 2006. When that failed and she was told the only other option was surgery followed by the fitting of a colostomy bag, she travelled to private clinics in Germany to undergo expensive experimental treatments, which involved such things as heating up tumours. Initially, she reported that she had been reassured her tumour had disappeared, calling it a 'miracle' – except tests shortly afterwards showed it to be larger than ever.[16] She was later inspired to make a documentary from her deathbed about her disappointment. In spite of six visits to clinics in Germany, she died in June 2009.

The European Commission's State of Health in the EU report from 2019 found the UK distinctly average when it came to healthcare. For preventable mortality, it put Britain fourteenth out of thirty countries (it included a handful of non-EU countries), above Belgium, Germany, Denmark, Austria and Finland, but behind France, Spain, Italy, Sweden and the Netherlands. Where Britain scored relatively higher was in the reach of its public health system. The NHS was available for irregular residents and there were no access problems for rural or peripheral populations. It was a little less good than many countries in persuading adults to be vaccinated against influenza or to have their children inoculated with the MMR vaccine.[17]

Britain also scored well on preventative medicine, spending more on this – 5 per cent of the health budget – than any other country. Whether this shows in the health of the population is another matter. The healthfulness of a country's population is not just a function of the effectiveness of its public health system, of course, but also of the habits of its people. On this, Britain is not exactly the healthiest place on Earth.

Britain's obesity levels are a source of national shame – or they ought to be. There seems to be a growing body of opinion that rails against 'fat-shaming' and which asserts that obesity is really just another disease and nothing to do with personal responsibility. 'Body weight, fat distribution, and risk of complications are strongly influenced by biology,' declared Professor John Wilding of the University of Liverpool and Vicky Mooney of the European Coalition for People Living with Obesity in the *British Medical Journal* in 2019, citing that two hundred genes were involved in influencing a person's weight. 'It is not an individual's fault if they develop obesity.'[18]

It is easy to blame the easy availability of junk food, but then we had chip shops serving chips fried in dripping long before we had pizza joints and fried chicken. Did Britons undergo some dramatic genetic change between 1993, when the obesity rate among adults was 15 per cent, and 2016, when that proportion had climbed to 29.5 per cent? Moreover, are Britons so genetically different from people in Japan, where the obesity rate is just 4.4 per cent, or the South Koreans, who have an obesity rate of 4.9 per cent?[19] The obesity-isn't-an-individual's-fault lobby takes us for fools. The rise in obesity is a very serious problem in Britain, and it will not be addressed by trying to free individuals from the personal responsibility they bear for their diets. It may well be that some people are more genetically disposed than others to put on weight, and that some people find it easier to stop eating than others. Yet, even so, when faced with an oversize pizza, it is an act of free will how much of it to eat. To eat to excess is as much a matter of choice as to smoke or take illegal drugs.

The UK's obesity rate is not quite in the league of the US, where 37.3 per cent fall into that category. Moreover, other European countries are not far behind. In France, 23.2 per cent of adults are obese, in Germany 25.7 per cent, Spain 27.1 per cent and in Italy 22.9 per cent. No European country can take pleasure from these figures. There is nothing inevitable about an advanced industrial society, with mostly sedentary jobs, running to fat. The experience of Asia shows that. Besides Japan and South Korea, Singapore has an obesity rate of 6.6 per cent.

Britain comes out badly, too, on deaths from illicit drugs, with 3.68 deaths per 100,000 in 2019, with Scotland pulling up the national average. This was higher than any European country, outside Scandinavia or the Baltic states; twice as high as France or Germany and four times as high as Italy or even the Netherlands, whose liberal drugs policy has led to 'coffee shops' openly selling cannabis in Amsterdam. Deaths attributed to cocaine use are especially high in Britain at 0.17 per 100,000 – three times as high as France, Spain or Germany. In Western Europe, only Sweden has a higher toll. Britain, though, has a far cleaner nose than the US, which saw 18.83 deaths per 100,000 from illicit drugs in 2019, with 2.31 from cocaine. Once again, it is Southeast Asia that sets an example, with deaths from illicit drugs in Japan at 0.27 per 100,000 in 2019, and those in South Korea at 0.16 per 100,000.[20]

On alcohol-related deaths, Britain fares quite well among other European countries, with 23.3 deaths per 100,000 in

2019 – a little higher than Spain or Italy but significantly lower than France (33.8 per 100,000) or Germany, which at 42.8 deaths per 100,000 has one of the highest death rates in the world. Where Britain does score well among its European peers is for its low rate of smoking. The percentage of adults who smoke fell from over 50 per cent in the 1970s to 15.4 per cent in 2020. In France, it was 33.4 per cent, Germany 22 per cent, Spain 27.7 per cent and Italy 23.1 per cent.[21]

When Covid-19 struck in early 2020, all the usual preoccupations of public health officials took a back seat. As the virus gripped Italy and Spain, Britain at first seemed removed from the crisis. In any case, Britain had just been declared to be the second best-prepared country in the world for a pandemic – after the US.[22] Here, at least, was an area in which Britain, supposedly, led Europe on health. By the third week of March, though, everything had changed. As Britons began to succumb to the disease, the rates of infection and death began to point in a wholly different direction; suddenly, it seemed that Britain was going to be one of the hardest-hit countries on earth.

Britain's Covid-19 Inquiry started in the autumn of 2023 with what seemed to be a distinct narrative: that the country had suffered especially badly during the Covid pandemic due to its failure to lock down early enough. When it came to the turn of the former prime minister, Boris Johnson, to appear in the hot seat, the counsel to the inquiry, Hugo Keith KC, put it to him that Britain had suffered the highest, or second highest depending on which dataset you chose, death rate in Western Europe. It was yet another case, so it seemed, of lumbering Brexit Britain failing where others had succeeded.

Yet it was an unfair charge. Statistics that looked only at deaths officially attributed to Covid-19 missed something rather important: there was never an internationally agreed definition of what constituted a Covid death. Was it someone who had quite obviously died as a consequence of being infected – or did it also include people who, while they may have caught Covid in their final days, had been close to death anyway? Public Health England (PHE) – the quango that had been in charge of collecting the statistics at the time – initially used an even broader definition: added to the toll was absolutely anyone who had died and who had previously, at some point in the past, contracted Covid. They were being included in the figures even if they had fallen off their bicycle after recovering from Covid three months earlier. As were people who had contracted Covid while being treated in hospital for other mortal conditions. As Carl Heneghan, Professor of Evidence-Based Medicine at the University of Oxford, pointed out, this would eventually mean, as Covid-19 became endemic, that almost everyone who died in England would eventually be recorded as a Covid death.[23] PHE subsequently changed its definition to anyone who had tested positive for Covid within twenty-eight days of their deaths – but still disregarded other causes.

No wonder Britain was coming out as a Covid-ridden hellhole in the early days of the pandemic. The more illuminating way to judge the death rate from Covid across countries is by looking at 'excess mortality' over a much longer period. This is defined as the number of deaths – from all causes – compared with the number of deaths which would have been expected, based on mortality data from the preceding years. This captures people who have died from conditions other than Covid but whose deaths had connected causes – for example, people who died of heart attacks because they were unable to get medical attention. On the other hand, it corrects for people who may have died of Covid but who were close to death from some other condition at the time they contracted the virus – they do not show up as 'excess deaths' because they would have died around the same time anyway.

The most comprehensive attempt to compare excess deaths around the world during Covid was undertaken by an international team of scientists funded by the Bill and Melinda Gates Foundation and published in the *Lancet* in April 2022. It looked at data from 191 countries and compared the number of deaths in 2020 and 2021 to the number who would have been expected to die during those years – based on data from previous years, adjusted for population growth, age profile of the population and so on.

The United Kingdom came out with an excess mortality rate of 126.8 per 100,000 – a little above the global average of 120.3, but below the Western European average of 140.0. Britain as a whole fared little differently from France (124.2) or Germany (120.5). But many countries fared much worse than did Britain. Spain had excess mortality of 186.7 per 100,000 and Italy 227.4.[24]

In other words, no, Britain was not an outlier where the virus was allowed to rip, thanks to an incompetent, reckless government, while others in Europe stayed safe. No European country came off well out of the pandemic. For countries which avoided high rates of mortality you have to look eastwards, to Japan (44.1 excess deaths per 100,000 in 2020 and 2021), South Korea (4.4) or Singapore (-15.8, meaning fewer people died than would have been expected during those two years had it not been for Covid). Australia had an even more negative rate of excess deaths, at -37.6 per cent per 100,000, but had the advantage of being relatively remote, and a long way from the seat of the infection; Asian countries were neither, and yet they achieved low rates of excess mortality without the hard lockdowns employed in Europe and Australia.

It was Italy, not Britain, which experienced overflowing A&E departments, with hospitals forced to allow over-65s to die without treatment in some cases. The country's

emergency units were still struggling four years later. In
January 2024, 1,100 patients were waiting to be admitted to
emergency wards in the Rome region alone, as a seasonal
rise in respiratory infections had overloaded the system.
While junior doctors in Britain had indulged in a six-day
strike to demand higher pay, doctors in Italy had worked
solidly through the Christmas period to provide what cover
they could.[25] But a far worse situation was on the horizon
in Italy, with a quarter of the country's 102,000 doctors due
to retire by 2025. Italy has been a lot less successful than
Britain in recruiting overseas doctors, not least because it
offers them substantially lower pay. In 2023, Italy's specialist
doctors were earning the equivalent of $82,000 a year, com-
pared with $156,000 in Britain and $175,000 in Germany. In
desperation, the Italian government turned to Cuba in 2023,
from where it planned to borrow 500 doctors.[26] As with many
European countries, Italy's public health system is being
propped up by medical staff from developing countries –
countries that could well do with the doctors and nurses for
their own citizens.

Covid-19 exposed weaknesses in healthcare systems all
around the world. The German system was widely admired
in Britain at the beginning of the pandemic, but it is appreci-
ated a little less so in Germany. An analysis by the American
German Institute think-tank summarised its failings.[27] On
paper, Germany seems to boast a lot of nurses – the third
highest number per head of population in Europe. It also
seems to have more ample beds than most countries – 776
per 100,000 population, compared with 240 per 100,000 in
Britain. But that didn't mean more nurses and more beds
were available when it mattered. When the pandemic struck,
emergency planners found themselves with a lack of central-
ised data on how many beds were available and where. The
NHS, parts of which still cling to fax machines, evidently isn't

the only healthcare system with a strange aversion to computers (although the NHS has actually become quite good at collecting data in recent years through NHS Digital).

As for Germany's apparent abundance of nurses, they were complaining of overwork even before the pandemic. When you look at the ratio of nurses to hospital patients, Germany flips to become the second worst in the EU, after Hungary. The problem is that German hospitals have a perverse financial incentive to treat patients in hospital when they might more effectively be treated as outpatients. The number of inpatient treatments in Germany rose by 15.4 per cent between 2000 and 2017, concluded the American German Institute, but not because medical needs justified it – it was thanks to hospitals undertaking unnecessary treatments in an attempt to rake in fees and keep themselves afloat.

Even so, German hospitals have fallen into a financially precarious state. According to the consultancy Roland Berger in a study in 2022, 70 per cent of Germany's six hundred largest hospitals – and 90 per cent of public hospitals – are in deficit. Moreover, the problem with staff overload has become worse thanks to large numbers of nurses quitting the profession.[28] That is exactly what we were told would happen in Britain as a result of Brexit, but it seems to be happening in Germany instead.

And in France. According to a paper by the French government's Directorate of Research, Studies, Evaluation and Statistics, two thirds of GPs have had to turn away patients because they have too many to cope with.[29] In some parts of the country, hospitals have had to close their out of hours A&E departments, while patients wait months for treatments such as rehabilitation after a stroke.[30] One of the reasons for a chronic shortage of doctors is that a cap on the number of medical students has starved the profession of new recruits from France itself – exactly the same as has happened in Britain.

Ireland doesn't have a universal public healthcare system – something which is proving a big barrier to the dreams of those who want a united Ireland. Half the population of Northern Ireland cite this as a factor in how they would vote in a theoretical referendum. Two thirds of the population of the Republic are obliged to pay for at least some services. Not that this helps to cut demand sufficiently to avoid the same sort of overcrowding problems which the NHS suffers from – even worse, in fact. In 2023, 121,526 patients – including 3,450 children – ended up being admitted to hospital without a bed to accommodate them. Many had to be treated on trolleys in corridors instead. In order to try to relieve pressure on hospitals, the government is introducing what it calls 'acute virtual wards', where people who might normally be admitted to hospital are instead left at home, their condition monitored remotely – a more extreme example of the online consultations that GPs surgeries in Britain are increasingly trying to force on their patients.

European public health systems are malfunctioning thanks to demographics and stagnant economies. Ageing populations are exerting ever greater demands and expectations for care, while European economies are no longer producing enough wealth to meet those demands. For now, Europeans continue to enjoy a high life expectancy, but the continent no longer stands out as it once did. In 1971, the UK had a life expectancy at birth of 72.2, growing to 80.7 in 2021. France went from 72.1 to 82.5 and West Germany/Germany from 70.9 to 80.6. Sweden had the longest-lived people in the world in 1971, reaching an average of 74.6 years. Now, Swedes (83.0 years) are outlived by the Japanese (84.8), Australians (84.5) and South Koreans (83.7). The latter lived to a mere 62.9 in 1971. The most dramatic gains in life expectancy have come in Southeast Asia, while the Chinese have extended average lifespans from 57.6 years to 78.2 years in half a century. The

US is the real laggard, though, with life expectancy increasing from 71.1 in 1971 to a relatively modest 77.2 fifty years later. Yes, the Chinese, on official statistics at least, are now living longer than are Americans.

With Europeans smoking more, taking more drugs and having far higher rates of obesity than Southeast Asia and many other parts of the world, and with their healthcare systems struggling to keep up, it won't be long before the continent starts to lose one of its most obvious claims to enjoy the highest living standards in the world. On this measure, however, the US is trailing far further behind.

In one sense, though, Britain did excel during the Covid-19 pandemic. As a special report by the European Court of Auditors in 2022 concluded, the UK got ahead of the rest of Europe in procuring and rolling out vaccines. It had begun procurement earlier. A UK vaccine taskforce was set up on 20 April 2020, two months before the EU procurement process began. Even so, many on the Remain side of the fence thought that Britain should throw in its lot with the EU; that we would get effective vaccines quicker and more cost-effectively that way. But that isn't exactly how things turned out. The UK managed to approve the first vaccine, produced by Pfizer in association with the German company BioNTech, and start rolling it out on 8 December, four days ahead of the US and earlier than any other country in the world. Rollout of the vaccine began in the EU on 26 December, after which progress was initially far slower than in Britain. By the end of March 2021, 46 per cent of the UK population had had at least one dose of a Covid vaccine, compared with just 13.2 per cent of the EU population.[31]

All governments that ordered vaccines while they were still being developed were taking a speculative risk. They had no idea whether the drugs would prove safe and effective or not, but they were prepared to put up the money in order to speed up development. The EU's procurement process was thwarted, however, by putting too much faith in one vaccine: that developed by French company Sanofi, in association with UK company GSK. In September 2020, the EU ordered 300 million doses – half as many again as its initial order for the Pfizer vaccine. Unfortunately, the Sanofi vaccine fell behind, with the first trials showing low rates of effectiveness. It was finally approved for use in the EU in November 2022, by which time most Europeans had been double or triple jabbed with a Covid vaccine and the pandemic was happily retreating into our collective memories. The EU had favoured the home team, but its bet had failed to pay off. Moreover, as the European Court of Auditors discovered, while UK and US contracts with vaccine manufacturers had included clauses demanding priority delivery, EU contracts had not, leading to its orders falling down the queue and the EU having to undertake the unseemly business of taking the manufacturers to court in an effort to try to speed up delivery.

In late January 2021, when it was falling far behind in the vaccination rate, the EU briefly proposed to place an export embargo on Pfizer vaccines manufactured within the EU – to prevent them, in other words, being sent to Britain. It was a remarkable act of hostility, which drew condemnation from both sides of the border in Ireland – a border which the EU had only weeks earlier been insisting must stay open, without border controls, for the sake of the Northern Irish peace process.[32] The proposal was quickly withdrawn, but it showed the nasty, protectionist side of the EU, quite at odds with the image of the spirit of enlightened cooperation which Remainers had been trying to portray. As so often, at its most challenging moments the EU had been found badly wanting.

12.

Education

Nowhere was Brexit felt more bitterly than on Britain's campuses. For many academics, the very concept of Brexit was not just an attack on the EU, it was an attack on reason itself. A vote for Brexit, claimed Professor Michael Arthur, President and Provost of University College London, two weeks before referendum day in June 2016, would damage the reputation of UK universities and lead to them slipping down the world rankings. It could also lead to the university losing a significant proportion of its undergraduates – 12 per cent of whom, at the time, were drawn from other EU countries. As if to prove his point, one of his students, a second-year archaeologist from Italy, had vowed to return home if Britain voted to leave. 'I will not associate myself with any country in Europe that does not recognise the importance of a united continent,' he told the *Guardian*.[1] Others feared that UK students would miss out on chances to study abroad as Britain withdrew from the Erasmus programme – an exchange programme which had been running since the 1980s.

Come the result, and the Ivory Towers were rumbling even

more with disgust. UK academics couldn't seem to let go of the idea that dim-witted Brexit voters had robbed them of their birthright to EU citizenship. In 2017, a University of Leicester study claimed that the referendum vote would have gone the other way if just 3 per cent more of the UK population had been university educated – the reasoning being that graduates were more likely to have voted to Remain.[2] 'Brexit caused by low levels of education, study funds', read the headline in a newspaper story carrying the findings. The researchers and headline writer might just have asked themselves whether the possession of a degree is simply a marker for age, given that there were relatively few universities in existence when today's septuagenarians were in their twenties. Those older voters – who voted Leave in much greater proportions than the young – were the ones most likely to have felt let down by the promises made about EU membership in the early days. A much less university-educated population, don't forget, voted two to one to remain in what was then the European Economic Community in the first referendum in 1975.

A study by the Bath University School of Management in 2023 went one further and claimed that Remain voters were, on the whole, more intelligent than Leave voters. On the back of a survey of 3,183 heterosexual couples (why gay people and those who currently do not have a partner were excluded it didn't say) it claimed that 73 per cent of people in the highest cognitive group voted Remain, compared with only 40 per cent in the lowest cognitive group. So there – scientific proof of what the liberal-left always felt in its gut to be true: that Brexit voters are thick.

To be fair to the author, Chris Dawson, he didn't quite state that in black and white, and recognised that some Brexit voters were in the highest cognitive group. But what he did claim was that Brexit voters may have been swung by campaigning material that was 'contradictory, false and often fraudulent, especially regarding the pro-leave side'. The last clause is quite an assertion, given some of the material put out by the Remain campaign, not least the claim by the Treasury – since proved to be hopelessly wrong – that a vote for Brexit would collapse the economy by up to 6 per cent and increase unemployment by up to 800,000 within two years.[3] Moreover, his study didn't appear to have asked the Leave voters exactly what inspired them to vote that way – rather crucial information if you are going to assert that voters have been misled. Actually, there was a very good reason why people who perform less well in cognitive tests may have voted for Brexit, and one that has nothing to do with their susceptibility to poor information. They are more likely to be employed in low-paid, elementary occupations – the very ones which were being undermined by the free movement of labour. They voted Brexit not because they are stupid, but because they quite correctly worked out that it was in their personal interests for Britain to leave the EU – just like the lorry driver I spoke to in 2022 who said he had hadn't seen a pay rise for years until Brexit, but had then seen his pay jump by 40 per cent in a few months.

But bitterness and disappointment of Remain-voting academics aside, is it even true that UK universities have suffered from Britain's departure from the EU? The scientists' fear that Britain would lose out on research money as a result of leaving the Horizon Europe funding programme was realised for a couple of years, while Britain's application for associate membership was held in abeyance (the EU used it as a bargaining chip during and after Brexit negotiations). During the hiatus, when Britain was not in Horizon, the UK government continued to fund research directly. But, on 1 January 2024, the UK rejoined the programme, giving it continued access to the programme's £95 billion of funding. Associate status of

Horizon is held by seventeen other countries outside the EU, including Turkey, Israel and New Zealand. Others, including Australia, Canada and Japan, have applied to join. Horizon, in other words, is becoming a global programme rather than simply a European one.

The Erasmus programme has spawned a successor – the Turing programme – which continues to offer opportunities to UK students to spend time abroad studying. It is not so generous as the Erasmus programme, in that it does not cover the cost of overseas students coming to Britain to study, but it is global rather than simply European, and so offers far wider opportunities.

Did Brexit lead to a collapse in overseas students? There was certainly a decline in the number of EU nationals coming to take up undergraduate courses in Britain. The numbers applying plunged by 40 per cent in 2021/22 and the numbers accepted fell by 50 per cent. The following year there was a further drop of 24 per cent in applications and 29 per cent in acceptances.[4] There is a very good reason for this. When Britain was in the EU, EU nationals were treated like home students when it came to charging tuition fees. This meant that they paid a maximum of £9,250 a year in English universities and nothing at all in Scottish universities – the Scottish taxpayer generously funded their education. Now, EU nationals are treated like any other overseas students, and can be charged the full cost of their courses.

But has this damaged UK universities? On the contrary, the overall number of overseas students who came to Britain to study has never been higher, with 679,970 enrolled in university courses in 2021/22. Students from outside the EU – who are nearly five times as numerous in the UK university system as EU students – have more than made up the difference. The contrast now is that all overseas students are paying a full commercial rate for their courses. The education of EU students has become an export industry rather than an expense to be borne by UK taxpayers

Did Brexit, as the President of UCL claimed it would, damage the reputation of UK universities? Hardly. The best of them continue to outshine their EU brethren. Take the *Times Higher Education* rankings, which judge the quality of research and teaching based on 134 million citations in 16.5 million research publications, as well as survey responses from 68,000 students. The top ten consists of Oxford, Cambridge and Imperial College plus seven US universities. The top EU university – the Technical University of Munich – weighs in at number thirty. The top hundred breaks down as follows: thirty-eight US, eleven UK and twenty-one EU,[5] with East Asian and Australian universities taking up most of the remaining places.

If you don't want to believe a ranking table that is based in Britain, then take a look at the rival Center for World University Rankings, which is based in the UAE and similarly looks at research citations, plus academic distinctions won by alumni and the number of graduates employed by large companies. Its own top ten consists of Oxford, Cambridge plus eight US universities. The highest EU university – Paris Sciences et Lettres – comes in at number twenty-one. The top 100 is made up of fifty US institutions, nine UK ones and sixteen from the EU.[6] To give a further idea of the reputation of the British higher education system and the soft power it wields – which is unlikely to be undone by Brexit – here is a remarkable statistic: in 2023, the leaders of fifty-eight countries around the globe had been educated at a UK university. That is nearly a quarter of the world. Not even dubious studies claiming that Brexit voters are stupid, put out by Britain's less-esteemed universities, has been enough to damage that reputation.

Meanwhile, French universities continue to do what they

do best: to provide latter-day Robespierres with the stage on which to act out their revolutionary fantasies. Ever since 1968, French universities have regularly been afflicted by student-led disruption. In 2009, students in Paris rioted in protest at education reforms, blockading their campuses and inspiring copycat protests and riots in Barcelona, Rome and several other Italian cities. In April 2022, students at the Sorbonne staged a sit-in, occupying several buildings because they didn't like either of the candidates who had made the final two for the run-off in the French presidential election. 'Since young people are concerned with environmental issues, with social issues, with antiracist, feminist and LGBTQ issues it is necessary to have a candidate to represent us,' claimed one of their spokespeople. The French electorate, needless to say, had had a choice of several left-wing candidates in the first round, but none had secured enough votes to make the run-off. In other words, the students were protesting against democracy itself – while, without a hint of irony, waving banners reading: 'We are all anti-fascists'.[7]

In March 2023, the student agitators were back in strength, with 90,000 turning out to join trade unions in protest against President Macron's plan to raise the retirement age from 62 to 64 (it is currently 66 in Britain and was 65 for most of the past century).[8] Two months later, they were occupying university buildings again, this time protesting against climate change – and were joined by students in Germany, Portugal, Belgium, demanding the immediate end of fossil fuels, without seeming to have much of a plan for how to avoid the economic collapse that would inevitably follow. In Athens, in 2021, students rioted in protest at government plans to end the so-called 'asylum law', a 1970s piece of legislation which prevents police officers from entering university campuses and which has been blamed for them becoming havens for drug-dealers, sex attackers, vandals and thieves – and driven many young Greeks to seek to study overseas in order to avoid the lawlessness.[9]

European universities too often give the impression of being places where the exchange of ideas and the sharing of wisdom takes second place to the dogmas of student politics. There seems to be a growing tendency among students that they should decide what should be taught and how. In 2022, students in Barcelona staged a sit-in demanding that all students be put on a compulsory climate change course, focusing on the evils of fossil fuels – raising the question of what they are doing at university at all, if they thought they knew more than their tutors? The university, however, acceded to their requests and the compulsory module was introduced from 2024. It is little wonder, with the students in control, that European universities have ended up punching well below their weight in research.

So much for universities, what about school education? Is the EU superior to Britain in that respect? Only, to judge by the OECD's PISA tests, in the case of Estonia. PISA – the Programme for International Student Assessment – aims to compare the academic performance of 15–16-year-olds across borders by setting standardised tests, which are taken in a minimum of 150 schools in each of the eighty countries in the system. In the 2022 rankings, UK students had a mean score of 489 in maths, 494 in reading and 500 in science. This put Britain equal fourth out of nineteen European countries in maths, third out of twenty-two countries in reading and equal fourth out of twenty countries in science. UK students comfortably outperformed those in France, Germany, Italy and Spain in all three areas. Finland, of whose education system great things are often said in Britain, outperformed Britain in science but not maths and reading. The only EU country that can claim consistently to have outperformed Britain was

Estonia, where students scored an average of 510 in maths, 511 in reading and 526 in science.[10]

As for the rest of the EU, it is trailing Asia badly. In 2022, the highest PISA scores were in Singapore (575 in maths, 543 in reading and 561 in science), Japan (536 in maths, 516 in reading and 547 in science) and South Korea (527, 515 and 528 respectively). Moreover, these three countries succeeded in maintaining pupils' performance even during the pandemic. Most other countries saw performance plunge between 2018 and 2022. UK children, however, suffered less than many in the EU – in spite of school closures which dragged on for months. In maths, UK children slipped 13 points between the two dates. French pupils, by contrast, slipped 21 points and German ones 25 points.

The underperformance of France's schools began well before the pandemic. A report by CNESCO – the government body that oversees standards in French schools, like Ofsted in Britain – reported that 10 per cent of pupils, equivalent to 100,000 each year, were leaving school without a single qualification to their name. They neither had a baccalaureate nor the more vocational Certificate d'aptitude professionelle (CAP).[11] Perhaps that is not altogether a surprise given that many of their teachers themselves struggle to pass a version of the CAP designed for educators. In 2022, only 557 applicants managed to satisfy the requirements for teaching maths – allowing the profession to fill a little over half the 1,035 places available. In physics and chemistry, only 209 passed, less than half the number required to fill the 425 vacancies. The failure to find enough suitably qualified candidates has led to a shortage of teachers, with 1,728 posts vacant in 2022 in Paris and the Ile de France alone.[12] Gaps have been filled with less-qualified staff. Even if pupils do have a suitable teacher, it doesn't necessarily mean they will get to attend lessons, as schools are rife with strikes due to teachers complaining of low pay. As for the pupils, they are too busy protesting or bullying each other – a survey in 2023 revealed that up to a million pupils in the country reported being bullied.[13]

France has a very high-minded attitude to school education, but the reality fails miserably to live up to the ideal. The academically demanding curriculum is a source of national pride, but therein lies the problem, according to Marie Duru-Bellat, a sociologist at the Paris Institute of Political Studies (also known as Sciences Po). 'In France a maths teacher will say he is a mathematician rather than a teacher,' she says. The idea that teaching is itself a valuable skill seems to be lost – former President Nicolas Sarkozy even closed down dedicated teacher training colleges, although they were later reopened by his successor Francois Hollande. Yet, even with a high-minded curriculum, the school system is failing the most able pupils as badly as the less able ones. According to educational psychologist Fabrice Bak, schools are not set up to cater for children who learn material quickly but then rapidly disengage if they are not kept challenged: 'The education system is sick from the inside,' he has written. Rather than address the issues of teacher shortages and children leaving school without qualifications, Emmanuel Macron's government has found a different priority in recent years: banning pupils from wearing to school a long Muslim dress called the abaya. 'When you walk into a classroom you shouldn't be able to identify the pupils' religion just by looking at them. I have decided that the abaya can no longer be worn in schools,' said the then newly appointed education minister Gabriel Attal, in September 2023, shortly before being kicked upstairs once again to become prime minister. He wasn't around when the deal came into force, provoking yet more strikes, as teachers in Paris banlieue refused to act as clothing police. Attal himself, needless to say, had attended an elite private school.

A dispassionate observer might say that the problem in

French schools has less to do with what pupils choose to wear and rather more to do with the weapons they are able to bring into school – as well as a failure properly to manage pupils who are known to have been radicalised by extremist groups. A month after Attal announced his ban on the abaya, a teacher was stabbed to death and another critically injured at a school in Arras, northern France, by a 20-year-old Chechen refugee, and former pupil, who had been identified by intelligence services as a threat and stopped a few days earlier, but was released.[14] It was merely the latest in a spate of such attacks. In 2020, a teacher, Samuel Paty, was stabbed by pupils and then decapitated by another Chechen refugee at a school in the Paris suburb of Éragny-sur-Oise, after showing cartoons of the Prophet Mohammed during an ethics class. Another teacher was murdered by a 16-year-old pupil at a school in the southwestern town of St Jean de Luz, in February 2023.[15] It may be the US with its high school and college shootings that has the worst reputation for violence in places of education, but France seems to be rapidly catching up.

In Germany, schools seem to be evolving into daycare centres but struggling when it comes to education. In 2021, more than seven in ten schools were offering what is known in Britain as 'wrap around care', with pupils allowed to stay for long hours while their parents are at work – up from one in ten in 2002. Parents have been keen to seize the opportunity, with 47.5 per cent of pupils enrolled for long days in 2021, up from 4.2 per cent in 2002. But what are they doing while they are at school? Not mastering their maths and German, it seems. According to the Educational Monitor kept by think-tank INSM, there was a 5 per cent decline in pupils' academic performance scores between 2013 and 2023, with only schools in the Saarland and Hamburg improving their performance. There were steep falls in Bremen and Baden-Württemberg. German schools, suggested the authors of the study, had failed to find a way to cope with the increasing number of migrant children – in 2021, 21.1 per cent of pre-school children were found to speak no German at home. Furthermore, fewer children seem to enjoy educational opportunities outside of school. In 2011, 39.2 per cent of pupils hailed from households that had more than a hundred books. By 2021, that had fallen to 30.9 per cent.[16]

Even before Covid-19, Italian schools were failing to hang onto their pupils. The country had grappled for years with high truancy rates, and students opting out of education after the age of sixteen. In 2017, 26 per cent of 15–34-year-olds were neither in education, work or training, higher than in any other EU country (in Britain it was 14 per cent).[17] In 2019, Italy had the second lowest proportion of 25–64-year-olds with a qualification beyond school, at 19.6 per cent; only the Romanian working-age population was less well educated.[18] But then came Covid, and Italy's schools tuned out for longer than any others in Europe, depriving children of thirty-five weeks of education time in the first year of the pandemic. Some pupils had no schooling for six months and then attended just forty-two days' worth of school between September 2020 and March 2021. Many didn't bother coming back at all. By 2021, one in five pupils in Naples aged under sixteen had dropped out of school altogether.[19] In Catania, Sicily, one Italian teacher lamented that just seven of her nineteen pupils had bothered to turn up for one lesson – this in a part of the country where some areas still have an illiteracy rate of 18 per cent. The failure to keep Sicily's children in school is at least good news for the mafia. 'The risk is that we may lose an entire generation to criminal gangs,' said the teacher.

Illiteracy is one thing that most developed countries have been able to forget about, with close on 100 per cent of their adult populations (allowing for adults with learning difficulties) able to read and write. Yet in parts of Southern Europe it lingers on. In Portugal, as recently as 2001, 9 per cent of the adult population was illiterate, rising to 16 per cent in the southern region of Alentejo. By 2021, that was down to 3.1 per cent, but still there is a big divide between men and women: even now, 4 per cent of adult Portuguese women cannot read or write.

Europe may claim historically to be the seat of the enlightenment, of science and reason. But, when it comes to education standards, it is slipping behind. Schools are underperforming and universities are training political activists rather than people who can think and reason for themselves.

13.

Older and Older

If the world were a family, Africa would be the trouble-some teenager – its population had a median age of just 18 in 2020. Asia and South America would be its elder siblings, each with a median age of 31. Australia comes next, at 33, then North America at 35 (the US is 38, with Mexico pulling the median age downwards). But as for Europe, it is old enough to be Africa's father. In 2020, the median age of people living in Europe was 42, that of European citizens 44.[1]

No European country is quite yet in the position of the world's oldest major nation, Japan, where the median age is 47, but most are fast going the same way. Some regions already do have a median age of over 50. Chemnitz in Lower Saxony, in the former East Germany, has the dubious distinction of being Europe's oldest region, followed by Sachsen-Anhalt, Mecklenburg. Brandenburg, also in Germany, Liguria and Sardinia in Italy, and Asturias in Spain.[2] Does it matter? For years, many thought not. A declining birth rate was seen as an environmental and social gain. It was seen as sign of female emancipation, and as the mechanism that would save us from a Malthusian reckoning with nature. Moreover, some countries, such as Italy and Spain, had a political objection to anything which encouraged families to breed, associating the idea with their fascist pasts.

But, suddenly, Europe is panicking about its demographic timebomb. In 2019, the European Commission for the first time appointed a commissioner with responsibility for demography. The Work-Life Balance Directive has tried to nudge the birth rate upwards in a very EU sort of way: by trying to ensure gender balance in parental leave and to outlaw the dismissal of employees on the grounds they are about to become parents.

In 2020 and 2021 – thanks only in part to the pandemic – Europe reached a milestone: its population fell for the first time in modern history. Pandemic over, the EU expects its population to resume growing until it hits a peak of 449 million in 2026, after which long-term decline will set in, falling to 441 million by 2050 and 416 million in 2100.[3] Yet the real problems have already begun, with the working-age population shrinking by 12 million between 2010 and 2020.[4] Europe is already beginning to suffocate beneath its pensions and social care liabilities, as ever fewer workers are forced to support an ever growing number of pensioners. In 2021, the over 65s made up 20.8 per cent of the population of Europe, with three people of working age for every citizen over 65. By 2050, the over 65s will make up 30 per cent of the population, with only two people of working age for every pensioner.

The imbalance between Europe's working and retired populations could be put right, to some extent, by raising the retirement age. But there seems little hope of that in the near future, not when French workers rioted in response to President Macron's attempt to raise the state retirement age from 62 to 64 in 2023. In spite of growing longevity, several European countries still have a retirement age of under

65 – an age at which it was set in Britain over a century ago (it is currently 66 in Britain and will rise to 67 by 2028). Greeks still retire at 62 and Italians at 64, even though those two countries having huge fiscal holes. At current rates, estimates the EU, the cost of pensions will be swallowing 26.7 per cent of European GDP by 2070.[5]

Europe's demographic crisis is worse than it at first appears, because it is currently masked by high rates of migration. Migration is keeping the median age of Europeans two years younger than it would otherwise be, which is helping to disguise the real problem at the heart of Europe's demographic timebomb: collapsing birth rates. To put it straight: Europe is slowly ceasing to breed.

To achieve a sustainable population in a modern country with low rate of infant mortality, it is necessary for a country to have a fertility rate – the average number of children that woman will bear in her lifetime – of around 2.1. In 1972, every Western European country achieved that bar West Germany (1.8) and Sweden (1.91). Yet, by 2022, not a single European country did. A couple came close: France and Ireland were both on 1.97. The UK was on 1.87. Some countries are breeding at little over half replacement rate. Remarkably, the most precipitous falls have been in Southern European countries where the fertility rate was highest half a century ago. Greece's fertility rate plunged from 2.55 to 1.31 between 1972 and 2022, Portugal's from 2.88 to 1.25. Sweden's fertility rate, on the other hand, remains exactly where it was in 1972, at 1.91.[6]

Birth rates would be even lower were it not for high levels of migration, because the migrant population in many countries has a significantly higher birth rate than the native population. In England and Wales, in 2022, for example, 30.3 per cent of live births were to a non-UK-born mother and 35.8 per cent of babies had one or both parents born overseas.[7] Many

Europeans have come to have a negative view of migration, yet their countries are relying increasingly on migrants simply to keep their populations from shrinking.

In its falling birth rates, Europe is not so different from the rest of the developed world. It is remarkable that of the forty-one countries that the IMF classified as 'advanced economies' in 2023, only one of them had a fertility rate greater than replacement rate: Israel, at 2.82. Birth rates in Asia have plummeted even faster than those in Europe. Japan had a fertility rate of 2.11 in 1972, falling to 1.53 in 2022; it fell even lower, to 1.31 at the beginning of this century. South Korea's fertility rate fell from 4.04 in 1972 to 1.39 in 2022, Singapore's from 2.84 in 1972 to 1.28 in 2022. Even India – which overtook China to become the world's most populated country in 2023 – is falling below replacement rate, with a fertility rate of 2.2 in 2022. Most of South America, too, has fallen below replacement rate, the fertility rate in Brazil plunging from 2.23 in 2001 to 1.65 in 2022. Only parts of Africa now have the very high fertility rates that were more or less universal in developing countries until recent times. Niger currently has the highest fertility rate in the world, at 6.86.

But of all continents, it is Europe where the problem of declining birth rates is most acute because it has the most aged population to start with – and also because it has the most developed social security systems. The greater the state support offered to pensioners, the bigger a fiscal problem an ageing population becomes. Remarkably, Europe's birth rate is collapsing in spite of social policies that are supposed to support families with young children. Policies on mandatory parental leave and childcare provision have failed to persuade people to start families.

The working age population is shrinking faster in some countries than in others. Facing the most acute crisis is Greece, where the number of people between fifteen and sixty-four is projected to fall by 40 per cent by the end of this century. With public finances still struggling to recover from the sovereign debt crisis of 2011, it is hard to see anything but fiscal disaster in the decades ahead. Things are not looking a lot better in Poland, where the working-age population is projected to fall by 35 per cent by 2100, and Italy, which is in for a 30 per cent fall.[8]

Britain is at least in a slightly better position than almost any other European country – it is one of only three where the working-age population is projected to rise over the course of the century. The other two are Norway and Sweden. Not only is the fertility rate in Britain holding up a little better than in most countries; migration to Britain is mostly of younger people who have long working lives ahead of them. Yes, supposedly anti-migration Britain actually has a policy of enlightened self-interest when it comes to opening its labour market to workers capable of boosting the economy.

Democratic governments do not order people to breed. But, at some point, they are going to have to start asking: how far are birth rates going to fall, how much of a problem is this going to be, and what, if anything, should we do about it? Changing social conditions have led many women to put off child-rearing until much later in life as they pursue careers. Many people no longer carry the expectation that they will start a family as earlier generations once did. The costs of raising children have risen sharply owing to high property prices; if you cannot afford more than a one-bedroom flat, you are unlikely to choose to start a family. There may be medical reasons, too: a study led by the Hebrew University of Jerusalem in 2023 found that sperm counts around the world have fallen by 50 per cent over the past half century, for reasons which remain obscure.[9] Some of these issues can and should be addressed by public policy. For many years, for example, planning policy in Britain encouraged the building

of one- and two-bedroom flats in the belief that elderly
homeowners would want to downsize, freeing up their family
homes for the next generation. But many don't want to do this,
and why should they? Planning policy should favour family
homes – and ones which ordinary people can afford; not
high-end homes packaged for the global investment market.
The tax structure – in Britain especially – is not friendly to
families, least of all to women who want to take career breaks
to look after young children. It would make a big difference if
children were to be granted a tax-free allowance which could
be transferred to their parents, allowing families to keep more
of their earnings. As for sperm counts, that is an issue that
demands greater official attention, in the same way as rising
rates of cancer among young people.

But there is a deeper malaise in Europe – which to some
extent is shared by North America. For some young people
it seems to be a virtue to refuse to breed, for the good of the
planet. 'The natural world is collapsing around us,' according to Blythe Pepino, a sometime pop singer who founded a
movement called Birthstrike, 'I couldn't bring a child into
that.'[10] The French have coined a term for it: collapsology,
the belief that human civilisation is doomed and therefore it
would be cruel to start a family. As Julie, a 23-year-old Swiss
puts it: 'Bringing children into the world where nature has
been destroyed ... Where our worries deal with managing
to breathe, and there is no way out ... I think it's unfair to
impose this on an individual who hasn't chosen it.'

One study found that between a third and a half of 16 to
25-year-olds in some European countries and the US were
hesitant to think about having children because of their worries over the climate, though the same fears did not extend to
developing countries like Zambia, where people found that
thinking about climate change made them keen to have more
children.[11]

European youth is stuck in a cycle of negativity, which was not shared by earlier generations, in spite of the far darker clouds that blotted their horizons. People who lived prior to the twentieth century did not refuse to breed on the grounds that it would be unfair to bring a child into a world where infant mortality was rife. The world wars of the twentieth century did not stop Europeans having children and nor did the Cold War and the threat of nuclear annihilation – indeed, the advent of the latter coincided with a baby boom.

It is one thing to change public policy, to remove disincentives to start a family. To tackle a belief system which sees humans as a curse on the planet and promotes the decline of the human population is quite another. At this rate, European civilisation is going to become the first in the world voluntarily to drive itself to extinction – although a long, painful decline lies in store before it reaches that stage.

14.

Democracy

Europe might not have the sparkiest economy, it might not have the power and influence it once had, but on one thing we are all invited to agree: Europe is a place of freedom and democracy, a relative haven of civilised values in an imperfect world. Take it from the Economist Intelligence Unit's Democracy Index, which claims the world had twenty-four 'full democracies' in 2022, fourteen of which were in Europe. European countries that didn't make the cut as full democracies almost all fell into the next category down, 'flawed democracies' – a twilight zone which, in the Economist Intelligence Unit's judgement, has, since 2016, included the United States. There seems to be little rationale as to why the US has been downgraded from a full democracy other, perhaps, than the outcome of the 2016 presidential election (although Joe Biden's America has failed to recover its position). West of Belarus (and Russia's Kaliningrad province) there is only one European country that falls into the Economist Intelligence Unit's third category, 'hybrid regimes' – Bosnia. None have sunk into the 'authoritarian' pit of the world, home to Russia, China, most of Africa and, drinking from the fetid pool right down at the bottom, Taliban-run Afghanistan.[1]

If you prefer, there is the Varieties of Democracy (or V-Dem) Index put together at the University of Gothenburg. This also divides countries into four categories for freedom and democracy. In 2022, it put thirty-two countries into the top group, 'Liberal Democracies', of which eighteen are in Europe. The UK is one of them, albeit with a score lower than many, for reasons that are not explained. Most other European countries are in the next group, 'Electoral democracies'. This includes most of Eastern Europe as well as Austria (there is nothing to explain why the latter is not counted as a liberal democracy). The V-Dem index has especially harsh things to say about Greece, which it describes as being on a 'slippery slope', not least thanks to the discovery that national intelligence services were phone-tapping a long list of the government's opponents, including investigative journalists.[2]

Or there is the Global State of Democracy Index, also established by Swedish academics, in which twenty-two of the top thirty places are awarded to European countries. The UK, once more, is among them – although there is a caveat. Brexit, it is explained, is 'revealing new social divisions and giving rise to a more populist brand of politics. Notwithstanding these developments, the UK's Global State of Democracy scores over the course of the past five years have remained relatively stable.'[3]

This phrase reveals rather a lot about the Global State of Democracy Index – and, indeed, the European attitude towards democracy in general. You might think that the holding of a referendum to decide an important matter, followed by a government executing the instructions of the people, would be regarded as the sign of a healthy democracy. But no, the whole process seems to be treated as something negative; democracy has just about survived in Britain, in spite of Brexit. 'Democracy' would have been better served, presumably, had the UK government not asked the people whether or not they wished to remain in the EU and simply made the decision for them, judging what was good for them.

It is little wonder that European countries score so highly in the indices mentioned above. The indices are all Eurocentric, turning on a concept of democracy that has evolved in Europe since 1945. The European model of democracy does not revolve around raw 'people power', as the word 'democracy' means if taken literally, but around a permanent infrastructure of rights laid down by lofty legal institutions. Consultation with the people is distinctly limited and conducted within strict boundaries: if a human rights court rules, say, that gay marriage or abortion is a right, then this becomes part of the permanent litany of rights, which cannot be challenged by anyone. Representatives of the people may be elected, but they may not breach those boundaries, even if that is what the majority of people want them to do. Any attempt to challenge established liberal values is denounced as 'populism' – which, in as much as it means anything, seems to mean political ideas that are popular but which the user of the word wishes were not.

It is remarkable that the profiles of European countries which appear on the Global State of Democracy website fail to mention the gaping democratic deficit which lies at the heart of the EU. The EU has an elected parliament, yet it exists solely to rubber-stamp legislation which has been generated by an unelected executive, the European Commission. Once approved by the parliament, the commission's directives must be incorporated into domestic law of member states. National governments and parliaments have little choice in this; whole areas of legislation affecting the lives of citizens of members states are effectively sprung on them with little public debate or scrutiny by elected representatives. The only real chance that citizens of member states have to influence EU-inspired laws is at the very early stages of a directive being drafted, when elected governments are able to lobby the commissioners. But, at that stage, it is very difficult for ordinary people, who are not part of some well-represented vested interest, to know what is going on.

During the Brexit negotiations, it was suggested that Britain could adopt a similar position to Norway, which is not a member of the EU but is a member of the single market. In Norway's case, rules are imposed on the country without any input from the country's government at all – 'diplomacy by fax' is how it used to be described, when that was the relevant communications technology. So why does Norway come out top in several of these democracy indices when its people have so little say over so many of the laws that affect them?

The tension between democracy and the EU's way of doing things was amply demonstrated by the EU's spat with Poland and Hungary. In 2017, the EU enacted Article 7 of the Treaty on the European Union for the first time, which allows for sanctions against member states that it determines have breached its founding values on human rights and respect for law and democracy. Poland's crime was that the ruling Law and Justice Party had sought to appoint and discipline judges. A Disciplinary Chamber, it ruled, was not sufficiently separate from government. In 2021, Poland and Hungary went on to rile the European Commission by passing laws to ban the depiction of homosexuality in books written for under eighteens. The laws were, in the words of European Commission president Ursula von der Leyen, 'shameful'.[4] Poland further upset the European parliament when its constitutional tribunal issued a ruling banning abortion for social reasons – although it was still allowed in cases where a pregnancy had resulted from rape or incest, where there were foetal abnormalities or where the mother's life or health was in danger. The parliament passed resolutions condemning the Polish law – even though abortion is not supposed to be a matter within its competence. When the Polish government sought to assert the primacy of national law over EU law, the European Commission started to withhold £57 billion of Covid recovery funds from the country.

Say what you like about Poland's Law and Justice Party – but is it really the role of a European Commission president with no popular mandate, or the European parliament, to start deciding what domestic laws a member state should or shouldn't have? As regards the EU's objections to the Polish government appointing judges to the country's supreme court, that is exactly what happens with the European Court of Justice – whose twenty-seven judges are appointed by the governments of each member state. The irony, though, was lost on the European Commission. It was somewhat odd, too, to hear the European Commission accusing Poland and Hungary of breaching 'democratic values'. It is very much an EU thing to use the words 'democratic values' when what it really means is a set of socially liberal values. In the case of Poland and Hungary, the people had voted for socially con-servative parties and had, as a result, ended up with socially conservative governments. That was democracy – whether you agreed with the outcome or not.

The EU has become far more assertive at poking its nose into the affairs of member states in recent years. As it hap-pens, Britain had its own law between the late 1980s and late 1990s which forbade councils from promoting homosexuality in schools – Clause 28 of the Local Government Act. Yet the EU did not seek to punish Britain for it or comment on it in any way. The law was eventually abolished by the UK parliament. The EU can hardly claim that a ban in schools on the promotion of homosexuality breaches the founding principles of the European Union because, when the then European Economic Community was founded in the 1950s, homosexuality was still illegal in one of the founding member states, West Germany – not something that Poland was attempting to do. The same is true of abortion, which was illegal in all six founding member states when the EU was created. The EU's disapproval of Poland and Hungary's laws on these two issues has grown out of a change in attitudes in Western European countries since the 1950s and a growing will to impose those attitudes on more conservative Eastern European states; it cannot be claimed to be among the union's founding principles.

The EU only really tolerates democracy when it gives the 'correct' answer. That much was clear when the people of Denmark voted narrowly against the Maastricht Treaty in a referendum in June 1992. The Danes were made to go back and vote again – with a series of opt-outs offered second time around. It happened again when Irish voters rejected the Treaty of Nice in 2001 – they, too, were made to vote again, this time with only very minor changes to the text, which were supposed to address fears that Ireland could lose its neutrality in times of war. When the EU attempted to pass a new constitution in 2005, both France and the Netherlands voted against it in referendums. This time, the French and Dutch governments weren't going to risk a second rejection, and the treaty was pulled. Or at least it was for a while. The proposed constitution was later reborn as the Lisbon Treaty, which was ratified by most of Europe's parliaments alone – without referendums. The Irish, however, were allowed a vote and chose to reject it, and guess what? They were made to vote again. Is it any wonder that EU member states have started electing 'populist' governments when their people have been treated with such contempt by the EU?

The EU is not, however, the only body involved in this

de-democratisation process: the European Court of Human
Rights (ECHR) approaches democracy in much the same
way. Europe's democratic deficit goes right back to the
ECHR's origins in 1950. You can find it by comparing the
texts of the United Nations' Universal Declaration of Human
Rights, signed in 1948, and the European Convention on
Human Rights, which was signed two years later and went
on to become the foundation on which the European Court
of Human Rights is built. In many ways these are very similar documents. Both assert rights to life, liberty, fair trial,
freedom of expression and association, the right to practice
religious belief. Both recognise the right not to be enslaved,
to join a trade union, to marry and have a private life. But it
is when you get to Article 21 of the UN document that you
notice a rather large hole in the European one.

Article 21 of the UN document states: 'Everyone has the
right to take part in the government of his country, directly or
through freely chosen representatives. The will of the people
shall be the basis of the authority of government; this will shall
be expressed in periodic and genuine elections which shall be
held by secret vote or by equivalent free voting procedures.'

You will look in vain at the European document for any reference to the 'will of the people', or to the idea that everyone
has the right to take part in the government of his country.
(Forgive the expression 'his country' in the UN document;
in the language of the time it was perfectly well understood
to refer to women, too). The only reference to elections in the
European Convention refers to members of the European
Commission of Human Rights, who were to be elected by the
Committee of Ministers from a list drawn up by the Bureau
of the Consultative Assembly – so not exactly the choice of
the people.

Not only is the European convention silent on democratic
rights, it adds some pretty stiff caveats to the right to free

expression, the right to hold opinions and to impart information. 'The exercise of these freedoms,' it states, 'since it carries with it duties and responsibilities, may be subject to such formalities, conditions, restrictions or penalties as are prescribed by law and are necessary in a democratic society in the interests of national security, territorial integrity or public safety, for the prevention of disorder or crime, for the protection of health or morals, for the protection of the reputation or rights of others, for preventing the disclosure of information received in confidence, or for maintaining the authority and impartiality of the judiciary.'

In other words, don't mess with the judges. Where the UN essentially trusted the people, the Council of Europe, which drafted the European Convention, treated them with deep suspicion. The UN declaration saw democracy as the ultimate guarantor of freedom; the European convention found every reason to suppress it. Why the difference? The UN declaration was heavily influenced by the United States; it was the work of the Commission on Human Rights, chaired by Eleanor Roosevelt, wife of the late president Franklin D. Roosevelt. The European Convention was the work of a group of European countries, many of which had just spent years occupied by Nazi Germany. They saw the 'will of the people' a little differently as the Nazis had risen to power by exploiting democratic institutions; their priority was to try to protect societies against demagogues, and put in place a permanent infrastructure of rights which – they hoped – would guard against fascism.

The difference in attitudes between the UN charter and the European Convention didn't matter so much when both were fairly basic documents containing a small number of provisions against which few people would disagree; it has become quite another matter now that the European Convention has sprouted numerous protocols not in the

original document. The turning point came in 1978, when
the ECHR first exercised the 'living instrument doctrine'
which had been written into the European Convention from
the beginning. This effectively gave its judges the right to
make up the law as they went along, based on the vague
principles contained within the convention. Needless to say,
none of the laws effectively created by the judges has been
put to public vote.

Nothing brought this out more than a judgement by the
ECHR, in April 2024, in favour of a group of elderly Swiss
women who claimed that their right to a family life had been
infringed by the failure of their country's government to do
more to tackle climate change. That failure, they alleged,
had helped cause a heatwave which had forced them to stay
indoors for days on end. 'This is something that comes up
all the time in human rights,' said Jessica Simon, the lawyer
who had brought the case, 'the conflict between the idea of
democracy as just what the people choose and democracy
as entailing some fundamental and universal rights which
matter irrespective of what the majority decides.'[5] That
rather begs the question: who decides what these 'fundamental and universal rights' should be? Who decides whether or
not the rights of a mother take precedence over the right to
life of an unborn child, or whether a public right to safety
takes precedence over the right of a criminal not to be
deported to a country when he might suffer harm? These
decisions seem to fall to small numbers of judges, who are
effectively writing their own opinions into law with no one
else allowed to challenge them. In the Swiss climate change
case, a handful of judges effectively decided to instigate a
human right to go outdoors during a heatwave – and to
assert that that right trumped all economic considerations.
Moreover, they ruled that the Swiss government was responsible for causing a particular period of hot weather – which

is somewhat tenuous given that there has always been hot weather and that Switzerland, in any case, is responsible for only a tiny proportion of global carbon emissions. What a democratic government has to do – but the ECHR saw no reason to do – is to balance risks and rights. It has to take into account the fact that, while slashing carbon emissions might be desirable for an environmental point of view, it can also heavily impact on citizens' wellbeing if, for example, it makes energy and food less affordable.

Britain certainly needs no lesson in democracy from the ECHR or from other European countries. It is easy to forget just how recent a phenomenon democracy is in much of Europe. In Eastern Europe, including the eastern third of Germany, it goes back only as far as 1989. Portugal was a fascist dictatorship until 1974, Spain until 1975. Greece was under a military junta from 1967 to 1974. Take into account the Nazi occupations and only four countries in Europe can claim to have been uninterrupted democracies for a century or more: the United Kingdom, Ireland, Switzerland and Sweden. EU countries may be vastly better places now than they were under their various authoritarian guises, but there remains in Europe, and especially among those who run the EU, an attitude which is distrusting of the people. So many of Europe's institutions are founded on the assumption that we, the people, need to be defended against ourselves; that, give us half a chance, and we will rapidly evolve into Nazis, anarchists, or descend into some other kind of mob-like rule. The growing use of the term 'populism' says it all. Although the term in its modern guise comes from the name of a nineteenth-century US political party established to represent farmers' interests, it is now attached, pejoratively, to any European politician who dares to stand up to the cosy consensus that has been established between political parties or elitist institutions. Isn't the whole point of democracy that you are supposed to seek popularity? Not, it seems, in the European worldview. Europe increasingly does not operate a system of democracy but one of kritarchy – rule by judges – and enlightened oligarchy.

15.

Soft Underbelly

The 2018 NATO summit in Brussels had not even got underway before US President Donald Trump, in typical bombastic fashion, had offended nearly every other delegate, including many on his own side. Germany, he told a pre-summit meeting with Secretary General Jens Stoltenberg, was a 'captive of Russia'. Stoltenberg muttered about his remarks being 'inappropriate' but Trump was having nothing of it, going on to threaten US withdrawal from NATO unless other members upped their contributions to the organisation. 'The US pays tens of Billions of Dollars too much to subsidise Europe, and loses Big on trade,' he later tweeted. 'On top of it all Germany just started to pay Russia, the country they want protection from, Billions of Dollars for their energy needs coming out of a new pipeline from Russia.' By the time German defence minister (and later president of the European Commission) Ursula von der Leyen had protested that Germany was the second largest supplier of troops to NATO exercises, and Chancellor Angela Merkel had tried to reassure the world that Germany had many diverse sources of energy, Trump had abandoned the conference and gone back to his hotel – though he did later return with smiles, and business was done.

Donald Trump might be obnoxious; his diplomatic skills left a little wanting. He is not necessarily the sort you would want at your dinner party, let alone your summit to discuss the security of an entire continent. But, all the same, it is hard to refute the point that he was making: that the US has been underwriting the defence of Europe for decades while many European countries themselves have been backsliding on their commitments, preferring to spend their cash on social programmes rather than on defence budgets. One of the conditions of NATO membership is that states agree to spend at least 2 per cent of GDP on defence. Yet, at the time of the 2018 summit, only four out of twenty-eight member states achieved this target: the US, which was spending 3.31 per cent of GDP, Greece on 2.38 per cent, the UK on 2.06 per cent and Estonia on 2.01 per cent. Five countries were spending less than 1 per cent of GDP, including Belgium on 0.88 per cent, Spain 0.91 per cent.[1] Germany was spending 1.23 per cent of GDP and France 1.78 per cent.

US presidents had been making this point – rather more politely – for many years, but without bringing about change. Only four years earlier, NATO members had agreed to put it right and hit the target by 2015. However, between 2014 and 2017, eleven countries actually reduced their defence budgets as a share of GDP. Belgium – the host of the 2018 summit – was happy to show off its culinary skills, boasting that the chef for the official leaders' dinner had grown the vegetables in his own garden. Yet, in the four years leading up to the summit, it had cut its defence budget in actual terms, let alone real terms. It was, to put it metaphorically, happy to rely on the US to defend its herb garden.

Outrageous though it may have been, Trump's intervention

did have some effect. By 2022, a further six countries had reached the 2 per cent target. But Germany, on 1.44 per cent, and France, on 1.90 per cent, had still failed to meet the requirement. Meanwhile, Trump was proved right on the other point he had made in Brussels. As soon as Vladimir Putin's tanks rolled into Ukraine, it became apparent that Germany's energy policy really was held captive by Russia. As Germany reluctantly accepted that it was going to have to boycott Russia's gas and oil, and even more so when Russia itself began to turn down gas supplies to Europe, the EU was sent into a mad scramble to secure energy supplies for the winter. Fortunately, help was at hand in the form of imports of liquified natural gas (LNG) from the US and Qatar. Facilities to receive the gas were hurriedly built on Germany's North Sea coast, and a very shivery winter was just about averted – although output from German factories had to be reduced, adding to the country's woes. Germany had shown itself to be reliant on the US not only for its defence but also for security of its energy supplies.

Given Germany's history, it might be excused for not building up armed forces on the scale of the US or other European countries – the world might well have worried if it had done. Indeed, until Germany was given back its sovereignty in 1990, there were strict limits on its military; what was then West Germany was restricted to an army of 500,000 men. Even so, you might hope that the country could mount a more convincing force than it has done at times in recent years. On a NATO exercise in September 2014, soldiers mounted a broomstick on an armoured vehicle for want of a machine gun. Four in ten of the German soldiers who participated were found to be lacking the pistols they would need in a real operation, while only 31 per cent of the machine guns that were supposed to be available actually were in use. The German ministry of defence explained that it was using what

it called a 'dynamic availability management system' and
that in a real deployment it would have thirty days to equip
its force properly.[2] Presumably, it had had rather longer than
that to prepare for a planned military exercise – and I am sure
that Vladimir Putin will have the decency to give appropriate
notice if he decides to roll his troops over the German border,
like he did over the Ukrainian one.

The lack of equipment in the 2014 exercise was no one-off.
In that year, Germany appointed a new defence minister,
Ursula von der Leyen. The appointment gave her career a
huge upwards jolt: five years later she was appointed president
of the EU Commission. Yet she left the German military – or
Bundeswehr – in just as feeble a condition as she had found
it. The Armed Forces Report, produced by the Bundestag for
the year 2018, described the Bundeswehr as a 'bureaucratic
monster' which was afflicted by an 'over-organisation of
everything and everyone' but which was failing to deliver the
goods. Hardly any of the Bundeswehr's Leopard 2 battle tanks
were operational. The navy had no tankers. Submarines were
defective. Fewer than half of its Eurofighters and Tornadoes
were in airworthy condition.[3]

When Vladimir Putin's tanks started to line up on the
Ukraine border, in January 2022, Germany's contribution
to the crisis was worse than useless. It refused to respond to
a plea for military hardware, offering 5,000 battle helmets
instead – an offer which led to the mayor of Kiev to retort that
the German Ministry of Defence 'does not understand that we
are dealing with a perfectly equipped Russian army that can
start the further invasion of Ukraine at any time. What kind of
support will Germany send next? Pillows?'[4] One possible mo-
tivation for Germany's lack of military aid later became clear:
in a memo leaked to the newspaper *Der Spiegel* in 2023, the
head of the German army, General Alfons Mais, complained
that his force had only 60 per cent of the equipment it needed.

Donating anything to Ukraine would presumably have left it even shorter.

Worse, the country placed an embargo on arms exports to Ukraine, making it more difficult to transport the equipment which other countries had offered, such as anti-aircraft and anti-tank missiles from the Baltic states. The UK was quick to offer weapons, but the first flights to take them to Ukraine had to be routed around Germany. A month later, the folly of Germany's position became clear when the invasion materialised as feared. It is sobering to think that if other Western European countries had responded as Germany had done, Ukraine could have been rolled over by Russia within a few days.

There was a similar lack of engagement in December 2023, after Houthi rebels in Yemen started attacking ships sailing through the Bab-el-Mandeb strait into the Red Sea, threatening to block off the only direct shipping route from Asia to Europe, through the Suez Canal. The following month, the US and UK took joint action against the rebels, but where was the rest of Europe? The Netherlands gave some logistical backing and signed a declaration of support. Germany and Denmark also signed the declaration, along with Australia, New Zealand, Canada, South Korea and Bahrain. But there was no support from France, Spain or Italy at all – in spite of their economies being reliant on shipping through the Suez Canal. Once again, Europe was happy for the US and Britain to do the dirty work without considering it necessary to sully their own hands.

Donald Trump reinforced the point he had made at the 2018 NATO summit with even more vigour, as he began his campaign for a second presidential term in early 2024. He told a rally in South Carolina that the leader of a 'big country' in Europe had once asked him what would happen if his country had failed to meet the 2 per cent NATO spending target and had then been invaded by Russia. Would the US still come to his country's aid? Trump said that he replied: 'You didn't pay? You're delinquent? No, I would not protect you. In fact, I would encourage them to do whatever they want. You gotta pay.'[5]

Joe Biden's White House described Trump's comments as 'appalling and unhinged', but once again they achieved what Trump had presumably intended them to achieve: they got Europe talking about its own defence and questioning whether it could defend itself in the event of the US withdrawing from NATO? Europe should not really have a problem in doing this. It possesses its own nuclear deterrent in Britain and France. It has a vastly larger economy than Russia and markedly superior technology at its fingertips; it ought to be able to afford significantly more – and better – kit for conventional warfare. A lot of Russian military hardware relies on Western-designed and -made components, which have found their way into Russian kit either through export for peaceful purposes (some of it was provided notionally for Russia's space programme) or through third countries. Russian rockets which have been dismantled after being fired at Ukrainian targets turned out to have US-made gyroscopes and a Russian air defence system used British-designed oscillators.[6] While it might be worrying that this equipment may be breaching Western sanctions, it is a sign that Russia is finding it difficult to keep up with Western military technology. Putin's failure to execute what he thought would be a rapid take-down of Ukraine has revealed a lack of organisation, planning and strategy. If Ukraine can keep back Russian forces, then the rest of Europe – assuming a united response in tune with NATO's dictum: an attack on one is an attack on all – should easily prevail.

On paper, NATO has significant superiority over Russia in terms of human resources, even without the US. The

Russians can muster 1 million regular servicemen and 2 million reserves. NATO currently has 3.14 million regular forces and 2.75 million reserves available, but even without the US it would still have 1.77 million regular forces and 1.95 million reserves.[7] But, as for military kit, it would be found wanting in some important areas. It is ahead in shipping, in sheer numbers. Russia has one aircraft carrier; NATO has 28 with the US and 8 without. Russia has 14 destroyers and 66 submarines; NATO 119 and 144 with the US, 25 and 75 without. But when it comes to a land and air battle, which you might think more likely in the context of a Russian invasion of a NATO country in Eastern Europe, a NATO without the US begins to look a little skimpy. Russia has 12,267 tanks; NATO 14,125 with the US and 7,513 without. Russia has 18,266 artillery guns; NATO 12,997 with the US and 8,754 without. Russia has 340 fighter aircraft; NATO 1,104 with the US and 643 without. Russia has 689 attack aircraft; NATO 728 with the US and 162 without.

The raw numbers, however, don't tell us everything. Before the Ukraine war, the International Institute for Strategic Studies (IISS) think-tank worked through possible scenarios of how war between Russia and the rest of Europe might evolve. One involved attacks on shipping, another a Russian invasion of Lithuania and parts of northeastern Poland, to unite the detached Kaliningrad province with the rest of Russia. For the latter, the results did not favour a US-less NATO, which , the IISS concluded, would struggle to deploy more than 30–50 per cent of its land forces within 180 days. While European NATO notionally has one hundred armoured brigades, three quarters of them are made up of obsolete tanks or other armoured vehicles – and so could not effectively be deployed.

Overall, it calculated, NATO would find itself short of 2,500–3,750 tanks and 432–960 artillery guns needed to mount an effective defence. There would also be a deficit of 264 fighter aircraft and 396 pilots, and between 50,000 and 62,000 soldiers. In all, to make up the capability gap with Russia, it would require extra defence spending by NATO's European members to the tune of $288–357 billion. As for the scenario of a sea battle, it would take extra spending of between $94 billion and $110 billion to make up the capability gap. To put this into context, NATO's European members spent a combined total of $264 billion in 2018. Had they all met the target of spending 2 per cent of GDP on defence, they would have spent an extra $102 billion.[8]

Not that the mere act of spending money is sufficient to ensure effective defence. Sadly, even when European militaries do spend money it is too often on things that don't actually improve defence, but are wrapped up in other policy objectives. Europe might be short of tanks, aeroplanes and soldiers but no one can say it is short of bureaucracy. Perhaps inevitably, the EU's military policy arm, the European Defence Agency, has drawn up a Climate Change and Defence Roadmap to try to keep tabs on the carbon emissions of military operations. Henceforth, all missions and operations under the auspices of the EU Common Security and Defence Policy (CSDP) must have environmental advisers. Moreover, there is now a mechanism to measure and assess the environmental footprint of missions 'with a view to optimise the use and management of energy, water and waste'.

'Climate change introduces new operational challenges,' it goes on to say, 'including the need to provide missions and operations with equipment that is effective under extreme weather conditions and technology that is more energy efficient.' Moreover, the EU is developing training modules for all armed forces within its remit 'integrating the climate dimension into mandatory CSDP ore-deployment training'.

For goodness' sake, if European defence equipment is not

already capable of performing in extreme weather there is little hope for Europe – it has learned nothing since Napoleon's long march back from Moscow. Climate change adds nothing to the conditions that European forces have not already encountered fighting in Afghanistan, Iraq, Bosnia and many other places in recent decades. While there is every reason to seek energy efficiency in military equipment – supplying an army with sufficient fuel is a fundamental logistic challenge – it is hard not to conclude from the above that fashionable political causes of the day have been allowed to creep into defence policy. It is not wrong to be concerned about climate change, but the prospect of an invasion of NATO countries is a somewhat more acute problem – and one which genuinely poses an immediate and existential threat. Something tells me that Vladimir Putin is a little less bothered about getting bogged down in these issues than are European forces. He won't be having to take a pause mid-battle, as it sounds as if European armies could well be in future, to plug in and recharge his tanks.

It is ironic that Europe's defence forces are so weak in spite of many countries clinging on to conscription far longer than the US (or indeed Britain, which abolished national service in the 1960s and hardly discussed it again until recent Conservative party proposals). There is a clear lesson from the past half-century for anyone who wants to learn it: that it is the smaller, professional armies made up wholly of people who want to be in the military that are the more effective in modern warfare. The antithesis is Russia, whose unwilling conscripts forced into battle in Ukraine have helped to bog down the army. Ten EU countries, plus Switzerland, still have conscription. The German defence minister, Boris Pistorius, has proposed to bring it back, after it was abolished in 2011. Drafting hundreds of thousands of unwilling young people into armed forces that already lack military equipment – and who, of course, would swallow resources in other ways, such as in their need to be fed and housed – does not look the most efficient strategy. But then is the proposal to reintroduce conscription really about creating an effective fighting force or about social objectives? An unnamed defence official suggested to the newspaper *Die Welt* that reintroducing conscription was about creating a 'stronger bond between society and the Bundeswehr' – making it more 'democratic' and 'at less risk of attracting a disproportionate number of applicants with a penchant for militarism'.[9] It strikes me as not altogether a bad thing to have armed forces made up of people with a liking for military life. Why should the military be used as a form of social engineering? A professional football manager doesn't, after all, try to democratise his squad by opening it up to a wide, representative cross-section of the population. He puts out a team made up of fully engaged athletes, who are good at tackling the other side for the ball and then putting it in the back of the opposition's net.

There might come a time, in a military emergency such as that which has befallen Ukraine, when conscription might become necessary. But, in the meantime, why aren't European governments looking to the US for inspiration as to how to run modern military forces: professional soldiers and an absolute focus on achieving technological superiority over potential enemies?

For too long, Europe believed in the 'peace dividend' – the idea that the Cold War was over, and so money could be freed up from military spending and spent on social programmes instead. Government after government in Britain and other European countries chipped away at their armed forces, calculating that voters would hardly notice if a few more soldiers were stood down, or tanks not replaced – but they would, of course, notice if the money was spent instead on schools, hospitals or welfare. In the early days, after the end of the Cold War, this may have been understandable. There was genuine hope that Russia was rapidly evolving into a Western-style democracy. Russia joined the Council of Europe, put itself under the jurisdiction of the European Court of Human Rights. It started to hold genuine elections – for a while. If you overlooked Chechnya and the odd political murder, the Russia of Boris Yeltsin – and even in the early days of Vladmir Putin – could almost seem a benign place. But the scales should have fallen from Europe's eyes after the invasion and annexation of Crimea in 2014, if not before. Yet, even after this date, the contract for the Nord Stream 2 pipeline was signed, putting Europe even more at the mercy of Russian gas supplies. Western defence spending continued to fall far behind the levels demanded of NATO member-ship. Britain has consistently been one of the higher-spending countries but, even so, we ended up for several years with a pair of aircraft carriers that had no aircraft. Even now, when they do have aircraft, none were able to be sent to the Red Sea to counter the first of the Houthi attacks on commercial shipping because of a shortage of naval personnel was holding back a support vessel.[10]

Western Europe has not been taking defence seriously since the end of the Cold War. That is beginning to change, but it has taken a big kick up the backside from a US president – and an invasion of Ukraine – to achieve that.

16.

Eastern Europe

S o far, much of this book has concentrated on the large economies of Western Europe – those that are the nearest competitors of Britain. But what about the EU's new eastern lands, the former Soviet bloc countries which joined the EU in 2004 and 2007? They, surely, are a great success, and an advert for the European way of doing things?

Enter any Eastern European country today and you will see societies and economies that are vastly different to how they were under communism from 1945 to 1989. The gentle revolutions of 1989 did not just bring freedom but wealth, too. The smoky Trabants have given way to Volkswagens. Hundreds of miles of new roads are indistinguishable in quality from those found in Western Europe. The streets of the main cities, once drab and deserted, now bristle with tourists.

Eight Eastern European and Balkan states are now classified as high-income countries by the IMF: the Czech Republic, Slovakia, Slovenia, Croatia plus the Baltic states. Poland is not quite there yet, although perhaps it deserves to be; its GDP per capita is already higher than Greece and

Portugal, which are classified as high-income countries. But, in many ways, Poland is the pin-up for the EU's eastward expansion – or at least it was until the spat between the Law and Justice government and Brussels. Not even that crisis, however, seems to have dented public support for EU membership in Poland – in 2023, it was running 85 per cent to 10 per cent in favour of continued membership, a proportion that has been largely unchanged over the past decade.

But how much of Poland's rapid rise is due to EU membership and how much of it is down to the end of communism and the country's renewed economic and political independence? Quite a lot of it is the former, according to the Polish Economic Institute, a think-tank that has tried to model what would have happened had Poland not joined. It has produced a dramatic answer. GDP per capita, it claims, is 31 per cent higher than it would be had the country stayed out.[1] It reached this conclusion by looking at Poland's growth in GDP per capita relative to that of the EU average – which grew from 40 per cent in 1990 to 50 per cent in 2004 and 78 per cent in 2021. Poland's GDP relative to the EU as a whole, it contends, grew more quickly after 2004 – when the country joined the EU – than it did beforehand.

But there are a couple of glaring issues here. Firstly, the EU's average GDP per capita inevitably took a downwards turn in 2004 when ten new members joined – most of them, like Poland, relatively poor former members of the Soviet bloc – so, naturally, Poland's GDP per capita as a proportion of EU GDP per capita took a corresponding upwards turn. Secondly, it ignores the stagnation of many EU countries following the financial crisis of 2008–9 and the sovereign debt crisis that followed – a stagnation which hardly paints the EU in a good light. If you compare outright growth in post-communist, pre-EU Poland with that post 2004, the Polish economy actually grew a little quicker when it was outside the EU: an average of 4.3 per cent a year between 1992 and 2003, followed by an average of 4.1 per cent a year between 2004 and 2019.[2]

It would be extraordinary if Poland had not gained some economic benefit from EU membership. The EU did, after all, spend €175 billion of structural funds in Poland between 2004 and 2020, plus another €18.3 billion courtesy of Jean Claude Juncker's Plan for Eastern Europe.[3] This was, according to the EU, 56 per cent of all public investment in Poland over that period. It helped build, among other things, 7,625 miles of new roads plus an extension of the Warsaw metro. Membership of the single market has also helped to expand trade. But not everyone is convinced that the EU can buy healthy, long-term economic growth in Poland simply by showering it with grants. The problem with Poland's recent growth, according to Jan Boguslawski, political economist at Sciences Po, is that so much of it has come in the form of foreign capital investment. The country has become what he describes as a 'dependent market economy', where foreign companies build factories in Poland to take advantage of cheaper labour. Those companies then repatriate a lot of the profits – while Poland's native businesses fail to flourish. Among the EU's Eastern European member states, he points out, there is only a single company that makes it into the largest 500 companies in the world: Poland's oil refinery, PKN Orlen.[4] Foreign investment is not a bad thing; it quickly brings wealth, offers good jobs and forces native industries to up their own game. But there comes a point when you really want homegrown investment to be running alongside, even taking over from, foreign investment. In Eastern Europe's case, this seems to be slow in happening.

Poland's early days as an EU member brought another problem: the brain drain of skilled workers travelling to work in Western Europe. While some of their earnings found their way back to Poland in the form of remittances – according to Statistics Poland, at the end of 2020 there were 1.3 million Poles working abroad, sending a collective €2.6 billion back home – it took them away from Poland's own economy and didn't always do a great deal to improve workers' skills or experience, as many were employed in the West doing low-skilled jobs for which they were over-qualified.

Poland was lucky that it did not stick to its original plan of joining the euro by 2007. Had it done so, the financial crisis of 2008–9 could have landed it in the same position as Italy, Spain and Greece. The country would first have enjoyed a boom as interest rates were sharply lowered. Then, come the crash, it would have been left desperately needing to devalue its currency in order to make its exports competitive again – but would have found itself unable to do so. In the event, the Polish zloty was allowed to devalue – it fell from over 4.5 zloty to the euro in 2004 to less than 3.5 in 2008. As a result, Poland prospered while eurozone economies suffered; indeed, Poland was the only country in Europe not to fall into recession in 2008–9. Poland has found excuses not to join the euro ever since, yet, under the terms of its entry to the EU, it remains under obligation to do so at some point in the future. So are the Czech Republic, Hungary and Romania. Bulgaria has an opt-out.

As for Poland, so for the other former Soviet bloc countries. All have been transformed in the past three decades after the fall of communism, but EU membership is only part of the story; indeed, several of these countries grew faster in the years prior to EU membership than they have done since – in spite of the billions of euros in structural funds that have been poured into them since joining. The Czech Republic is argu-ably the biggest success story from EU expansion, growing by an average of 2.2 per cent in the years 1992–2003 and by 3.9 per cent from 2004–19. Hungary, like Poland, grew a little faster in the same pre-EU period (an average of 2.4 per cent) than it did after EU entry (average of 2.3 per cent).

The Baltic states grew rampantly during the 1990s (with a blip in 1999, in the case of Estonia and Lithuania). They did so by rapidly liberalising their economies and going out of their way to attract overseas investors. In 1994, Lithuania popularised the concept of a 'flat tax', which gave it one of the lowest tax rates for high earners anywhere – at 33 per cent. Low earners had a favourable tax regime, too: the personal tax-free allowance was initially set at just over twice the national minimum wage. Over the years, Lithuania reduced its flat tax rate, reaching 24 per cent by 2008 – irritating some academics who advocate progressive taxation, but helping to attract wealthy individuals and catapult the country into the club of high-income nations.[5] Between 1996 and 2003, the Lithuanian economy grew by an average of 5.9 per cent a year. That was all of Lithuania's own doing, prior to EU membership.

The Baltic States carried on growing rapidly in the first years of EU membership, yet went on to suffer especially harshly in the 2008–9 crash – each collapsed by 14 per cent in 2009. Since then, they have recovered to healthy growth, but not in the same league as in the early years after communism. Between 2004 and 2019, the average rate of growth in Lithuania was 3.5 per cent. It is a similar story in Slovakia, which grew by an average of 4.1 per cent per year between 1993 and 2003, then enjoyed a rollicking first four years in the EU, growing by an average of 7.4 per cent from 2004–8. Since it joined the euro on 1 January 2009, growth has been a lot more pedestrian, averaging 2.3 per cent over the next decade. Indeed, since joining the euro, Slovakia has had one of the lowest rates of growth in Europe.

No one really has any idea of what would have happened had the former Soviet bloc countries not joined the

EU – whether they had joined the European Free Trade Association (EFTA) instead, formed their own bloc or gone it alone. But one thing is for sure: EU membership has failed to address one of the enduring problems for all Eastern European countries: corruption. If the EU is about anything, it is supposed to be the promotion and adoption of common, high standards. Yet it doesn't seem to be working well when it comes to rooting out poor behaviour in public and commercial life. According to the annual Corruption Perceptions Index, Eastern Europe is lagging badly behind Western and Northern Europe. On a score out of 100, where zero means everything is corrupt and 100 means no corruption at all, Denmark and Finland take the top two places of all countries globally in the 2023 survey, with scores of 90 and 87 respectively. Germany comes 9th on 78 and Britain and France are tied in 20th place on 71. Hungary comes out 76th in the world on 42, behind Cuba, China, Senegal, Ghana and Jamaica. The problem in Hungary seems to be getting worse. As Transparency International puts it, 'using the coronavirus epidemic as an excuse, the budget deficit has inflated largely due to the expansion of public investments for political purposes and for the enrichment of cronies, as well as election spending'. The Hungarian public do, however, appear to be becoming a little fed up with the way power is exercised in the country. In February 2024, the country's president, Katalin Novak, was forced to resign after pardoning the former deputy director of a children's home who had coerced children into retracting claims that they had been abused by the director. The scandal did not prevent the director receiving an eight-year jail sentence, but it did irritate the public, who held a mass protest in Budapest.[6]

Other Eastern European countries are scarcely any better. Bulgaria was given a score of 43, Romania 46, Slovakia 53 and Poland 54. Italy, perceived as the most corrupt country in Western Europe, is on 56. Of the former Soviet bloc, only Estonia – on this measure – seems to have addressed the issue, with a score of 76.[7]

It is reasonable to say that all Soviet bloc countries inherited a deep cultural problem from communism: corruption was at times vital to survival, given that in some cases food and other goods could only be obtained on the black market. Such things take a long time to tackle when they become so embedded in society. However, EU membership has not helped by showering countries with generous development funds and keeping poor accounting records of how those funds are spent. As we have already seen, the Common Agricultural Policy (CAP) subsidies are an open invitation to fraudsters. The EU's climate policies, too, have provided other opportunities for fraud, not least the Emissions Trading Scheme set up to give industry a financial incentive to reduce emissions. Polluting businesses were granted carbon credits – effectively licenses to pollute – which could be traded. Those who failed to trim their emissions were forced to purchase credits from those that had. The first incarnation of the scheme collapsed as the prices of the credits crashed, but not before it had generated a massive VAT fraud which saw €10–20 billion stolen. In 2016, the founder of a Polish carbon broker, Consus, was jailed in France for his own part in the scheme.[8] That was €10–20 billion which could have been used investing in clean technology but was instead siphoned off from government budgets via a half-baked and poorly administered carbon credit scheme.

17.

Setting a Great Example

It is little wonder that most Eastern European member states have been unable to shake off their reputations for corruption when the problem seems to stalk Brussels. In 2022, the Belgian police arrested Eva Kaili, the Greek vice president of the European parliament, along with former Italian MEP Antonio Panzeri and two others, in connection with allegations that Qatar had bribed EU officials in order to win influence over EU policy-making – allegations which Qatar denies. A police operation had recovered €1.5 million in cash, some in Panzeri's flat and some in a suitcase carried by Kaili's father. Panzeri – who after leaving the European parliament had set up a campaign to bring human rights abusers to justice – was charged with corruption, money laundering and participation in a criminal group, and later confessed in a plea bargain.[1] Kaili was also charged with corruption and money laundering but a year later the investigation seemed to have stalled, and Kaili's lawyers were claiming that Belgian police had wrongfully removed her immunity from prosecution that she enjoyed as an MEP. This immunity can be revoked on the vote of a European parliament committee and also by police in cases where someone was caught in the act of committing a crime, but Kaili maintained the money being carried by her father had nothing to do with her.[2]

The obvious question here is: why on Earth do MEPs have immunity against prosecution? Surely, it is a fundamental principle of democracy that everyone is equal before the law, and that the people who make laws are subject to them like everyone else? OLAF, the EU's anti-fraud office (yes, it really does share its name with the German chancellor) complained that for months it wasn't even allowed access to the European parliament in order to investigate the scandal.[3] What does it say about an organisation when it won't even allow its own anti-fraud agency to set foot in its own building?

There seems long to have been a culture in the European parliament of MEPs thinking they are above the law, none more so than in expense claims. The UK parliament can hardly claim to have a clean nose, given the expenses scandal of 2009 when MPs were found to have used their parliamentary expenses to have bought duck houses, cleared the wisteria from the chimneys of their country homes and so on. But the extravagance of expense claims by MEPs is on a different scale entirely. Peter Skinner, who served as a Labour MEP for Southeast England from 1999 to 2014, claimed a remarkable £480,000 in expenses during his time in parliament – £100,000 of which was later found to be fraudulent. While it had notionally been claimed for support staff, it had actually been spent on jewellery, a honeymoon and other luxuries. He was jailed for four years in 2016.[4] Ashley Mote, who was elected as a UKIP MEP, managed to claim nearly £500,000 in fraudulent expense claims in just six years. Remarkably, he had been allowed to remain an MEP despite an earlier conviction for benefit fraud in Britain, in 2007. He was jailed for five years in 2015.[5]

They were not alone. An investigation by a group of European newspapers and websites found that, between 2019 and 2022, 108 MEPs were forced to pay back a total of €2 million in expenses that had been wrongfully claimed. An analysis of sitting MEPs found that twenty-three of them – 3 per cent of the total – had criminal convictions. A quarter of all MEPs had had some kind of blemish, such as being forced to pay back expenses or censure for some kind of misbehaviour that had stopped short of criminal conviction. They ranged from an Estonian MEP who sold a lost smartphone he had found while working on a ferry; to a Polish MEP who added an extra 340 km on his car mileage claims every time he drove from Poland to Brussels; and to Greek MEP Ioannis Lagos who was jailed for fourteen years in 2021 for being a member of a criminal organisation. Unbelievably, he was allowed to continue as an MEP in spite of his conviction, and continued to take part in debates by accessing them remotely in his prison cell.[6]

It is little wonder, with MEPs setting such an example, that EU structural funds are rife with companies and individuals that have their fingers in the till. A report by the OECD in 2019 estimated that every year at least €390 million are misappropriated from EU funds. Examples it cited included a street lighting firm which invented fictitious companies in order to submit fake bids which made its own bids look good value for money, a cartel of motorway construction firms which had agreed to submit artificially inflated bids in order to farm out work between themselves, and a road maintenance company which would close roads to make it look as if work was going on but where no work was actually done.[7]

In its report for 2022, OLAF said it had investigated 250 cases of fraud and irregularities, recommending that €426 million of misused EU funds be recovered and claiming that its investigations had prevented a further €197.9 million from being misappropriated. Sixteen investigations involved the EU's own staff, one case involving €275,000 claimed by parliamentary assistants for work that was not actually done. The report presents a portrait of a Europe full of chancers and conmen flogging smuggled cigarettes, adulterated honey and poor quality wine that had been poured into empty bottles of fine wine recovered from restaurants.[8] The above, however, were estimates just for money misappropriated from EU funds and people cheating on EU tariffs. A vastly higher figure has been put on the wider problem of fraud in Europe. In 2016, a report for the European parliament by the RAND Corporation estimated the overall cost of fraud – including social and economic costs, loss of tax revenues to member states and so on – at between €179 billion and €990 billion per year. Of this, it said €5 billion was lost to EU procurement. The answer to tackling this, according to the European parliament – which was the whole purpose of commissioning the study – was more EU integration.[9] Indeed, the above figures were claimed to be the cost of what the report called 'Non-Europe' – i.e. failure to integrate wholly. Considering the record of MEPs and their officials, it must be somewhat questionable that yet more people doling out yet more billions of euros of taxpayers' money, while claiming immunity from prosecution, would really solve the problem.

The RAND report failed to find any positive influence on tackling corruption from membership of the EU. 'Member states that had high levels of corruption in 1995 continued to do so in 2014,' it concluded. Over that period, the same pattern had persisted, with high levels of corruption in Eastern Europe plus Italy, with relatively low levels in Western Europe, and the lowest levels in Scandinavia.

In its 2022 report into the EU's budget, the European Court of Auditors reported fourteen cases of suspected fraud.

But that must only be the tip of the iceberg because, for example, it only inspected a sample of eighty-eight recipients of direct payments under the CAP – out of 5.9 million claims across the EU. Among those eighty-eight recipients, however, it detected six minor errors and one major one – where an Italian landowner had claimed payments for a lemon grove that did not exist.[10] It is not clear from the report whether inventing an entire lemon grove even qualified as what the European Court of Auditors defines as fraud or whether it was dismissed as a mere 'error'.

The court estimated an error rate of 4.2 per cent in EU budget spending in 2022, up from 3 per cent in 2021. Given that the EU spent €196 billion over the course of the year, this means there is €8.2 billion worth going out of the door when it shouldn't be. It is a figure that has been steadily rising in recent years, from €2.6 billion in 2018. It was enough for the court to issue an 'adverse opinion' on budgetary expenditure, declaring that the level of error was 'material and pervasive'. Ironically, the highest rate of 'error' was in projects which came under the banner 'cohesion, resilience and values'.

Then there is the cosy relationship between the EU and the many vested interests that have their claws dug deeply into its skin. The EU's rules on public procurement sum up a lot of what is wrong with the bloc. In 2014, it introduced new rules which were supposedly going to widen and democratise the award of contracts for government work, to improve value for taxpayers' money and, in particular, to open up new opportunities for the small and medium enterprises (SMEs) which are the bedrock of fast-growing economies. The result? A system that ended up rewarding a small pool of favoured suppliers even more than it did before. Between 2011 and 2021, the average number of bidders for each government contract across the EU fell from 5.7 to 3.2, and the proportion of public contracts that attracted only a single bid jumped from 23.5

per cent to 41.8 per cent. In some places it was far higher: in the Peloponnese in Greece, 66.5 per cent of contracts were awarded after just one company bid. How did a reform designed to achieve one objective end up achieving the exact opposite? Businesses interviewed by the European Court of Auditors told the same story again and again: the reforms had doubled the administrative procedures involved in putting in bids. The length of time it took for public bodies to go through the procurement process increased by 50 per cent to ninety-six days. In many cases, SMEs no longer had the resources needed to submit bids, and stayed out of government work. It paid them to stick to private sector contracts, where the rules were much simpler.[11]

The Court of Auditors' report also hints at a strong band of nationalism among public authorities in some countries, especially France, where a mere 1 per cent of public contracts were awarded to non-French bidders. While it is natural that large countries will award more of their contracts to native bidders than small ones – almost 30 per cent of public sector contracts in Luxembourg went to overseas firms – French public authorities notably award only half as many contracts to foreign bidders than do German ones, in spite of the latter having a far larger economy. It may be related that France also seems to lead Europe in the number of occasions where it did not pick the lowest bids for government work: only 10 per cent of contracts went to the lowest bidder, compared with over 60 per cent in Germany and nearly 100 per cent in Slovakia. So much for the ideals of the single market – somehow, it is still jobs for the garçons.

As we will see in a moment, there is one country whose turnaround in its fortunes in modern times was built on a very firm and comprehensive battle against corruption, which quickly established it as a safe and reliable place to do business, helping to funnel overseas investment onto its territory.

It is an area in which the EU is failing badly. Europe might not have the most corrupt nations on earth but it is certainly carrying a very big problem, which it ought to have tackled properly long before now.

18.

Conclusion: How can Britain Escape the EU's Low Trajectory?

As we have seen in so many ways, the club of European nations is not an enviable place to be just at the moment – whether you are Britain or a EU member state. Europe has become a global backwater; a region that once led the world in economic development and scientific progress, but which now seems economically stagnant and strangely wary of new things. It has regulated whole industries out of existence – or at least has forced them overseas. Its preoccupation with achieving net zero territorial greenhouse emissions is leading to a cascade of industries leaving the continent. While Europe might pride itself on its social values and quality of life, the growing and glaring differential in growth rates between Europe and more dynamic parts of the world is slowly undermining these ideals. Social tensions are growing; organised crime spreading to once peaceful places.

As for Brexit, five years on it is hard to see what the fuss was all about. It has not been a disaster, in spite of the continuing claims that UK growth has been harmed. The UK has not done worse than other comparable European economies; claims that it would have done better within the EU are based on fantastical assumptions that it would have outper-formed France and Germany had it stayed within the EU. It is true that friction in trade between Britain and the EU has increased, and life has been made hard – if not impossible – for companies which once exported small amounts of goods across the Channel. But the overall effect on the economy has been much exaggerated.

Yet, at the same time, it is hard to see what has really been achieved by leaving the EU. A handful of trade deals have been done with countries, such as Australia, which would not have been done otherwise – not that this has pleased some vested interests, notably UK meat producers, who fear com-petition from Australian rivals as tariffs and other barriers are steadily lowered over the next fifteen years. Britain has begun to diverge from the EU in the emerging industry of gene editing, which the EU continues to suppress through its over-precautionary approach but towards which Britain has adopted a more enabling attitude. However, in other areas, the UK continues to dream up new economy-crushing regu-lations. We continue to have a labour market and corporate laws that are inflexible compared with US standards.

Overall, Brexit might be said to be a score draw – albeit it a low-scoring one. It is akin to a dull 1–1 encounter between two minor league sides on foggy Tuesday evening in November, from which many people leave ten minutes early and every-one wanders home with a sense of disappointment. We surely can – and must – do better.

Part of the problem is that while a majority of the UK population voted for Brexit there was little in the way of agreement as to why we were leaving. According to the official Leave campaign – which was chosen by the Electoral Commission from several candidates – the main issue was one of sovereignty, as underscored by its slogan 'Take Back Control'. Several of the leading figures in the campaign, such as Boris Johnson and Michael Gove, had a fairly liberal attitude towards migration and trade. Their views could be summed up by the words that appeared on the cover of the *Spectator* magazine before the 1975 EEC referendum and again in 2016: 'Out – and into the world'. The idea was not to isolate Britain but to free it from a bloc which they saw as narrow interfering and protectionist, and to carve a more open relationship with the entire globe.

Yet, for many who voted for Brexit, the overriding issue was migration. Anyone who voted for Brexit thinking that it would close off our borders must now be feeling bitterly cheated. In 2022, net migration to the UK was 745,000, falling slightly to 672,000 in the twelve months to June 2023.[1] This is three times as high as the levels recorded in the early 2010s – levels which helped build the case for an in/out EU referendum in the first place.

The motivations of the economically liberal Brexiteers and those more interested in reducing migration are utterly at odds and are irreconcilable. In the immediate aftermath of the Brexit referendum, however, neither school of thought was put in charge of Brexit negotiations. After the resignation of David Cameron as prime minister, the job of carving out a new deal was left to his successor, Theresa May – who had campaigned for a Remain vote. Her lack of enthusiasm for the entire project, combined with an absence of clear instruction from a referendum result, which had merely asked people to make a binary choice between leave and remain, goes a long way to explaining why the whole withdrawal process was such a mess, and why it ended up pleasing hardly anyone. It has reaffirmed my belief that referendums should only ever be used in one clear circumstance: where a government is seeking approval for constitutional changes that it wants to bring about and for which very clear and detailed proposals have been published. If Britain were to leave the EU, the way it should have happened is for a party to have won a general election on a manifesto which promised to negotiate Britain's departure – followed by a referendum when it had agreed the terms of that departure. Instead, what we ended up with was a prime minister daring us to vote for something which he himself didn't want, which he personally claimed would be a disaster – and something which, to boot, nobody really knew what form it would end up taking.

But it is hardly worth revisiting all this now. We have left, and that is that. There is little support for a low-profile Rejoin movement. Even Lord Mandelson, who made the case for remaining in the EU as passionately as anyone, has dismissed the prospect of Britain going back into the EU, saying that neither the UK public nor Brussels has any appetite for it, and calling for the aspirations of Remainers to stop at closer ties with the EU.[2] The government of Keir Starmer, which came to office in July 2024, has confirmed that it will not be seeking to rejoin either the EU, single market or customs union.

The challenge now is to derive some advantage from Brexit. This will not be achieved by emulating the EU, by turning Britain into its endlessly orbiting satellite. It will re-quire Britain to achieve escape velocity, to break away from its regulatory pull. But, so far, we have made little effort to do so. Even some of those who, during the Brexit referendum campaign, seemed to be advocating the model of 'Singapore-on-Thames' seemed reluctant, when they found themselves in political office following Brexit, to bring it about. Boris Johnson proved a far more interventionist prime minister than his history suggested he would be – quickly resorting

to big government during the Covid pandemic. It wasn't
normal times, yet it is still notable that he expanded the state
markedly, leaving Britain with its largest tax burden since
the 1960s (it would subsequently rise to its highest levels since
the 1940s under his successor-but-one, Rishi Sunak). Michael
Gove proved to be no deregulator when he returned to government after Brexit – on the contrary, he was one of the
chief advocates for vaccine passports during the Covid-19
pandemic, and he introduced new planning requirements
and extra taxation for holiday lets in an unashamed effort to
reduce their number – despite their being a vital part of the
tourist industry. When even the avowed advocates of a low
tax, low regulation post-Brexit Britain turn out not really to
believe in it, what hope is there for achieving that vision?

Nevertheless, at some point, a UK government is going to
have to make a priority of economic growth. It is the lack of
growth which is imposing tensions in society, making many
people feel cheated. Union battles, arguments over tax and
spending, often revolve around the issue of how the national
cake is divided; yet the bigger issue is the size of the national
cake to begin with.

A government which addresses the lack of growth needs
to start by asking: what is it that has helped faster-growing
economies of the world to outstrip Europe in recent decades? Firstly, the US. The US does have one advantage over
Britain and Europe in that the dollar is the world's reserve
currency. It has allowed the US to shower its economy with
stimulus packages without having to worry so much about
bond markets losing faith in US government debt – global
investors were always going to carry on buying the dollar, re-
gardless of the size of the US national debt. But as we've seen
there is a big difference in how the US sought to stimulate its
economy during and after Covid-19. While Britain paid for
millions of workers – 9 million at the peak – to stay at home

and do nothing under the furlough scheme, US workers were treated much more meanly – many of them laid off without any furlough payments (though they did receive welfare). On the other hand, the US sought to boost the economy more generally, allowing growing businesses to became huge job-creating machines as the pandemic passed, hoovering up workers who had lost their jobs. In Britain, the government ended up bailing out businesses which would have gone bust in the absence of the pandemic; perversely, 2020 saw the lowest number of company insolvencies in three decades, in spite of the economy shrinking by 20 per cent in a single quarter.[3] The UK approach kept workers stuck in unproductive jobs and capital tied up in unviable businesses; the US, by contrast, saw workers and capital reallocated to growing industries.

However, the gulf between the US and European economies was growing wider well before the pandemic. What happened during Covid-19 echoed a more general difference between the US and Europe. As already noted, US employment law is far less geared towards protecting particular jobs, and far more geared towards incentivising businesses to create jobs; easy to hire and easy to fire, if you like. However hard European unions might fight to preserve jobs, if Britain wants to grow like America, it is going to have to free up its labour market and sweep away the more restrictive labour laws which were imposed on it during its membership of the EU.

So, too, will Britain have to find some way of encouraging entrepreneurs to grow their companies rather than selling out at the earliest opportunity. It is not that Britain does not produce good ideas; but again and again companies that show promise of becoming engines of growth choose to sell out to foreign competitors before they have had chance to reach anything like the size of America's tech giants. If we want tech giants we need to be asking: why is it that they are struggling to raise capital in Britain? The City of London is one of the world's great financial centres, and yet it does not seem to be serving UK industry well.

The European approach to boosting the economy is to try to pick winners. In 2023, the EU announced a €43 billion fund to try to spark the development of a European microchip industry. It is part of an EU Chips Act which seeks to double the EU's market share of the global microchip industry to 20 per cent, making the continent less reliant on Taiwan.[4] If it goes anything like Europe's efforts to develop a state-sponsored electric car battery industry, EU taxpayers should have a deep fear of what will happen to their money. In a fast-evolving area like chip manufacture it will be rather easy to waste money building factories to pump out yesterday's products – and miss the boat on technologies which will render them obsolete. What the US does brilliantly is not to shower public money on companies that appeal to government officials (although Biden's administration in particular has done its fair share of that) but to create the conditions in which start-up companies can raise capital, find premises, hire and fire staff without having regulators breathing down their necks. Most start-ups will fail – and there will be no point in propping them up – but that doesn't matter if just a handful of companies manage to clamber out of the economic primordial soup and prosper. The culture of US business – which includes the attitudes of state regulators – accepts and celebrates the 'creative destruction' which allows good ideas to feast on the entrails of the bad. The European approach – to try to preserve every last factory for fear of what will happen to the workers if it closes – is a recipe for misallocation of resources. There are successes from the European way of doing things: the Airbus consortium is slowly overhauling troubled Boeing in the airliner market. But we will get a lot further if we change the relationship between government and business, in order to stop the former trying to decide which are the promising ideas, to be showered with public money and ministerial lobbying, and instead limit government's role to creating the right regulatory, legal and financial environment in which ideas can battle it out between themselves.

Then there is the matter of energy prices. You can't really expect European industries to prosper when they are paying four times as much for their gas and electricity than their US competitors. And neither can you blame that huge differential entirely on Vladimir Putin. For years, while Europe has been setting unrealistic net zero targets and taking a fundamentalist approach to achieving them, the US has put energy security and affordability before all else. And, yes, this happened as much during Barack Obama's presidency as it did during Donald Trump's term of office between 2017 and 2021. As mentioned earlier, while European countries all but banned fracking and derided it as a part of a 'legacy' fossil fuel industry, the US embraced it, with the result that the US is now the world's largest producer of oil and gas. Thank God, for Europe's sake, that the US did take this line. Europe has exchanged reliance on Putin's Russia with reliance on the US. Ironically, in rejecting the case for a shale gas industry, countries like Germany have ended up with something far dirtier and more carbon intensive: it has been forced into reopening coal mines. The US has cut its carbon emissions sharply – albeit from a high level – by switching from coal to gas.

Things are changing. By the spring of 2024, European countries appeared to be going back on their promises to decarbonise the electricity sector by 2035 by commissioning 72 gigawatts' worth of new gas power plants to balance intermittent and unreliable wind and solar.[5] This includes Britain. Yet we continue to run towards a cliff edge created by unrealistic targets. While Europe deprives itself of affordable, reliable energy, the US and China are using their far cheaper energy to help collar the market in green technologies. The European approach seems to be to set ambitious decarbonisation targets, tax dirty industries out of existence and chuck money at half-baked technologies in the hope that they will rapidly improve in time to allow you to hit your targets. In the US and China, the emphasis is on giving green technologies the space and time to prove themselves, in the hope that they will naturally displace their dirtier forebears without having to curtail lifestyles and compromise economic growth. The problem of carbon emissions will be solved when technologies emerge that are not only cleaner but genuinely cheaper, too. They will then sell themselves; they will not have to be forced on an unwilling population.

The US is very far from a model society. Its public health system is sporadic and expensive, with poor outcomes when you look at the population as a whole. It is riven with social tensions. The poor, too often, drop through the net. Its once liberal universities have been infected with intolerance.

Moreover, the apparent health of the US economy disguises the presence of a large pool of potential but inactive labour. This is also true in Britain, where a growing rate of economic inactivity has attracted increasing concern since the pandemic. Notionally, Britain has one of the lowest rates of unemployment in the developed world: 3.9 per cent in January 2024 compared with an EU average of 6.0 per cent. However, that tells us far from the whole story. Of the working-age population – those aged between 16 and 64 – 9.2 million, or 21.8 per cent, were not in any kind of work in March 2024, a figure which has increased by 700,000 since the pandemic.[6] Among 16–24-year-olds, 851,000 – 12 per cent of the total – are neither in education, employment or training.[7] Yet look at the US's rate of economic inactivity and it is – surprisingly – even worse, at 25.2 per cent in the third quarter of 2023.[8] That is a massive section of the population which could be generating wealth but for one reason or another is failing to contribute.

We don't have to emulate the US; in many respects we could be doing better. What about another possible model for post-Brexit Britain, one on the other side of the world, which cropped up during the Brexit referendum campaign: Singapore? We heard over and over again from some quarters of how we were going to turn ourselves into 'Singapore on Thames'. So just what is Singapore? No country perhaps in history has grown so rich, so quickly. From a third world country with slums and high unemployment upon gaining its independence in 1965, Singapore burst quickly into the bracket of middle-income countries and then out the other side to become one of the world's richest countries. In 2022, it was second only to Luxembourg in terms of GDP per capita, adjusted for purchasing power parity (PPP) – i.e. taking into account local living costs – with each resident producing $127,606 per annum.[9] Moreover, it has consistently scored highly on the UN's Human Development Index, which takes into account health and education as well as economic living standards. In the third quarter of 2023, unemployment stood at just 2.8 per cent, while the economy was growing at an annualised rate of 2.2 per cent. That is low compared with a growth rate which has often exceeded 10 per cent over the past sixty years, yet Singapore has never run into the wall which some once rapidly growing economies have done, such as Japan.

For all Singapore's success, the idea of Britain emulating it in some way aroused remarkably negative emotions among many in Britain. Some see the small city state as a corporate dystopia – 'Disneyland with the death penalty' as someone once memorably put it. According to the then Labour Party leader Jeremy Corbyn in 2017, the Conservatives were intent on turning Britain into a 'Singapore-style low wage tax haven'.[10] Characteristically, Corbyn – who by contrast has lionised the socialist basket case of Venezuela – was wrong on both counts. Singapore is certainly not low-waged (see above), and nor is it a tax haven. Personal income taxes are fairly low – the top rate in 2024 was 24 per cent. So too is corporation tax, at 17 per cent.[11] But they are not in tax haven territory. Surely, a country which has pulled itself up so far, so quickly, deserves better than to be dismissed as a possible model for Britain, so just how did Singapore manage to transform itself?

Singapore had little in the way of natural resources, but what it did have was a strategically important position on the world's shipping routes and also air routes. Its first prime minister – and the only person to hold the job in the first twenty-five years of its life as an independent country – Lee Kuan Yew, unashamedly set out to construct an economy based on inward investment. The strategy was quite plain: to become, by tackling corruption and creating a stable banking and legal environment, the safe option for Western businesses wanting to expand into Asia. Singapore set out to be Hong Kong, but cleaner, and without the threat of being handed over to China when Britain's colonial lease ran out. While Singapore's city-state image might lead those unfamiliar with the country to assume its economy is all about finance – about shovelling money around in tall, glass tower blocks – Singapore simultaneously built-up manufacturing industries from scratch, beginning with clothing and rapidly expanding into higher value areas. To attract business, the government created an Economic Development Board whose functions went beyond Western bodies that go under such names. It nurtured businesses and helped find them premises, as well as taking them through very easy-to-understand regulation – the exact opposite of the EU's tortuous legislative environment where rules frequently conflict. The government paid Western corporations to educate and train the workforce, concentrating on a technical education. Trade union excesses were suppressed by rolling unions into one, state-sponsored union, the National Trades Union Congress.

Singapore is not, however, the haven of red-in-tooth-and-claw capitalism which many – critics and advocates alike – believe it to be. It has a compulsory savings scheme, the Central Provident Fund, into which citizens must pay a quarter of their earnings. While it might have a passing resemblance to Britain's National Insurance contributions, there is a very, very large difference: a Singaporean's contributions go into a dedicated, personal pot, which can be called upon for housing, education, medical care and retirement. Remarkably, 80 per cent of the population live in social housing. There was nothing laissez-faire about Singapore's programme to clear the slums in the 1960s onwards. Land was compulsorily purchased and developed by state corporation. In time, residents were allowed to buy ninety-nine-year leases on their homes, but there are strict limitations as to whom the leases can be sold. From its beginnings, Singapore's housing programme has imposed national and racial quotas on housing blocks to prevent the development of ghettos.

Like several of the world's wealthiest countries, the Singapore government runs a sovereign wealth fund – two in fact – to capture commercial value for the state and to ease the burden on the taxpayer. One of the wealth funds, Temasek, invests in many of Singapore's own companies, while the other, the Government of Singapore Investment Group (GIC), invests more internationally. Between them, they produce enough income to cover around 20 per cent of government expenditure, while their value acts as collateral for public debt, allowing the government to borrow at lower rates than most countries.

But there is a dark side. There is no way that I would risk

writing a book like this were I Singaporean. While notionally
a democracy, only one party – the People's Action Party – has
been in power in sixty years. That it has remained in power
for so long might not be entirely unconnected with the government's propensity for suing its critics, be they protesters,
journalists or, in some cases, opposition politicians. A one-
party state does not make for a healthy society. Singapore has
been well governed by the only three prime ministers it has
had since independence; the trouble will come when one day
it finds itself less well governed, and it proves hard to dislodge
the ruling party. There are some charming leftovers from
British colonialism in Singapore, like Raffles hotel; one less
charming hangover is the noose. The country still uses the
death penalty, not just for murder but for small-time drug traffickers like 45-year-old Saridewi Djamani, executed in July
2023 after being caught five years earlier bringing 30 grams
of heroin into the country.[12] Much as I abhor the soft attitude
towards hard drugs in Britain and Europe, Singapore's extreme penal code is a blot on its otherwise strong claims to
be a civilised country. Surely, there is a middle way between
the laissez-faire attitudes to hard drugs which have turned
the Netherlands into Europe's narco-state and the putting to
death of minor drugs traffickers.

Britain doesn't, of course, have to emulate any particular
country, but bearing in mind the experiences of two very
different countries whose economies have consistently outgrown Britain and Europe in recent decades, let's try and
construct a blueprint for a Britain which is capable of pulling
away from the rest of Europe and achieving a long term,
higher trajectory of growth. Firstly, how to attract investment?
As the Singapore experience shows, it is not handouts and
bribes which matter so much as a clean and safe, politically
stable environment in which to do business. Achieve that and
you are halfway there. Add low taxes and straightforward,

well-targeted regulation and you have a very attractive environment in which to do business.

Britain already has a big advantage in being a stable democracy – even if it sometimes seems to us otherwise. Its legal system is strong. Its taxes are not the highest, but corporation tax, in particular, could be lower. Corporation tax receipts grew substantially between 2010/11 and 2019/20, from £43.0 billion to £63.5 billion – in spite of the rate being reduced from 28 per cent to 19 per cent. When corporation tax is higher than competitor countries, companies divert profits away from Britain; when it is lower, they start diverting profits towards Britain. Since 2023, the corporation tax rate has been jacked up again to 25 per cent – the full results of which have yet to become clear.

Britain is not, sadly, free from corruption. On the contrary, too few questions have been asked over the years as oligarchs and others sought to use London as place to launder money. There should be no tolerance of this, and no reason not to tackle it. In 2016, the anti-corruption campaign group Transparency International reported that one in ten properties in the London borough of Kensington and Chelsea was owned by companies registered in 'secrecy jurisdictions' such as the British Virgin Islands. That doesn't prove that their purchase was to aid money laundering, but it is a somewhat unhealthy sign of how much London property is being purchased as assets by buyers who appear to feel a need to keep their identities private – as opposed to ordinary residents who just want somewhere to live.[13] A report by the Treasury and Home Office four years later suggested that little had changed: London property was still being bought up by overseas-registered companies. Moreover, the guards against money laundering were not properly in place – estate agents advertising homes with a guide price of over £5 million were supposed to register with HMRC for guidance on how to

check the provenance of the funds used to purchase those
properties, but only half had done so.[14]

One of the areas in desperate need of reform is UK company law. It is far too easy to set up a company without need to
prove identity, residence or any evidence of business activity
taking place – easier, as some have pointed out, than getting
a library card, for which a utility bill is often required. All
you need is a credit card and five minutes of your time. UK
company registration is being systematically abused in order
to serve criminal interests. During one three-month period,
between April and June 2022, 200,000 companies were registered at Companies House. Sadly, it wasn't a sudden rush of
entrepreneurialism, as closer inspection showed. Ninety-five
companies were found to be registered at sixty-five houses in a
single Herefordshire street, many apparently by Romanians.
A further hundred companies were registered, by Chinese
people, to a single semi-detached house in Orpington – the
bewildered owner of which knew nothing about them.[15] It
was not necessarily all indicative of major crime – one of the
reasons for Chinese to set up a UK companies appears to be
to facilitate getting money out of China, which has been made
difficult by Xi Jinping's government. Most who use UK companies as vehicle for doing this have probably never set foot
in Britain. Yet the abuse of UK company law makes Britain
seem like a haven of lawlessness. It should not be possible
to set up a company without having to produce documents,
present yourself for a face-to-face interview and prove that
you actually have an intention of conducting a legal business
activity. This is one instance where we could do with a bit
more regulation.

As for regulation more generally, Britain has yet to make
any serious effort to diverge from EU laws. There are some
ways in which it should not seek to diverge. EU product standards are well established. There is little to be gained from

allowing noisier lawnmowers and more energy-consuming kettles in Britain – even if they were desirable, it would provide unnecessary complication and expense, and manufacturers would likely stick with EU standards anyway. But there are many other regulations that could be relaxed to great benefit. Development of land is still compromised by EU-era rules regarding habitats and nitrate emissions. It is not that anyone wants to trash the environment, but something is wrong when it gets to the stage – as it did in 2022 – when, according to the Housebuilders' Federation, construction of 120,000 new homes was being held up by rules demanding that developers prove their new homes would have zero effect on local nutrient levels.

Housing, indeed, has become a huge barrier to Britain's economic vibrancy. Prices are far too high, and too much of the housing stock has been monopolised by global investors – many of them resident in Singapore, as it happens. In many parts of the country, it is unaffordable even to rent a decent home. This makes it far harder for people to move around the country to look for work in the manner which Americans take for granted. The UK government has tried to dissuade overseas investors from buying up large numbers of housing units through imposing high taxes. But far more drastic action is required. Britain should go back to what it was doing in the post-war years, and which Singapore has also done: build new towns on land that has been compulsorily purchased by development corporations. It doesn't have to be social housing. Buy land at agricultural value, grant it planning permission then sell off plots to developers, using the uplift in value to build roads, sewers, schools and other infrastructure, and housebuilding levels could be greatly increased as well as prices lowered. At the moment, that uplift in value is almost all being captured by lucky landowners. As for tackling speculators, this could be easily achieved by writing a simple condition into the deeds of a large proportion of new homes, which states that these properties can only ever be used for the purposes of owner-occupation. A similar approach should be used to provide premises for expanding businesses. At the moment, Britain has a planning system which is mostly reactive: a business finds land, submits planning application and planners – often after interminable delays – make a decision. If Britain wants to attract business investment, it needs to turn this around and adopt a system in which businesses can quickly be matched-up with sites that are pre-approved and ready for development. By all means, we should debate where development should take place, environmentalists must be consulted and so on. But then land should be zoned and infrastructure put in place so that sites are available – quickly – for those businesses which need them.

Britain should seek to move away from European-style company regulation and adopt more US-style rules. If companies want to close factories or lay-off employees, there should be few barriers to them doing so. Trying to force businesses to hang on to obsolete jobs merely ensures the misallocation of capital. Just look at Britain's railways, which have spent much of the past few years paralysed by frequent strikes as unions try to prevent rail companies running trains without guards – a practice which already happens on a third of UK trains and has been employed since the 1980s, with no reduction in safety. The role of guards on trains, indeed, was made redundant by signalling improvements in the mid-nineteenth century (their original role was to run back down the line in the event of a breakdown to warn any following trains and prevent a collision). Nor is there any need in modern metro services to employ drivers. Driverless technology has been in existence since the 1980s, and there are over a hundred metro lines in the world which operate without a single driver – Singapore among them.

Worse, UK rail operators are obliged, when they take over franchises from other operators, to continue to employ the same staff on the same terms, under Transfer of Undertakings laws – a classic piece of EU law that makes it extremely difficult for a new operator to improve services or efficiency, and which undermines the whole purpose of private operation. Britain's railways would be better off under a single state company which invests in full automation of lines when the density of operation justifies it. The 'open access' arrangements whereby private operators can instigate services not currently being provided by the state operator should be retained, however.

Should government subsidise businesses with grants, sweeteners and other enticements? In Britain, as in many countries, the government has been doing this for decades – and earning a very poor return, usually because it has been done for the wrong reasons, such as to prop up failing businesses for fear of job losses. That said, there is a case for public investment, where, say, there is a public interest in new technologies being developed, but where the likely rewards might not come early enough to attract private investment. Such a case might be in novel forms of renewable energy or in nuclear fusion. Britain cannot and should not attempt to outgun the US on this, which is splashing $890 billion through the Inflation Reduction Act to subsidise green technologies. But where the UK government does invest in new technology, it shouldn't simply hand over grants; it should take a stake in growing companies, creating the nucleus of a UK sovereign wealth fund which could help fund public spending, and tax cuts, in the future. That is what the wealthiest countries – Singapore and Norway among them – have done. They are in a vastly better fiscal position than is Britain.

As for the state, as for individuals: a savings culture would do Britain a lot of good. Why not do away with our dishonest, non-existent 'National Insurance' fund and replace it with a compulsory savings scheme in which individuals retain ownership and control of their personal pot of money, to be used for retirement as well as other defined purposes, such as education and healthcare? Britain could take a lesson from Singapore, too, on education. It was a technical-based education, well-tuned to the needs of the economy, which made a huge difference in Singapore. In Britain, and across Europe, we have gone in the other direction. There is little correlation between university courses on offer and the careers which are available at the end of it. Europe trains students for political activism – and then finds itself short of engineers and doctors.

Something is going to have to be done about the growing numbers of people of working age who are not in work, education or training. Ideally, the government should simply abolish unemployment. Rather than pay benefits for people to do nothing, those who cannot find work elsewhere should be offered three days a week of work at the national minimum wage, with no restrictions on what they can do on the other four days and no deduction from their wages for taking other work. There would be plenty of tasks for them: from caring jobs to filling in potholes; there are all manner of things which simply are not currently getting done at the rate they need to be. The obligation on people to turn up somewhere and do some work would keep them connected with the discipline of employment, while the freedom to do other work on the side would eliminate the welfare trap, where some people can find themselves worse off by taking a job because they lose more in withdrawn benefits than they gain in earnings. Moreover, it would tackle rampant benefits fraud. Britain has experimented before with demanding that people work for their benefits. In 1996, the then Conservative government introduced a pilot scheme called 'Project Work' in which 6,800 benefits claimants in Hull and Medway were asked to go through thirteen weeks' intensive job hunting, followed by thirteen weeks of compulsory work. The result? While 920 of them found work, a far higher number – 3,100 – simply stopped claiming – quite possibly because they were already employed and the obligation to turn up for a job would have exposed their fraudulent claims. Maybe some of the claimants lived abroad, or didn't even exist. Either way, the scheme was so successful that it even impressed the commentator Polly Toynbee, not one normally given to praising Conservative governments. The pilot scheme, however, died a death when John Major's government was defeated by Tony Blair in 1997.[16]

Is there some way that Britain could combine the energy, individualism and love of freedom of America with the discipline and sense of purpose of Singapore? I am not sure how much of the above is saleable to a UK public at the moment, given the deep ructions in society, the misplaced admiration for the European Union which exists in many people and the attraction that the comfort blanket of protectionism and closed borders still holds for many Brexit voters. But I am sure that such a hypothetical country would be a winner. And of one other thing I am certain, too: the upheaval of Brexit will have been in vain if we don't at least try to do something different to the rest of sclerotic Europe.

Notes

Introduction

1. 'Estimating excess mortality due to the Covid-19 pandemic: a systematic analysis of Covid-19 related mortality, 2020–21', *Lancet*, 16 April 2022
2. www.dw.com, 20 February 2020
3. *Financial Times*, 14 October 2022
4. Jonathan Portes, *New Statesmen*, 8 November 2022
5. Tweet by @julianHjessop, 15 October 2022
6. www.destatis.de, 27 August 2024
7. BBC archive, 18 January 1973
8. *Guardian*, 6 December 2023

I.

1. *Financial Times*, 15 January 2024
2. 'Gross Domestic Product: chained volume measures, seasonally adjusted', Office of National Statistics (ONS)
3. 'Claimant Count and Vacancies Time Series', ONS
4. Reuters, 29 September 2023
5. Bureau of Economic Analysis, www.bea.gov.uk
6. *Financial Times*, 2 February 2024
7. www.lemonde.fr, 6 February 2024
8. *Financial Times*, 11 January 2024
9. 'Public service productivity, UK: 1997 to 2022', ONS, 17 November 2023
10. Calculations from www.data.worldbank.org

11. www.ourworldindata.net, from Maddison Project database
12. Maddison Project database, www.rug.nl
13. 'Industrial Production by Country', www.ec.europa.eu
14. 'Production in December 2023', www.destatis.de
15. www.ceicdata.com
16. *Financial Times*, 26 September 2024
17. www.whatcar.com, 27 September 2023
18. *Daily Mail*, 4 November 2023
19. *Financial Times*, 22 January 2024
20. *Daily Telegraph*, 5 March 2024
21. *Daily Telegraph*, 13 March 2024
22. *Guardian*, 1 December 2023
23. 'Industrial Electricity Prices in the IEA', Department for Energy Security and Net Zero, 30 November 2023
24. www.ourworldindata.org, from EMBER data
25. *Financial Times*, 19 February 2024
26. *Financial Times*, 6 February 2024
27. *Daily Telegraph*, 30 January 2024
28. www.insee.fr
29. www.data.worldbank.org
30. Bloomberg, 3 June 2020
31. European Trade Union Institute, www.etui.org
32. www.yle.fi, 31 January 2024
33. 'Absence for Work Due to Illness', OECD data
34. *Daily Telegraph*, 26 February 2024
35. 'Average Annual Hours Actually Worked per Worker', OECD data
36. *World Nuclear News*, 19 December 2022
37. *Financial Times*, 27 January 2024
38. 2023 EU Industrial R&D Investment Scorecard
39. *The Times*, 3 February 2024
40. EY Global IPO Trends, 2023
41. www.bbc.com, 14 September 2023

2.

1. *Daily Telegraph*, 3 February 2015
2. *New Scientist*, 5 October 2015
3. 'Genetically Modified Crops Global Market Report 2023', The Business Research Company, January 2024

4. 'Genetically Modified Crops and Sustainability', www. geneticliteracyproject.org, 15 November 2022
5. Regis, *Golden Rice: The Imperilled Birth of a GM Superfood*, John Hopkins University Press, 2019
6. *Financial Times*, 27 February 2024
7. *Forbes Magazine*, 22 April 2010
8. 'Natural Gas Prices in Europe, Asia and the United States', International Energy Agency
9. www.ieefa.org, October 2023
10. www.bbc.com, 9 December 2023
11. www.dw.com, 12 June 2023
12. www.euronews.com, 24 January 2024
13. *Daily Telegraph*, 10 May 2023
14. 'Public service productivity, UK 1997 to 2022', ONS, 17 November 2023
15. www.bbc.com, 5 July 2019
16. 'Unemployment Rates', www.oecd.org
17. CNN, 2 February 2024
18. 'Employment by country of birth', ONS, 13 February 2024
19. www.ijmuk.org
20. Global Slavery Index, www.walkfree.org
21. www.bbc.com, 28 July 2018
22. www.cps.gov.uk
23. www.migrationobservatory.ox.ac.uk
24. *Daily Mail*, 30 July 2013
25. *Daily Mail*, 12 July 2013

3.

1. www.business.yougov.com
2. Stein and Santini, 'The Sustainability of "Local" Food: a review for policymakers' , *Review of Agricultural, Food and Environmental Studies*, vol. 103, 2022
3. *Guardian*, 23 March 2008
4. Ibid.
5. www.policy.trade.ec.europa.eu
6. 'Trade (% of GDP)', www.data.worldbank.org
7. 'Europe: Market Access and Barriers to Trade', www.ahdb.org
8. www.bbc.com, 11 January 2021
9. www.bbc.com, 13 January 2021

10. www.britishpoultry.org.uk
11. Reuters, 23 May 2024
12. *Financial Times*, 19 March 2024
13. 'Could the EU's ban on palm oil in biofuels do more harm than good?', www.weforum.org, 8 October 2019
14. 'Land used for European biofuels could feed 120 million people daily', www.transportenvironment.org, 9 March 2023
15. www.euractiv.com, 31 January 2024

4.

1. Speech to the Bank of the Netherlands, 14 January 1999
2. *Guardian*, 13 August 2002
3. 'Housing in Ireland: from crisis to crisis', National University of Ireland, SSRN online journal, January 2015
4. *Guardian*, 6 February 2008
5. www.data.worldbank.org
6. www.ec.europa.eu

5.

1. 'Rail Market Monitoring Report', Autorite de Regulation de Transports, 2021
2. www.bundesrechnungshof.de, 15 March 2023
3. Sky News, 31 August 2020
4. AP News, 13 July 2023
5. *El Pais*, 2 January 2019
6. *Guardian*, 14 September 2016
7. www.international-railway-safety-council.com
8. European Transport Safety Council, www.etsc.eu
9. *Daily Telegraph*, 24 March 2002
10. 'Global Traffic Scorecard 2022', www.inrix.com
11. *Daily Telegraph*, 20 July 2009
12. International Road Federation
13. www.dw.com, 29 October 2021
14. www.dw.com, 31 October 2010
15. 'Global Airport Ranking', www.airhelp.com
16. www.euronews.com, 25 July 2023
17. www.researchoutreach.org, 11 April 2022
18. *Guardian*, 17 August 2018

19. 'The State of US and European Broadband Prices and Deployment', Progressive Policy Institute, August 2021
20. 'Broadband Coverage in Europe 2022', European Commission
21. *Guardian*, 22 May 2023
22. 'Universal Postal Service Must Modernise', Ofcom, 24 January 2024

6.

1. www.bbc.com, 4 February 2018
2. www.shelter.org, 14 December 2023
3. www.bbc.co.uk, 1 February 2024
4. 'Eighth Overview of Housing Exclusion in Europe 2023', www.feantsa.org
5. Ibid.
6. Ibid.
7. 'Housing Costs and Affordability', Department for Levelling Up, Housing and Communities, 14 December 2023
8. 'Housing in Europe 2023', Eurostat
9. *Daily Telegraph*, 1 March 2024
10. www.bbc.co.uk, 3 October 2023
11. www.cbsnews.com, 3 October 2023
12. 'Assessing House Prices: Insights for "Houselev", a dataset of Price Level Estimates', European Commission, July 2019
13. www.destatis.com
14. www.bbc.co.uk, 28 February 2024
15. www.ourworldindata.org, from IHME data
16. www.bbc.com, 16 December 2022
17. *Guardian*, 21 March 2019
18. *Observer*, 9 April 2023
19. *Journal of Forensic Sciences*, vol 48, no. 3, May 2003
20. 'Large Housing Estates of Berlin', *Housing Estates in Europe*, 15 August 2018
21. 'The Role of Green Space in London's Covid-19 Recovery', www.rics.org, 5 October 2020
22. 'How Green Are European Cities?', European Environment Agency, 1 February 2022

7.

1. *Sunday Times*, 8 September 2019

2. www.globalinitiative.net
3. AFP, 11 May 2022
4. 'Serious and Organised Crime Threat Assessment 2021', www.europol.europa.eu
5. *Daily Telegraph*, 10 April 2024
6. 'Crime Index by Country 2023 Mid-Year', www.numbeo.com
7. 'Interactive charts on Homicide', www.ourworldindata.org, from UN Office on Drugs and Crime
8. *New European*, 9 September 2020
9. www.France24.com, 4 July 2012
10. *Le Monde*, 21 July 2022
11. 'Sharp Increase in Knife Crime Since 2010', www.bra.se, 19 December 2023
12. 'Suspects of Crime Among Persons With Domestic and Foreign Backgrounds', www.bra.se
13. www.nltimes.nl, 18 February 2024
14. *Guardian*, 28 February 2024
15. www.dw.com, 27 February 2024
16. *Daily Telegraph*, 4 January 2024
17. *Daily Telegraph*, 8 January 2024
18. *Daily Telegraph*, 9 January 2024
19. *Spectator*, 30 September 2023
20. www.coe.int, 7 December 2023

8.

1. *Guardian*, 25 August 2021
2. www.itv.com, 24 February 2023
3. *Daily Mail*, 24 January 2024
4. www.greekreporter.com, 25 May 2019
5. *Independent*, 22 January 2018
6. *The Connexxion*, 23 August 2023
7. 'Global dietary quality in 185 countries from 1990 to 2018 shows differences by dation, age, education and urbanicity', *Nature*, 4 September 2022
8. *The Times*, 1 January 2024
9. *Financial Times*, 17 October 2016
10. *Guardian*, 27 April 2022
11. www.ourworldindata.org, using World Bank data
12. *Politico*, 24 January 2020

13. *Daily Telegraph*, 7 August 2023
14. emerging-europe.com, 26 February 2021
15. 'Brexit: Food Prices and Availability', House of Lords Report, 2017
16. 'The European Union One Health 2022 Zoonoses Report', European Food Safety Authority and European Centre for Disease Prevention and Control, 12 December 2023
17. *Farmers Weekly*, 7 June 2016
18. *New York Times*, 17 September 1990
19. 'The UK's Agri-Food Trade Policies One Year On From Brexit', *EuroChoices*, August 2022
20. *The Netherlands Agricultural Sector in International Context*, 2023 edition, Wageningen University and Research
21. Common Agricultural Policy: key graphs and figures, www.agriculture.europa.eu
22. *Guardian*, 16 November 2023
23. *Daily Telegraph*, 24 January 2024
24. www.agreste.agricultural.gouv.fr
25. *Le Monde*, 8 February 2023
26. www.apnews.com, 15 February 2024
27. www.dw.com, 18 January 2024
28. *Guardian*, 28 December 2019
29. 'Food Production to Supply Ratio', ONS, 3 November 2023

9.

1. *Guardian*, 27 January 2016
2. *The Ecologist*, 25 January 2016
3. *Independent*, 27 March 2018
4. 'UK Regulation After Brexit', Brexit and Environment, October 2022
5. BBC Future Planet, 12 October 2023
6. *Le Monde*, 10 April 2023
7. www.rfi.fr
8. *Guardian*, 10 January 2023
9. www.dw.com, 17 May 2018
10. 'European Waters Assessment of status and pressures', European Environment Agency 2018
11. 'Water Quality by Country', www.worldpopulationreview.com
12. 'Air Quality in Europe – 2018 Report', European Environment Agency

13. www.umweltbundesant.de, 14 December 2018

14. Reuters, 12 August 2022

15. BBC, 10 December 2015

16. www.rfi.fr, 19 July 2017

17. www.theweek.com, 15 July 2019

18. 'Evaluation of Public Policy to Combat the Proliferation of Green Algae in Brittany', Chambres Regionales et Teritoriales des Comptes, July 2021

19. www.eea.europa.eu

20. 'Circular Economy: definition, importance and benefits', www.europarl.europa.com

21. www.unearthed.greenpeace.org, 21 October 2018

22. www.theworld.org, 13 January 2016

23. 'What are the main destinations of export of EU waste?', www.ec.europa.eu

24. www.bbc.com, 2 July 2021

25. www.eurowildlife.org, 28 February 2012

26. World Resources Institute, www.wri.org, 28 June 2022

27. *Sunday Times*, 7 January 2018

28. 'Illegal Building in Italy: too complex a problem for national land policy?' *Cities*, vol. 112, May 2021

29. www.theconversation.com, 27 July 2018

30. Clark, *Not Zero: How an Irrational Target Will Impoverish You, Help China (and Won't Even Save the Planet)*, Forum, 2023

31. www.zerotracker.net

32. *Financial Times*, 26 May 2023

33. 'GHG displacement factors of harvested wood products and the myth of substitution', *Nature*, 27 November 2020

34. www.sustainableplastics.com, 21 July 2023

35. www.ineos.com, press release, 20 February 2024

36. *Daily Telegraph*, 20 February 2024

37. *Financial Times*, 27 February 2024

38. 'Renewable Energy and Jobs: Annual Review 2023', www.irena.org

10.

1. 'Hate Crime: the Facts Behind the Headlines', Civitas, October 2016

2. *Guardian*, 7 September 2016

3. *Guardian*, 28 June 2016

4. www.independent.co.uk, 22 June 2021

5. BBC, 4 October 2016

6. 'Hate Crime, England and Wales 2022 to 2023', Home Office, 2 November 2023

7. Golec de Zavala et al., 'The Relationship between the Brexit Vote and Individual Predictors of Prejudice: Collective Narcissism, Right Wing Authoritarianism, Social Dominance Orientation', *Frontiers in Psychology*, vol. 8, 2017

8. www.kcl.ac.uk, April 2023

9. 'Being Black in the EU – Experiences of People of African Descent', European Agency for Fundamental Rights, 25 October 2023

10. *Financial Times*, 6 February 2024

11. 'Experiences and Perceptions of antisemitism: second survey on discrimination and hate crime against Jews in the EU', European Union Agency for Fundamental Rights (FRA), 2018

12. *Guardian*, 17 December 2012

13. www.blog.lse.ac.uk, 16 November 2018

14. www.politico.eu, 17 August 2017

15. *The Times*, 25 February 2014

16. '"We Just Want Some Rights!" Migrant care workers demand rights in Austria', Amnesty International, 2021

17. 'Out of Sight: migrant women exploited in domestic work', European Union Agency for Fundamental Rights, 2017

18. 'Protecting migrant workers from exploitation in the EU: workers' perspectives', European Agency for Fundamental Rights, 2019

19. 'Statistics on migration to europe', www.commission.europa.eu

20. Annual asylum statistics, 2022, www.ec.europa.eu

21. 'Asylum in the EU: Facts and Figures', European Parliament, 2021

22. Annual asylum statistics, www.ec.europa.eu

23. 'How many people do we grant asylum to?', Home Office, 29 February 2024

24. BBC, 2 April 2015

25. *Guardian*, 19 March 2024

26. BBC, 4 September 2020

27. BBC, 5 January 2016

28. www.dw.com, 31 December 2020

29. 'Manifesto for Germany: the political programme of the Alternative for Germany', 12 April 2017

30. www.dw.com, 18 January 2017

31. www.dw.com, 10 October 2021

32. Euronews, 30 November 2021
33. *Financial Times*, 19 November 2021
34. BBC, 17 January 2022
35. BBC, 18 April 2018
36. *Washington Post*, 6 April 2023
37. *Guardian*, 26 October 2022
38. BBC, 1 May 2012
39. www.dw.com, 17 October 2021
40. *Spiegel International*, 31 January 2013
41. Anne Applebaum, *Washington Post*, 13 November 2017
42. AP, 12 December 2023
43. *Daily Express*, 7 February 2024
44. www.oecd.ilibrary.org
45. *Daily Telegraph*, 2 August 2017
46. *Daily Mail*, 25 March 2024
47. BBC Future Planet, 12 October 2023
48. *Guardian*, 15 August 2008

II.

1. *Guardian*, 14 June 2016
2. *Guardian*, 21 September 2017
3. *Today*, BBC Radio 4, 2 November 2017
4. NHS workforce statistics, June 2017
5. NHS workforce statistics, June 2023
6. 'The NHS budget and how it has changed', King's Fund, 20 September 2023
7. 'Has Brexit affected the UK's medical workforce?' Nuffield Trust, 27 November 2022
8. *Guardian*, 8 January 2023
9. www.dw.com, 18 December 2022
10. www.aa.com.tr, 11 January 2023
11. www.nltimes.nl, 18 December 2019
12. www.ourworldindata.com
13. www.ourworldindata.com, from the 'Global Burden of Disease' database maintained by the Institute of Health Metrics and Evaluation (IHME)
14. Choi et al 'Global comparison of cancer outcomes: standardisation and correlation with healthcare expenditures', *BMC Public Health*, vol. 19, 2019

15. Ibid.
16. *Daily Mail*, 16 May 2009
17. 'State of Health in the EU Companion Report 2019', European Commission
18. *Brtish Medical Journal*, 17 July 2019
19. IHME data
20. Ibid.
21. Ibid.
22. 'Global Health Security Index 2019', www.ghsindex.org
23. BBC, 20 July 2020
24. 'Estimating excess mortality due to the Covid-19 pandemic: a systematic analysis of Covid-19-related mortality, 2020–21', *Lancet*, 16 April 2022
25. www.euronews.com
26. Reuters, 4 October 2023
27. www.americangerman.institute, 1 November 2021
28. www.rolandberger.com, 8 September 2022
29. www.drees.solidarites-sante.gouv.fr, 25 May 2023
30. www.euronews.com, 29 June 2022
31. 'Special Report 19/2022: EU Covid-19 vaccine procurement', EU Court of Auditors, 12 September, 2022
32. www.bbc.com, 30 January 2021

12.

1. *Guardian*, 3 June 2016
2. www.independent.co.uk, 7 August 2017
3. See chapter 2
4. 'International Students in UK Higher Education', House of Commons Library, 20 November 2023
5. University Rankings 2024, www.timeshighereducation.com
6. www.cwur.org
7. www.france24.com, 14 April 2022
8. *Guardian*, 28 March 2023
9. *Guardian*, 11 February 2021
10. PISA 2022 Results, www.oecd-ilibrary.org
11. www.thelocal.fr, 8 December 2017
12. www.lemonde.fr, 27 August 2022
13. www.euronews.com, 28 September 2023
14. www.bbc.com, 13 October 2023

15. www.bbc.com, 22 February 2023
16. INSM Educational Monitor 2023, www.insm.de, 30 August 2023
17. *Financial Times*, 13 November 2018
18. 'Quality of Life Indicators', Eurostat, 2019
19. www.politico.eu, 8 June 2021

13.

1. www.weforum.org, 27 February 2020
2. Eurostat yearbook, 2023
3. 'Declining Birth Rate in Europe: addressing the demographic emergency', Institut Jacques Delors, July 2022
4. *Financial Times*, 14 January 2020
5. www.weforum.org, 27 February 2020
6. www.ourworldindata.org
7. 'Births by Parents' Country of Birth 2022', ONS
8. Data hub www.spectator.co.uk, 31 January 2024 (from ONS and Eurostat figures)
9. 'Temporal Trends in Sperm Count', *Human Reproduction Update*, vol. 29, issue 2, March–April 2023
10. *Victoria Derbyshire Show*, BBC2, 4 March 2019
11. 'Climate Change, mental health and reproductive decision-making: A systematic review', PLOS Climate, 9 November 2023

14.

1. Democracy Index 2022, www.eiu.com
2. Democracy Report 2023, www.V-Dem.net
3. www.idea.int
4. *Guardian*, 15 July 2021
5. www.dw.com, 10 April 2024

15.

1. www.nato.int, press release, 26 June 2022
2. *Newsweek*, 19 February 2015
3. www.bundestag.de, 29 January 2019
4. *Bild*, 26 January 2022
5. www.bbc.co.uk, 11 February 2024
6. 'Operation Z: the Death Throes of an Imperial Delusion', Royal

United Services Institute, April 2022
7. www.armedforces.eu
8. 'Defending Europe: scenario-based capability requirements for NATO's European members', *International Institute for Strategic Studies*, 10 May 2019
9. www.dw.com, 24 February 2024
10. *Daily Telegraph*, 12 January 2024

16.

1. 'How Poland Benefits From the Single Market', Polish Economic Institute (www.pie.net.pl), July 2023
2. From World Bank data
3. 'Growing Together: EU Support to Poland since 2004', www.commission.europa.eu
4. www.politico.eu, 22 June 2023
5. 'Flat Rate Personal Income Tax in Lithuania, Romania and Hungary: a revolutionary idea without revolutionary outcomes', *Journal of European Social Policy*, vol. 32, issue 1, 13 August 2021
6. www.bbc.com, 17 February 2024
7. Corruption Perceptions Index 2023, www.transparency.org
8. www.euractiv.com, 18 July 2016

17.

1. *Financial Times*, 17 January 2023
2. *Financial Times*, 10 December 2023
3. www.politico.eu, 6 June 2023
4. www.bbc.com, 29 April 2016
5. *Daily Telegraph*, 12 July 2015
6. www.thejournal.ie, 31 January 2024
7. 'Fraud and Corruption in European Structural and Investment Funds', www.oecd.org, 2019
8. OLAF report, 2022
9. 'The Cost of Non-Europe in the Area of Organised Crime and Corruption', RAND corporation, 2016
10. '2022 EU audit in brief', European Court of Auditors
11. 'Special report 28/2023: Public procurement in the EU', European Court of Auditors

18.

1. 'Long-term international migration, provisional: year ending June 2023', ONS, 23 November 2023
2. *Guardian*, 27 March 2024
3. 'Company Insolvency Statistics, October to December 2020', The Insolvency Service, 29 January 2021
4. Reuters, 18 April 2023
5. *Daily Telegraph*, 27 March 2024
6. 'Labour market overview', ONS, March 2024
7. 'Young people not in education, employment or training, UK: February 2024', ONS
8. 'Short-Term Labour Market Statistics: Inactivity Rates', www.oecd.org
9. www.worldbank.org
10. *Sophy Ridge on Sunday*, Sky News, 22 January 2017
11. www.iras.gov.sg
12. www.bbc.com, 28 July 2023
13. *Financial Times*, 6 April 2016
14. *Guardian*, 21 December 2020
15. *Spectator*, 19 November 2022
16. *Independent*, 27 February 1997

Index